Modern and Contemporary Poetry and Poetics

Series Editor
David Herd
University of Kent
Canterbury, UK

Founded by Rachel Blau DuPlessis and continued by David Herd, *Modern and Contemporary Poetry and Poetics* promotes and pursues topics in the burgeoning field of 20th and 21st century poetics. Critical and scholarly work on poetry and poetics of interest to the series includes: social location in its relationships to subjectivity, to the construction of authorship, to oeuvres, and to careers; poetic reception and dissemination (groups, movements, formations, institutions); the intersection of poetry and theory; questions about language, poetic authority, and the goals of writing; claims in poetics, impacts of social life, and the dynamics of the poetic career as these are staged and debated by poets and inside poems. Since its inception, the series has been distinguished by its tilt toward experimental work – intellectually, politically, aesthetically. It has consistently published work on Anglophone poetry in the broadest sense and has featured critical work studying literatures of the UK, of the US, of Canada, and Australia, as well as eclectic mixes of work from other social and poetic communities. As poetry and poetics form a crucial response to contemporary social and political conditions, under David Herd's editorship the series will continue to broaden understanding of the field and its significance.

Editorial Board Members:
Rachel Blau DuPlessis, Temple University
Vincent Broqua, Université Paris 8
Olivier Brossard, Université Paris-Est
Steve Collis, Simon Fraser University
Jacob Edmond, University of Otago
Stephen Fredman, Notre Dame University
Fiona Green, University of Cambridge
Abigail Lang, Université Paris Diderot
Will Montgomery, Royal Holloway University of London
Miriam Nichols, University of the Fraser Valley
Redell Olsen, Royal Holloway University of London
Sandeep Parmar, University of Liverpool
Adam Piette, University of Sheffield
Nisha Ramaya, Queen Mary University of London
Brian Reed, University of Washington
Ann Vickery, Deakin University
Carol Watts, University of Sussex

More information about this series at
http://www.palgrave.com/gp/series/14799

Stephan Delbos

The New American Poetry and Cold War Nationalism

palgrave
macmillan

Stephan Delbos
Department of Anglophone Literatures and Cultures
Charles University
Prague, Czech Republic

ISSN 2634-6052   ISSN 2634-6060   (electronic)
Modern and Contemporary Poetry and Poetics
ISBN 978-3-030-77351-9   ISBN 978-3-030-77352-6   (eBook)
https://doi.org/10.1007/978-3-030-77352-6

© The Editor(s) (if applicable) and The Author(s), under exclusive licence to Springer Nature Switzerland AG 2021
This work is subject to copyright. All rights are solely and exclusively licensed by the Publisher, whether the whole or part of the material is concerned, specifically the rights of translation, reprinting, reuse of illustrations, recitation, broadcasting, reproduction on microfilms or in any other physical way, and transmission or information storage and retrieval, electronic adaptation, computer software, or by similar or dissimilar methodology now known or hereafter developed.
The use of general descriptive names, registered names, trademarks, service marks, etc. in this publication does not imply, even in the absence of a specific statement, that such names are exempt from the relevant protective laws and regulations and therefore free for general use.
The publisher, the authors and the editors are safe to assume that the advice and information in this book are believed to be true and accurate at the date of publication. Neither the publisher nor the authors or the editors give a warranty, expressed or implied, with respect to the material contained herein or for any errors or omissions that may have been made. The publisher remains neutral with regard to jurisdictional claims in published maps and institutional affiliations.

Cover illustration: Erika Pino / Getty Images

This Palgrave Macmillan imprint is published by the registered company Springer Nature Switzerland AG.
The registered company address is: Gewerbestrasse 11, 6330 Cham, Switzerland

CONTENTS

1 Introduction — 1

2 Raw Americans: The Persistence of *The New American Poetry*'s National, Binary Model of Anglophone Poetry — 11

2.1 *I Sold the Best Minds of My Generation: The Material Success of* The New American Poetry — 13

2.2 *Collecting Poetry, Courting Controversy: American Poetry Anthologies since* The New American Poetry — 19

2.3 *The New Poets Versus the New Poetry: The Binary of Academic and Avant-Garde* — 27

2.4 *Our Avant-Garde:* The New American Poetry *and the Deconstruction of Transatlantic Anglophone Poetry* — 40

2.5 *Bards of the White Citizens' Councils: Gender and Race in* The New American Poetry — 46

3 Behind Enemy Lines: *The New American Poetry* as a Cold War Anthology — 53

3.1 *Divided Together: Literary Life in Cold War America* — 54

3.2 *Another Bunch: Obscurity and Alienation in Post-war American Poetry* — 71

3.3 *Weapons of the Cold War:* The New American Poetry *and* The New American Painting — 78

vi CONTENTS

4 The Community of Love: *The New American Poetry* and Revolutionary Relationships in Cold War America 87

    4.1 Particularly Vulnerable: Gay Poets in The New American Poetry 90

    4.2 Freedom from the Pursuit of Insane Objectives: The Cold War Community of Love 98

    4.3 I Love My Love: The New American Poetry*'s Reconsideration of Traditional Relationships* 109

    4.4 A Social Feeling: Beyond Formal Divisions in Post-war American Poetry 125

5 This Thing Is Most National: Nationalism and Assimilation in *The New American Poetry* 131

    5.1 Poems and Passports: The New American Poetry*'s Nationalist Conception of Post-war Anglophone Poetry* 132

    5.2 American in the Wider Sense: Reading The New American Poetry *Transnationally* 144

    5.3 Red, White and Recognizable: The Design and Title of The New American Poetry 157

    5.4 The Decisive Defining Factor: Donald Allen's Construction of American Poetry 161

6 Post-war to Post-truth: Reassessing the American Avant-Garde Canon 167

    6.1 Hallucinations of Homogeneity: The New American Poetry*'s White, Male Legacy* 169

    6.2 A Degree of Variation: Form and Subjectivity in Avant-Garde American Poetry 179

7 Conclusion: The Slow Collapse of the Formalist Framework 193

Appendices 199

Bibliography 213

Index 231

CHAPTER 1

Introduction

What is American poetry? This simple question had many contradictory answers during the Cold War, when a response revealed as much about politics as poetics. This was a period when the personal became political and arguments about poetry and national policy overlapped. Conservative critics in the 1940s and 1950s who favored received forms over formally experimental poetry not only showed their politics in negative reviews of such poetry, they used poetry reviews to promote their politics. Cold War arguments about what made poetry *poetry* were also disputes over what made Americans *American*. While Donald Allen's anthology, *The New American Poetry 1945–1960* (1960), is generally interpreted as a rejoinder to these conservative tendencies, the reality—like so many aspects of the Cold War—is not so simple.

Allen's book is involved in Cold War politics and poetry in complex ways that have mostly been overlooked, as criticism of American poetry since 1945 has tended to focus on form and, more recently, race, gender and identity. This shift had started by 1960, the year Grove Press published Allen's anthology and Robert Lowell described American poetry as a competition between the cooked and the raw.[1] In the years following

---

[1] Robert Lowell, "National Book Award Acceptance Speech," *The National Book Awards*, http://www.nationalbook.org/nbaacceptspeech_rlowell.html#.Vllc7_mrTIU, May 1, 2015.

© The Author(s), under exclusive license to Springer Nature Switzerland AG 2021
S. Delbos, *The New American Poetry and Cold War Nationalism*, Modern and Contemporary Poetry and Poetics, https://doi.org/10.1007/978-3-030-77352-6_1

1

World War II, American poetry and culture underwent dramatic changes and discussions of both were often acrimonious and divisive. In this context, a poem was never just a poem. These confluences of poetry, politics and propaganda should enrich our discussions of this writing. Yet, while post-war American culture, from abstract expressionism to jazz, film and theater, has been reexamined within the framework of Cold War cultural politics, *The New American Poetry*, one of the most influential poetry anthologies of the century, has been overlooked.

More than 25 years ago Charles Bernstein wrote, "the Cold War and the U.S.'s new hegemonic global role would be a more obvious context for a sociohistorical reading of the New American Poets."[2] His essay was based on a talk at the New School for Social Research given on February 15, 1990,[3] and published in 1991, during the dramatic final days of the Cold War. At that time, when Cold War mentalities, constructions and divisions were still very much in the air, the Cold War certainly should have seemed an obvious context in which to read Allen's anthology and its historical moment. The Cold War was more of an everyday reality for Americans in the early 1990s than it is in 2021, even given the fact that some commentators believe we are now experiencing a second Cold War[4] and others argue that the first Cold War never truly ended.[5] But in 1991 the Cold War still loomed too large to distinguish all of its contours. At that time there was also a lack of primary documents concerning both Allen and his anthology as well as, crucially, American cultural warfare during the Cold War. As a result, very few scholars took up Bernstein's suggestion.

Studies of American Cold War poetry published since the early 1990s, such as Edward Brunner's insightful *Cold War Poetry* (2000), deal with *The New American Poetry* only in a cursory manner.[6] But we now have previously unavailable tools to explore this context, and we also have

---

[2] Charles Bernstein, *A Poetics* (Cambridge: Harvard University Press, 1992), 206.

[3] Bernstein, 231.

[4] Dmitri Trenin, "Welcome to Cold War II," *Foreign Policy*, March 4, 2014, https://foreignpolicy.com/2014/03/04/welcome-to-cold-war-ii/, January 9, 2018.

[5] Andras Schweitzer, "This isn't the start of a new cold war – the first one never ended," *The Guardian*, December 13, 2016, https://www.theguardian.com/commentisfree/2016/dec/13/cold-war-never-ended-west-russia, March 12, 2018.

[6] Even a book that is otherwise as rewarding as Stuart D. Hobbs's *The End of the American Avant Garde* incorrectly refers to Allen's anthology as *New American Poets*. Stuart D. Hobbs, *The End of the American Avant Garde* (New York: New York University Press, 1997), 136.

1 INTRODUCTION 3

important new points of view, including transnational literary studies, which have developed over the past two decades. Reconsidering this crucially influential anthology from a transnational perspective and the vantage point of the twenty-first century widens our framework of interpretation, allowing us to interrogate much about *The New American Poetry* that has been taken for granted, including the seemingly simple designation of "American" poetry. In the process, the Anglophone poetry that emerged after World War II can be read within a global context, both enriching and complicating our understanding of it.

But were Cold War politics truly germane to Allen's editorial decisions, and if so, how are these influences visible in the anthology? On February 10, 1961, Allen wrote a letter to Charles Olson, narrating an event that had taken place the day before:

> Then yesterday at the drugstore I heard the druggist say to three cute young bobbysoxers who were sipping icecream sodas: 'Don't you girls do anything but eat icecream sodas and go to school?' And they said immediately, 'Yes, we fight communism.'[7]

These girls wittily turned political discourse against a hectoring older man. But the moment also captures the way that ideology pervaded everyday life in the years following World War II, evoking the environment in which *The New American Poetry* was conceived, published and interpreted. If the concept of fighting communism was on the minds of young girls in 1961, Allen himself, on other levels, was also immersed in the politics of his time.

Allen was perspicacious regarding poets who would soon become central to the American canon, yet it is striking how much *The New American Poetry* did not predict or seems to have ignored, including the Civil Rights Movement and feminism, both of which would burst onto the national stage in the 1960s after more than a decade of development. Instead, Allen's anthology reflects some of the early Cold War's most troubling characteristics, including American nationalism, conservatism and imbalances of gender and race. *The New American Poetry* is a Cold War anthology, influenced by this period of intense nationalism, repressive heteronormativity and contested borders, and such a reading of the book provides us with a new perspective on both it and the American poetry of

---

[7] Donald Allen to Charles Olson, February 10, 1961, Box 93, Folder 6, Donald Allen Collection, MSS 3, Special Collections & Archives, UC San Diego Library.

the period. Our contemporary conception of American poetry as split between traditional and avant-garde or free verse and formal, as well as the association of American poetry with innovation and British poetry with tradition, and the sense that white men have been responsible for poetic innovation since World War II—all of which Allen's anthology perpetuated—are therefore grounded in the politics and cultural atmosphere of the Cold War. A reconsideration of Allen's anthology also reorients our thinking about the American avant-garde from World War II until today.

Like Allen's anthology, Lowell's binary of cooked and raw has become famous for its seemingly astute summary of the post-war landscape of American poetry. The connections and the contrasts between the post-war avant-garde and that of the early twenty-first century are evident in Vanessa Place's poem "No More," published in the March 2013 issue of *Poetry*. In it, Place writes: "No more songs of raw emotion, forever overcooked,"[8] commenting, like Lowell, on the poetry of her contemporaries while repudiating both sides of the Lowellian binary. In so doing, Place suggests that the dominant framework for comprehending the norms and limits of American poetry needs to be destroyed, or at the very least that it is no longer relevant.[9] Yet the very existence of Place's statement and the apparent need for this repudiation suggest how pervasive Lowell's model, and by extension the framework for American poetry established shortly after World War II, still is. The line of influence from conceptual writing through language poetry back to the post-war avant-garde as represented by Allen's anthology is not difficult to distinguish.[10] The conceptual writer Craig Dworkin has described how he and his contemporaries have been

---

[8] Vanessa Place, "No More," *Poetry.org*, March 2013, https://www.poetryfoundation.org/poetrymagazine/poems/56142/no-more, November 18, 2017.

[9] Perhaps this is what Place meant when she said, "conceptualism wants to put poetry out of its misery." See: Burt Kimmelman, "Who is There?: Revisiting Michael Brown's Autopsy Report and Reassessing Conceptual Poetry Two Years after 'Interrupt 3,'" *Dispatches from the Poetry Wars*, August 25, 2017, http://dispatchespoetrywars.com/commentary/2017/08/revisiting-michael-browns-autopsy-report-reassessing-conceptual-poetry-two-years-interrupt-3-burt-kimmelman/, January 25, 2018.

[10] Burt Kimmelman clearly traces the lineage of influence from conceptualism to language poetry, *The New American Poetry*, and the objectivists in his essay "*The New American Poetry*'s Objectivist Legacy: Linguistic Skepticism, the Signifier, and Material Language." See: John R Woznicki, *The New American Poetry: Fifty Years Later* (Bethlehem: Lehigh University Press, 2013), 221. Similarly, Charles Bernstein suggests that World War II affected poets of the language movement who were born during the war. Charles Bernstein, *A Poetics* (Cambridge: Harvard University Press, 1992), 193.

1 INTRODUCTION 5

directly inspired by the post-war avant-garde, including Charles Olson's essay "Projective Verse," first published in 1950 and republished in *The New American Poetry*.[11] Critics such as David Kaufmann have cited the egalitarianism at the heart of conceptual writing and the way that Kenneth Goldsmith "equates the poet and the nation,"[12] suggesting the subjectivity that guides a project like *Seven American Deaths and Disasters* but stopping short of identifying the American nationalism at its core, which stems in large part from Allen and the post-war moment.

Allen's anthology has also recently been cited as a precursor to racial and gender imbalances in contemporary anthologies and the twenty-first century avant-garde.[13] Examining these controversies and the way they intersect with *The New American Poetry* brings this study of Allen's anthology up to date, providing an opportunity to reform our understanding of the contemporary avant-garde in a wider context and encouraging a confrontation of the charges of racism and white privilege that have been leveled against some contemporary critics as well as conceptual writers like Goldsmith and Place with a knowledge of their roots in the practice and presentation of the post-war avant-garde.

Several critics have done important work on *The New American Poetry*, specifically Alan Golding in his groundbreaking writing on anthologies and canonization and his illuminating research in the Allen archives, which first brought to light crucial context for Allen's conception of the anthology in the 1990s. More recently, John Woznicki gathered a group of

---

[11] Craig Dworkin describes conceptualism's interest in "the potential of writing that tries to be 'rid of [the] lyrical interference of the individual as ego' (as Charles Olson famously put it)." Craig Dworkin, "The Fate of Echo," in *Against Expression: An Anthology of Conceptual Writing*, eds. Craig Dworkin and Kenneth Goldsmith (Evanston: Northwestern University Press, 2011), xliii. Another example of the post-war avant-garde's influence on conceptual writing comes from Trisha Low, who studied "Uncreative Writing" with Goldsmith at the University of Pennsylvania. She suggests that the "formal tic" of "timestamping," or recording the exact time of composition in a particular work, "is a gesture which Conceptualism itself borrowed from the New York School." Trisha Low, "On Being-Hated: Conceptualism, the Mongrel Coalition, the House That Built Me," *Open Space*, May 20, 2015, https://openspace.sfmoma.org/2015/05/on-being-hated-conceptualism-the-mongrel-coalition-the-house-that-built-me/, December 28, 2017.

[12] David Kaufmann, *Reading Uncreative Writing: Conceptualism, Expression and the Lyric* (Cham: Palgrave Macmillan, 2017), 32.

[13] See, for example: Cathy Park Hong, "Delusions of Whiteness in the Avant-garde," *Lana Turner*, http://www.lanaturnerjournal.com/7/delusions-of-whiteness-in-the-avant-garde, October 28, 2017.

contemporary critics to examine the legacy of Allen's anthology 50 years after its publication. These are foundational texts in the study of *The New American Poetry*. This book builds on that scholarship and adds several crucial new points of view. It considers Allen's anthology in a transnational framework, acknowledging important recent developments in the study of literature. This book also utilizes new discoveries in Cold War studies that can help create a literary, sociological and historical context for Allen's work that is not visible in his archives and has not been available for scholars until recently. This shows how poets on both sides of the so-called anthology wars were reacting to the same systemic conditions in American society, complicating categorical narratives.

The recent publication of correspondence and biographies of several important poets in Allen's anthology and the post-war milieu has also unearthed rich material to draw from when creating a more complete picture of *The New American Poetry* and its immediate impacts, as well as the conditions from which it emerged. The following chapters supplement these publications with original, unpublished interviews from some of the major figures of post-war American poetry, including Edward Field, Joanne Kyger, Donald Hall, Robert Pack and Basil and Martha King. Their invaluable first-hand accounts enrich this study and support its arguments.

We are now in a better position than ever to reassess *The New American Poetry* and its impacts, as well as its contemporary utility or obsolescence. On the one hand, *The New American Poetry*'s framework seems irrelevant, as American poetry is far more pluralistic today than it was in 1960. And yet we cannot so easily dismiss this anthology which has played a key role for succeeding generations of poets and critics. Revealing the problematic richness of *The New American Poetry* and its context requires examining it from many angles. This is the task of the following chapters. Proceeding from the late 1950s, when Allen was beginning to conceive of his anthology, this study examines the Cold War milieu in which *The New American Poetry* was created, the book's success as a publishing project for Grove Press, its reception among critics, poets and anthologists, its nationalist and conservative presentation of liberal poets who had revolutionary ideas about society, love and relationships, its gender and racial imbalances, and its problematic legacy today.

Chapter 2 establishes the framework for the study, introducing arguments about *The New American Poetry* that will inform the rest of the book. This chapter examines the material success of Allen's anthology and its influence, both on subsequent American poetry anthologies and on the way we think about Anglophone poetry today. Three effects of the anthology are highlighted. The first is the perpetuation of a division in American poetry between academic and avant-garde. The second is the conflation of American poetry with innovation and British poetry with tradition. The third effect is rooted in the anthology's inclusion of few women and poets of color, which has contributed to the sense that innovative American poetry has mostly been created by white men. These effects provide different points of view from which to examine *The New American Poetry* and are taken up individually in the following chapters.

Chapter 3 examines the social, historical and political context in which Allen created and published his anthology to argue that *The New American Poetry* is rooted in the Cold War. The chapter highlights some of the crucial divisions and anxieties of literary production in the period, including debates about whether poets belonged in the academy and the myopia of mainstream critics concerning poets not affiliated with universities or major presses. Utilizing documents, publications and correspondence from this period, the chapter also shows how violent political rhetoric crept into American life during the 1950s, including discussions of poetry, as American culture was used as propaganda, a weapon of the Cold War. Of central importance here is *The New American Painting*, a touring exhibition of abstract expressionist paintings that was secretly funded by the CIA in 1958 and inspired Allen at a crucial moment in his development of the anthology. This connection between Allen's anthology and Cold War cultural warfare is an important supplement to our consideration of *The New American Poetry* as a document of the counterculture.

Chapter 4 examines Allen's description—in a letter to Robert Duncan in 1959[14]—of "the community of love" as the most important unifying quality of *The New American Poetry*. The chapter first highlights the homosexual subtext of this exchange between two gay men during a period known as the "Lavender Scare," which was especially repressive toward homosexuals.[15] Then, tracing the subversive political connotations of this phrase back to their origins, the chapter uses Allen's words as a

[14] Donald Allen to Robert Duncan, November 3, 1959, TL: 1, 1959–1964, Box: 77, Robert Duncan Collection, PCMS-0110, The Poetry Collection of the University Libraries, University at Buffalo, The State University of New York.

[15] David K. Johnson, *The Lavender Scare: The Cold War Persecution of Gays and Lesbians in the Federal Government* (Chicago: University of Chicago Press, 2004), 8.

starting point for a consideration of the changing nature of relationships in Cold War America and reveals that while many of the poems in the anthology do not appear to address political issues, they do in fact express radical approaches to relationships and marriage that put them at odds with the country's prevailing conservative tendencies. Examining the specifically communist and communalist connotations of the phrase "the community of love," the chapter reveals the complex ways that Allen and his anthology interacted with Cold War culture, politics and society and also puts focus on the liberal content of many of the poems in *The New American Poetry*.

Chapter 5 investigates the nationalism of Allen's anthology, as manifest in the title and the American flag cover image, as well as Allen's introduction and editorial policy. The chapter argues that these elements fit *The New American Poetry* into the renewed sense of nationalism in the United States during the Cold War. Of note here is how Allen's definition of "American" shifted and contracted during the time he was editing the book, partially due to the influence of Charles Olson. The chapter also argues that by following up on the initial success of this anthology with other publications using similar titles and cover images, Allen created a consensus about innovative poetry as specifically American while at the same time suggesting that formal poetry was old fashioned and tied to the British tradition. Reading *The New American Poetry* from the transnational perspective allows us to recalibrate many of the anthology's large claims, precipitating revisions of our ideas about American and British poetry alike.

Chapter 6 connects Allen's anthology with the twenty-first-century American avant-garde by juxtaposing the composition of the book with contemporary discussions about the exclusion of women and people of color from the discourse. This chapter traces the roots of the current racial and sexual homogeneity of experimental American poetry back to *The New American Poetry*, examining the unfortunate history of exclusion in the American avant-garde and also suggesting ways the anthology has played a role in the critical discourse on American poetry and the relationship between form, content and identity since being absorbed by the mainstream and the academy. Examining *The New American Poetry*'s continued influence with a knowledge of its Cold War context shows how Allen's conception of American poetry was conditioned by the very culture he was pushing back against, and it also suggests that many critics continue to base their conception of avant-garde writing on an aesthetic, form-based model that Allen's anthology helped establish and which is no longer relevant, in large part because it does not take into account writers who are more concerned with identity and social issues than traditional formal mastery or experimentation.

The book concludes by arguing that the dominant critical framework for Anglophone poetry as it was established after World War II, with *The New American Poetry* as a primary model, is on the verge of collapse because it does not accurately represent the increasing diversity of American poetry. The laudable diversification and decentralization of Anglophone poetry make it unlikely that we will again see a hierarchical poetic canon or such authoritative anthologies as *The New American Poetry*. Ideally, however, future anthologies and conceptions of the canon will do away with national divisions in favor of a more inclusive framework that also takes into account the vital contributions of women and people of color and does not seek to separate concepts of form and content.

A more general note on the way that I use terms like "American poetry" is required. One argument of this study is that breath-based and colloquial poetry was not exclusively the innovation of American poets in the years following World War II. So when dealing with English-language poetry that was not restricted to the United States, the adjectives "Anglophone poetry" and "English-language poetry" are typically utilized. And while the transnational standpoint of the book would suggest that the terms "US" and "American" poetry are misleading, limiting or even meaningless, these are generally used to refer to the category of American poetry which is taken for granted by most readers. In such cases these usages should be understood as convenient signposts when the distinction is not essential for the argument. The following chapters provide alternatives for the obfuscating simplicity of cooked versus raw, academic versus avant-garde and American versus the rest of the world, terms that have become too common in discussions of poetry. These clichés, left unquestioned, discourage our comprehension of the crucial intersections of poetry, politics and culture.

In a letter to Donald Allen in May 1958, when the editor was still in the early stages of developing and designing *The New American Poetry*, Allen Ginsberg wrote: "The anthology also sounds like an undreamt of early windfall miracle. It should be a great bomb & clear the air almost

10   S. DELBOS

immediately of all the doubting critical bullshit."[16] How right and wrong he was. Neither Ginsberg nor Allen could have anticipated just how significant an effect *The New American Poetry* would have and how controversial it would look in the twenty-first century. It is extraordinary that a poetry anthology is still cited so often more than 60 years after its publication. And although it did not win over the staunchest conservative critics, the anthology did immediately make it much harder to ignore the work of younger poets like Ginsberg who were just beginning their careers in the late 1950s. This seemingly comprehensive and well-edited anthology from a press as significant as Grove brought these poets a level of promotion most of them had not experienced before. It was indeed an impressive salvo in what soon become known as the anthology wars. But like all powerful explosives, *The New American Poetry* caused collateral damage, something we have only recently been able to comprehend. The negative effects the anthology and its legacy have had on women, poets of color and innovative non-American poets who have been excluded from the critical narrative should give any reader pause and inspire a detailed reexamination of the anthology's liberal and liberating reputation.

American poetry has not been the same since *The New American Poetry*. This study does not attempt to return the discourse to the conditions that prevailed before Allen's vital anthology was published but rather to revisit the origins of the current discourse to uncover its roots and resonances in Cold War America, so that we may move beyond the brilliant shadow *The New American Poetry* has cast. Only then will the path be cleared for new, more comprehensive ways of writing about poetic innovation since 1945. Reinstating Allen's anthology in its volatile cultural context and unpacking the motivations—at times conflicting and unconscious—that led the editor to conservatively nationalize an international development of innovative poetry written in English while at the same time embracing the cultural liberalism of formal experimentation and socially subversive opinions adds depth and subtlety not only to our reading of the poems in the book but to the way we conceive of English-language poetry in the second half of the twentieth century and beyond.

---

[16] Allen Ginsberg to Donald Allen, May, 1958, Box 10, Folder 15, Donald Allen Collection, MSS 3, Special Collections & Archives, UC San Diego Library.

CHAPTER 2

Raw Americans: The Persistence of *The New American Poetry*'s National, Binary Model of Anglophone Poetry

The New American Poetry 1945–1960 has been referred to as "germinal,"[1] "groundbreaking,"[2] "epoch-making,"[3] a "watershed,"[4] a "hegemonic force,"[5] a "cornerstone,"[6] and "indispensable."[7] According to the publisher and the editor, it has sold more than 100,000 copies, sometimes at a rate of several thousand per year,[8] making it one of the most highly praised and economically successful anthologies of post-war American poetry. This alone should motivate a closer examination of the anthology

---

[1] Alan Golding, "Black Mountain School," *The Princeton Encyclopedia of Poetry & Poetics* (Princeton: Princeton University Press, 2012), 144.

[2] Douglas Messerli, *From the Other Side of the Century: A New American Poetry 1960–1990* (Los Angeles: Sun & Moon Press, 1994), 31.

[3] Ron Silliman, *Silliman's Blog*, June 11, 2007, http://ronsilliman.blogspot.com/2007/06/donald-allen-theres-no-such-thing-as.html, May 15, 2015.

[4] Martin Duberman, *Black Mountain: An Exploration in Community* (Evanston: Northwestern University Press, 2009), 412.

[5] David Clippinger, *The Mind's Landscape: William Bronk and Twentieth-century American Poetry* (Newark: University of Delaware Press, 2006), 184.

[6] Tom Clark, *Charles Olson: The Allegory of a Poet's Life* (Berkeley: North Atlantic Books, 2000), 288.

[7] "The New American Poetry," *The Academy of American Poets*, http://www.poets.org/poetsorg/book/new-american-poetry-1945-1960, May 15, 2015.

[8] *The New American Poetry, 1945–1960*, University of California Press, http://www.ucpress.edu/book.php?isbn=9780520209534, May 1, 2015.

© The Author(s), under exclusive license to Springer Nature Switzerland AG 2021
S. Delbos, *The New American Poetry and Cold War Nationalism*, Modern and Contemporary Poetry and Poetics, https://doi.org/10.1007/978-3-030-77352-6_2

and its effects. Deepening our understanding of Donald Allen's editorial decisions and the context in which they were made and challenging received ideas of "cooked" and "raw"[9] American poetry with social, political and thematic considerations bring us to a more comprehensive and more accurate reading of the poetry of the mid-twentieth century and beyond. Doing so means attending to the Cold War context and a transnational rather than a national point of view, questioning the critical assumptions behind our perception of the anthology and examining how it has influenced the discourse on Anglophone poetry for nearly 60 years. Ultimately, this leads us to interrogate whether the precedents the anthology set remain useful for understanding poetry written in English since World War II.

Beginning with a brief consideration of the material success of *The New American Poetry*, this chapter focuses on three key effects of the anthology. The first is the persistent binary between "cooked" and "raw,"[10] namely that American poetry consists of two camps, one of which is formal, traditional and impersonal while the opposing camp is free verse, energetic and self-expressive. This binary stems from Allen's anthology more than any other publication and has set the pattern for subsequent anthologies since 1960. The second impact examined here is the conflation of so-called academic poetry with formal, conservative poetry in the British tradition, which is rooted in the widespread interpretation of *The New American Poetry* as an equal and opposite reaction to *The New Poets of England and America* (1957), edited by Donald Hall, Robert Pack and Louis Simpson, as these two anthologies taken together were mistakenly considered a complete picture of the Anglophone poetry of the period. The third effect examined in this chapter is the impact of the anthology's inclusion of few women and poets of color, which resonates with contemporary concerns about racism and sexism in the American avant-garde, a legacy that largely originated with *The New American Poetry*. These three effects inform the arguments of subsequent chapters. Beginning with a consideration of the anthology's material success and its economic impact on the poets included, this chapter initially recasts *The New American*

---

[9] Robert Lowell, "National Book Award Acceptance Speech," *The National Book Awards*, http://www.nationalbook.org/nbaacceptspeech_rlowell.html#.Vllc7_mrTIU, May 1, 2015.

[10] Robert Lowell, "National Book Award Acceptance Speech," *The National Book Awards*, http://www.nationalbook.org/nbaacceptspeech_rlowell.html#.Vllc7_mrTIU, May 1, 2015.

Poetry as a publishing project like any other, showing the book as it was before it became a milestone.

2.1 I Sold the Best Minds of My Generation: The Material Success of *The New American Poetry*

On April 6, 1958, Donald Allen, working freelance for Grove Press, wrote to publisher Barney Rosset with a proposal entitled "re: Publishing poetry." In it, he outlined the possible advantages of publishing contemporary poets in a series through Grove: "I am trying to think of some way to package and present volumes of the newer poets we have been considering and wonder if some such plan as this might not have some advantages."[11] The series was to focus primarily on contemporary poets but would also include the work of older writers such as Herman Melville. Allen goes on to describe short, quarterly volumes presenting single poets. In his notes for the letter to Rosset, Allen writes that such a series would "get us other books by poets but also build name of press."[12] On July 30, 1958, Rosset responded to Allen with a contractual agreement for "an anthology of modern American poetry."[13]

It is difficult to piece together the conversations that took place between April and July as the contract was drawn up and the exact details of Allen's project were confirmed and developed, and as Allen's initial idea for a series of publications coalesced into a single anthology.[14] But it is important to note that the monument that is *The New American Poetry* was first a product from a single editor and a publisher that depended on sales for its existence. Allen's correspondence over the next two years bears this out, as does the amount of work he put into compiling and editing the

[11] Donald Allen to Barney Rosset, April 6, 1958, Box 75, Folder 2, Donald Allen Collection, MSS 3, Special Collections & Archives, UC San Diego Library.

[12] Donald Allen to Barney Rosset, April 6, 1958, Box 75, Folder 2, Donald Allen Collection, MSS 3, Special Collections & Archives, UC San Diego Library.

[13] Barney Rosset to Donald Allen, July 30, 1958, Box 75, Folder 2, Donald Allen Collection, MSS 3, Special Collections & Archives, UC San Diego Library.

[14] At this time Allen was also planning another anthology, international and historical in scope, titled *The Modern Tradition: An Anthology of Modern Poetry, 1800–1960*, which remained unpublished. In his notes for the project Allen wrote "During recent years I've grown more and more interested in the way the modern poets have created their own tradition. This is a continuing process, of course, and it includes a number of writers of earlier periods, Dante and Shakespeare, for instance." Box 88, Folder 1, Donald Allen Collection, MSS 3, Special Collections & Archives, UC San Diego Library.

14   S. DELBOS

anthology, which necessitated him leaving his post as editor of *The Evergreen Review* in the summer of 1959 to devote more time to the project.[15] By November of that year, Allen would write to Gregory Corso: "I am broke and won't have any money for the antho [*sic*] until March or April, when I'll pay the poets their advances on the poems. Am having to work very hard to pay the rent and keep up because the anthology took me so long to complete when I should have been doing other things."[16]

It wasn't until November 6, 1959, after the anthology had gone through numerous permutations, that Allen could write:

> Great fatigue and lassitude hitting me intermittently since Monday when I delivered the antho [*sic*] completed and ready to roll… In the end the antho [*sic*] came to 400 pages, a solid chunk of something. I find it hard to believe, but we'll see. By making it much larger than the estimated 320, I will be in the hole financially in March when I pay the poets the advances. So I am thinking of asking that I be permitted to use the poetics statements for free, plus biographies of course.[17]

Allen would not be in the hole financially for long; *The New American Poetry* was a resounding success in more ways than one. The anthology provided a steady and lasting stream of income for Allen and the poets included and established Allen's reputation as a canny editor. The book was certainly a success for Grove Press, selling, according to Allen's later estimate, 750 copies per month in the first year,[18] and 3000 to 5000 copies annually while remaining in print for two decades.[19] It would be brought out again by The University of California Press in 1999.[20] As of June, 1961, it had sold 13,111 paperback copies and 858 hardback copies,

---

[15] Donald Allen to Edward Dorn, August 10, 1959, Box 9, Folder 12, Donald Allen Collection, MSS 3, Special Collections & Archives, UC San Diego Library.

[16] Donald Allen to Gregory Corso, November 30, 1959, Box 10, Folder 16, Donald Allen Collection, MSS 3, Special Collections & Archives, UC San Diego Library.

[17] Donald Allen, November 6, 1959, Box 93, Folder 5, Donald Allen Collection, MSS 3, Special Collections & Archives, UC San Diego Library.

[18] Donald Allen, Box 74, Folder 9, Donald Allen Collection, MSS 3, Special Collections & Archives, UC San Diego Library.

[19] Donald Allen, Box 74, Folder 6, Donald Allen Collection, MSS 3, Special Collections & Archives, UC San Diego Library.

[20] Donald Allen to Marjorie Perloff, August 24, 1996, Box 93, Folder 12, Donald Allen Collection, MSS 3, Special Collections & Archives, UC San Diego Library.

according to Allen.[21] In 1961 in England alone it sold 490 copies, attesting to its international reach.[22] Summing up, publisher Barney Rosset said: "[*The New American Poetry*] sold and sold... It taught poetry to a whole generation of young kids."[23]

Allen was not a full-time employee of Grove Press, and correspondence reveals his financial struggles as he balanced freelance breadwinning with an editorial project that was constantly enlarging in scope. What he thought would be a project of six months took three years, nearly exhausting him physically and economically in the process. But the struggle would pay off. Not only did *The New American Poetry* jumpstart Allen's career as an editor, first at Grove Press and later at his own publishing companies The Four Seasons Foundation and Grey Fox Press, it also allowed him to parlay one success into many other related publications, including *New American Story* (1965), *The New Writing in the USA* (1967), *The Poetics of The New American Poetry* (1973) and *The Postmoderns: The New American Poetry Revised* (1982).[24] The royalties for sales of *The New American Poetry* in the two decades after its publication are as follows: [25]

1960: $2964	1961: $807.27	1962: $1153.60	1963: $890.56	1964: $1048.84
1965: $1254.99	1966: $1631.65	1967: $2188.65	1968: $2649.62	1969: $1997.33
1970: $1277.83	1971: $848.96	1972: $662.96 (six-month period)	1973: $1130.09	1974: $999.97
1975: $1254.46	1976: $850.54	1977: $1185.89	1978: $687.22	1979: $780.05
1980: $552.70				

[21] Donald Allen to Robert Duncan, November 4, 1961, TL: 1, 1959–1964, Box: 77, Robert Duncan Collection, PCMS-0110, The Poetry Collection of the University Libraries, University at Buffalo, The State University of New York.

[22] Donald Allen, January 25, 1963, Box 74, Folder 6, Donald Allen Collection, MSS 3, Special Collections & Archives, UC San Diego Library.

[23] Loren Glass, *Counterculture Colophon: Grove Press, The Evergreen Review, and the Incorporation of the Avant-Garde* (Stanford: Stanford University Press, 2013), 64.

[24] It was also very likely the success of *The New American Poetry* that inspired Barney Rosset and Grove Press to offer a $10,000 advance to Allen and George Butterick when editing *The Postmoderns: The New American Poetry Revisited* (1982) compared to the $1000 advance Allen received from editing *The New American Poetry*. See: Box 75, Folder 2, Donald Allen Collection, MSS 3, Special Collections & Archives, UC San Diego Library, and Ralph Maud, *Poet to Publisher: Charles Olson's Correspondence with Donald Allen* (Vancouver: Talonbooks, 2003), 47.

[25] Box 74, Folder 6, Donald Allen Collection, MSS 3, Special Collections & Archives, UC San Diego Library.

16   S. DELBOS

While these numbers do not rival those of a best-selling novel, for an anthology of poetry they are impressive. The royalties were not all Allen's but would trickle down to the poets included, each of whom was paid an advance of $2.50 per page of type on the date of publication.[26]

For a poet like Charles Olson, whose work is featured prominently, the anthology's brisk sales meant a steady if not astounding income. Olson contributed 38 pages to *The New American Poetry*, which earned him a royalty in 1961 of $80.94 minus a $25 advance from Allen, leaving a balance of $55.94. The following year 4988 copies of the paperback edition sold, netting a 7.5 percent royalty of $1103.60, which, together with $50 from special sales, made a total of $1153.60, earning Olson $76.76. In 1963, the payments were $1.56 per page for the poetry, earning Olson $59.28. By 1965, the sale of 5671 copies in the previous fiscal year earned all poets $2.20 per page and a total of $83.60 for Olson. This rose considerably in 1967, when Olson earned $146.30, and even more the following year, when he earned $177.08.[27] Adjusted for inflation, this 1968 payment would be worth $1358.39 in 2021.[28] Not bad for a poet.[29]

---

[26] See: Ralph Maud, *Poet to Publisher: Charles Olson's Correspondence with Donald Allen* (Vancouver: Talonbooks, 2003), 47. Allen wrote: "This will be his share of the publisher's advance to me against royalties (which will be 10% of the retail price of all copies actually sold of the hard-bound edition, and 7 ½% of the retail price of all copies actually sold of the paper-bound edition. The royalty on copies sold as remainders will be 10% of the price received by the publisher, and no royalties will be paid on copies sold below manufacturing costs). In other words, I propose to pro-rate two-thirds of all royalty payments to me to the poets, keeping one-third of royalty payments as my editorial fee. I also propose to pro-rate on the same basis all other payments made to me, such as book club sales, sale of the book to a British publisher, etc. (I will not, of course, participate in any payments to poets for reprinting poems in magazines, etc.)... The advance payment of $2.50 per page of the anthology to each poet will be his share of the publisher's advance to me of $1000 (actually that works out at something better than two-thirds to the poets, as you can see). This advance payment more than covers the royalty payments due on anticipated sales of 5000 copies within the first year (we hope!) at about $1.95 per copy paper-bound... Each poet is to receive two free copies of the anthology on date of publication. He may order additional copies of the anthology from the publisher at a discount of 25% from list price."

[27] All figures accessed in the Charles Olson Research Collection, Archives & Special Collections at the Thomas J. Dodd Research Center, University of Connecticut Libraries.

[28] Bureau of Labor Statistics, CPI Inflation Calculator, http://www.bls.gov/data/inflation_calculator.htm, February 10, 2019.

[29] Not bad, but not life-changing either. As Martha King has said: "[Publishing in *The New American Poetry*] wasn't going to change their life the way that being a star painter would change your life so you could buy a house in the Hamptons. The people in *The New American*

2 RAW AMERICANS: THE PERSISTENCE OF *THE NEW AMERICAN...* 17

Some contributors were unsatisfied with Allen's proposed rate, however. Robert Duncan voiced early concerns about the payments, which were the cause of one of his first (of many) hesitations regarding the anthology. Duncan wrote to Allen in 1958 referring to "the Criterion and Faber anthologies – not to mention Caetani,"[30] who offered higher payments than what Allen proposed. He went on to state that a payment of "fifty cents a line will be acceptable," which would have been extremely lucrative for the poets.[31] Attempting to quell Duncan's fears, Allen responded in July:

> The recent *New Poets*[32] anthology paid, I am told, $4 per page (small type and a crowded page), with a somewhat higher fee going to Lowell and Wilbur. The *New Poets* payments were based on the assumption that the anthology would sell some twenty thousand. I cannot be so sanguine for the anthology I project; we'll be fortunate if we sell 10,000 in a period of several years. In other words my payments to the poets are scaled according to the advance Grove will pay me on their sales expectations. There is no magical way the rate of payment can be made to rise to the level of the Princess Caetani! If you insist on a higher rate of payment, then I shall have to severely restrict the amount of space I devote to your work – which I very much do not wish to do since I hope to show you as one of the 4 major poets of the decade.[33]

Allen's humble sales projections here are contradicted in a later letter to Duncan, in which he says sales of just over 13,000 are "rather disappointing," as he had hoped to sell 20,000 copies of the anthology by the second year.[34] But it was not only Duncan who complained about Allen's rate of

---

Poetry didn't suddenly get into *The New Yorker* and *The New York Times.*" Martha King, Personal Interview, Telephone, April 8, 2018.

[30] These references to "Caetani" and "the Princess" refer to Marguerite Caetani, Princess of Bassiano, who owned and edited the literary journal *Botteghe Oscure* in Rome.

[31] Robert Duncan to Donald Allen, July 12, 1958, Box 9, Folder 9, Donald Allen Collection, MSS 3, Special Collections & Archives, UC San Diego Library.

[32] This refers to *The New Poets of England and America*, edited by Donald Hall, Robert Pack and Louis Simpson, which will be discussed more below.

[33] Donald Allen to Robert Duncan, July 17, 1958, TL: 1, 1959–1964, Box: 77, Robert Duncan Collection, PCMS-0110, The Poetry Collection of the University Libraries, University at Buffalo, The State University of New York.

[34] Donald Allen to Robert Duncan, November 4, 1961, TL: 1, 1959–1964, Box: 77, Robert Duncan Collection, PCMS-0110, The Poetry Collection of the University Libraries, University at Buffalo, The State University of New York.

payment, which, according to James Broughton, did "not necessarily compete with the best-paying reviews."[35] Allen also received complaints from New Directions on behalf of Lawrence Ferlinghetti.[36] But ultimately, all of the included poets consented, and they received varying levels of compensation for their work. Given the anthology's numerous reprints over the years, they likely received more in the long run than they expected.

As an editor with years of experience, Allen was very much aware that in order for his anthology to be published he first had to successfully pitch the project to Barney Rosset. He also would have known that his reputation was in some ways tied to the anthology, which would explain why Allen "worked meticulously, and he went to great pains to investigate the poetic scene, inquiring after new poets, buying all the magazines, going to all the poetry readings and events manqué."[37] Indeed, Allen's archive shows that he was a voracious reader, always staying in touch with new developments. Building on his own knowledge and experience, Allen also engaged in detailed correspondence with many of the poets who would be included in the anthology, seeking their guidance, suggestions and assistance in designing the book that would become *The New American Poetry*. Ultimately it was a successful literary and commercial endeavor whose high sales were a precursor to its outsized influence.

Considering the material success of *The New American Poetry* grounds this examination of the anthology in social reality rather than theory or form and lays the groundwork for an examination of the subjective editorial choices that became the basis of a critical model of Anglophone poetry. This helps to establish the cultural and social context in which Allen was editing, a context that will be examined more closely in later chapters. Though *The New American Poetry* began as a poetry anthology like any other, its influence on both the practice of Anglophone poetry and the critical discourse about it has been extraordinary. Nowhere is this more evident than in subsequent American poetry anthologies.

---

[35] James Broughton to Donald Allen, September 1, 1959, Box 10, Folder 3, Donald Allen Collection, MSS 3, Special Collections & Archives, UC San Diego Library.

[36] James Laughlin to Donald Allen, Box 92, Folder 30, Donald Allen Collection, MSS 3, Special Collections & Archives, UC San Diego Library.

[37] Amiri Baraka, *The Autobiography of LeRoi Jones* (New York: Freundlich, 1984), 160.

2.2 Collecting Poetry, Courting Controversy: American Poetry Anthologies since *The New American Poetry*

The New American Poetry did more than expand the wallets of its contributors. Its presence can be felt even today in the discourse on Anglophone poetry and in the design of and expectations for American poetry anthologies. Bold in its formal iconoclasm, the anthology helped establish a two-camp model of American poetry that many subsequent anthologies have either mirrored or sought to refute.[38] While numerous poetry anthologies refer directly to Allen's, others, like A. Alvarez's *The New Poetry* (1962), make use of Allen's rhetoric of newness or, like Ron Silliman's *In the American Tree* (1986), utilize Allen's geographical style of organization, grouping poets based on region. This brief survey of some of the most significant anthologies of the last 60 years shows how Allen's vision of American poetry and his organization of it have remained influential. Rather than attempting to cover all of the anthologies published since 1960, the purpose here is to sketch the dominant trends of Anglophone poetry anthologies since Allen's by using several examples.[39]

One of the first anthologies to bear the marks of Allen's influence was in England: A. Alvarez's *The New Poetry*. Beyond the similarity of the title and the Jackson Pollock painting on the cover of the second edition (which connects to Allen's poets, whom he suggests are influenced by abstract expressionism in his introduction to *The New American Poetry*),[40]

---

[38] This chapter focuses primarily on American anthologies, with some from the United Kingdom mentioned as well. But the influence of Allen's anthology is not limited to both sides of the Atlantic. Murray Edmond cites several recent anthologies in New Zealand that have been influenced by *The New American Poetry*. See: Murray Edmond, "Trade and True: Anthologies Fifty Years after Donald Allen's *The New American Poetry*," *ka mate ka ora: a new zealand journal of poetry and poetics*, March 2010, http://www.nzepc.auckland.ac.nz/kmko/09/ka_mate09_edmond.pdf, February 8, 2019.

[39] A whole chapter might be dedicated to the influential anthologies edited by Jerome Rothenberg, including *Technicians of the Sacred*. See for example, the April 1, 1979, letter from Rothenberg, perhaps the most significant anthologist since Allen, to Allen: "If I haven't said so before – directly to you, that is – the original anthology has been a key work for me, as a model of what a really contemporary anthology can be and what it can do: not only the right time & place but the composition of the book itself, unquestionably one of the models for my own work..." Jerome Rothenberg to Donald Allen, April 1, 1979, Box 3, Folder 2, Donald Allen Collection, MSS 3, Special Collections & Archives, UC San Diego Library.

[40] Donald Allen, *The New American Poetry 1945–1960* (New York: Grove Press, 1960), xi.

Alvarez's essay "Beyond the Gentility Principle," which introduced his anthology, called for British poets to write from personal extremes that would scratch away the veneer of etiquette he thought was keeping them from writing well about contemporary life. Crossing national lines in this anthology of British poetry by including Robert Lowell and John Berryman at the beginning of the book, Alvarez suggested that British poetry was too tied to morality and gentility and would do well to take on the raw energy and naked self-exploration of poets such as Berryman and Lowell. Justin Quinn has written that Alvarez in a sense refused to correctly read the Beat poets and especially Allen Ginsberg, who was certainly writing from a place beyond gentility.[41] David Wheatley has also commented on this aspect of the anthology: "a reader of Donald Allen's *The New American Poetry* (1960) might find Alvarez's American line-up trading on a gentility principle of its own."[42] There are distinct connections between these two important anthologies but also clear divisions, specifically regarding the belief in a shared British and American tradition.[43] By borrowing from *The New American Poetry* in some ways and contradicting it in others, Alvarez's anthology shows that the dominant narrative about the co-dependence or independence of British and American poetry was still very much up for grabs in the early 1960s.

One of the first American anthologies to show Allen's influence was *A Controversy of Poets* (1965),[44] edited by Paris Leary and Robert Kelly, who were seeking to turn the discourse away from "movements, schools or regional considerations"[45] and back to the poem. The result is more inclusive than *The New American Poetry*, yet, as Ron Silliman has pointed out, the anthology "manifestly reflect[s] the perceived & passionately felt militancy of the various New American tendencies."[46] This is especially clear in

---

[41] See Justin Quinn, *Between Two Fires: Transnationalism and Cold War Poetry* (Oxford: Oxford University Press, 2015), 105–07.

[42] David Wheatley, *Contemporary British Poetry* (London: Palgrave, 2015), 9.

[43] Allen's influence on British poetry certainly did not cease with Alvarez's anthology. *Children of Albion: Poetry of the Underground in Britain* (1969), edited by Michael Horowitz and dedicated to Allen Ginsberg, documented formally experimental, voice-based poetry in England.

[44] For now leaving aside Donald Hall and Robert Pack's *New Poets of England and America: A Second Selection* (New York: Meridian, 1962), which will be examined in later chapters.

[45] Paris Leary and Robert Kelly, *A Controversy of Poets* (New York: Anchor Books, 1965), I.

[46] Ron Silliman, *Silliman's Blog*, October 9, 2002, http://ronsilliman.blogspot.com/2002/10/what-does-it-mean-to-rethink-poetry-of.html, May 15, 2015.

2 RAW AMERICANS: THE PERSISTENCE OF *THE NEW AMERICAN...* 21

the anthology's two postscripts, each written by one of the editors. Taken together, they seem to deny the two-camp model and yet insist upon its existence. As Paris Leary writes:

> This is an anthology in tension: it is designed to bring together poets who have heretofore sat at different tables, to see if there can be any conversation... The reader should be compelled by this anthology to ask questions and to read further for his answers. Is there a "new" poetry in rebellion against a "traditional" poetry? If so, what is new about the rebels and of what tradition are the Establishment stewards? Happily we no longer use the words "beat" or "academic" to describe American poems, but we must go further.[47]

Leary goes on to suggest that terms like "academic" are useless because supposedly non-academic poets such as Charles Olson and Robert Duncan were writing erudite and arcane poetry drawing on numerous literary, cultural and mythological traditions. This is certainly true, but Leary's declaration that terms like "academic" and "beat" were no longer used was wishful thinking, like his belief that the reading public could "go further." Poets, critics and readers would be mired in these divisions for decades to come.

Where Leary suggests that formal divisions were no longer useful, Kelly seems to contradict his co-editor, protesting the continued use of traditional form in American poetry:

> Literally perverse to me is the presumption of the fatuity of some poets who choose to hum in the measures of Donne or Herbert about important human issues to a generation that has experienced Auschwitz, Nagasaki, Algeria, and the Congo. That is pure escapism, and can catch only the saturated ears of an audience attuned to the reviews and the world of little-magazine infighting... More deeply, it is a betrayal too of the very achievement of the masters they follow, those masters who, whatever else their businesses, sang in their own voices in their own time.[48]

The New American Poetry did not invent the debate between formal and free verse, but it did perpetuate the debate, and *A Controversy of Poets* weighed in on it, explicitly positioning itself in relation to the two-camp

[47] Leary and Kelly, 560.
[48] Leary and Kelly, 564.

model and politicizing poetic form. This stance would remain prevalent for American poetry anthologies, even as the tables that Leary mentioned began to turn.

By the late 1970s, the division in American poetry would become more defined. While the work of many of the poets in *The New American Poetry* gained a wide readership and once-controversial figures such as Allen Ginsberg found places in the academy, voice-based free verse came to characterize much of the poetry written in the United States and Britain. Numerous formal poets, including Robert Lowell, W. S. Merwin and James Wright, moved away from received forms, with Wright writing as early as 1969 that "rhymed iambics" were something that "no fashionable poet would be caught dead writing these days."[49] As Langdon Hammer writes, discussing this period: "The formalism that had been the dominant style when [James] Merrill began writing was becoming an increasingly eccentric pursuit, displaced by the free verse of the creative-writing programs and the impersonal writing of Language Poetry."[50] But two groups are necessary for a division, and there were certainly many poets, like James Merrill, who continued to write in received forms. This led to the development of two very different movements in American poetry, the new formalists and the language poets, both of whom sought to move beyond, or at least push back against, what by then had become known as the work of "the New American poets." It was in this climate that Eric Torgersen declared a "Cold War in Poetry" in the pages of *The American Poetry Review* in 1982.[51]

During the 1980s, poetic form continued to be politicized in interesting ways. Back in 1965 Kelly had suggested it was perverse to write in received form about modern atrocities. Two decades later, Diane Wakoski would refer to the new formalism as un-American. Her essay "The New Conservatism in American Poetry," published in 1986, is fascinating, as this liberal, free-verse poet makes the same accusations made by conservative critics in the 1940s and 1950s against poets not writing in form.[52] The sense that free verse rather than formal verse is specifically American was,

---

[49] Anne Wright and Saundra Rose Maley, eds., *A Wild Perfection: The Selected Letters of James Wright* (New York: Farrar, Strauss and Giroux, 2005), 352.

[50] Langdon Hammer, *James Merrill: Life and Art* (New York: Alfred A. Knopf, 2015), 748.

[51] Eric Togerson, "Cold War in Poetry: Notes of a Conscientious Objector," *American Poetry Review* 11 (July-Aug. 1982): 31–34.

[52] See Alan Filreis, *Counter-Revolution of the Word* (Chapel Hill: University of North Carolina Press, 2008).

2 RAW AMERICANS: THE PERSISTENCE OF *THE NEW AMERICAN...*

as I argue below, a result of Allen's anthology and the way it helped conflate British poetry with tradition and American poetry with innovation.

This reversal, combined with language poetry's desire to move away from the voice-based writing of *The New American Poetry*, summed up by Robert Grenier's essay "On Speech" published in 1971, in which he famously exclaims "I HATE SPEECH,"[53] suggests that both free-verse poets like Wakoski and Language Poets had reduced the complex social and poetic legacy of Allen's anthology to formal considerations above all. Thus, by the mid-1980s, both language poets and new formalists could present themselves as rebellious outsiders reclaiming the language from the meaningless, overly subjective, traditional and/or experimental barbarians. Timothy Steele consolidated this sense with his study *Missing Measures: Modern Poetry and the Revolt Against Meter* (1990), as did editors Mark Jarman and David Mason with their anthology *Rebel Angels: 25 Poets of the New Formalism* (1996). Allen summed up these developments in a letter to Marjorie Perloff in 1996 regarding *The Postmoderns*, published in 1982:

> Some twenty years had elapsed since the 1960 pub. of NAP and the whole poetry scene in the US had undergone a transformation. Many of the "outsider" poets in 1960 now were on faculties of Colleges & universities with several volumes of verse in print and their reputation securely established. Meanwhile a new generation of poets had matured and poetry readings, poetry publications, books & mags had proliferated; there were even govt. grants to poets, small press publishers, distributors, etc. So that the revising of NAP required a very different perspective: a good deal of what had seemed intriguing and original in the early Beat days, now no longer held much interest. At the same time the many stalwart imitators of the original NAP poets, esp. O'Hara, now seemed quite uninterestingly un-new.[54]

[53] Ron Silliman, *In the American Tree* (Orono: National Poetry Foundation, 2007), xvii.

[54] Donald Allen to Marjorie Perloff, August 24, 1996, Box 93, Folder 5, Donald Allen Collection, MSS 3, Special Collections & Archives, UC San Diego Library. Further evidence of the effect of *The New American Poetry* on American poetry can be found in Allen's comments to George Butterick in 1977: "I think that it would be impossible to do a NAP today. In 1959 it was possible because there was a development emerging in all its varied glory and there were fewer poets that [*sic*] to be taken into account and naturally fewer poems that had to be considered. Even so that was a considerable job! Today it seems to me we can only aim at a well-designed teaching tool." Donald Allen to George Butterick, March 18, 1977, Box 14, Folder 7, Donald Allen Collection, MSS 3, Special Collections & Archives, UC San Diego Library.

Allen wasn't the only one to feel this way. Language poetry claimed affinity with the poets in Allen's anthology, but most practitioners believed that speech-based poetry had run its course. Silliman's *In the American Tree* (1986) is the first comprehensive collection of these poets. Silliman references *The New American Poetry* at several points in his introduction,[55] divides his anthology into sections labeled "West" and "East," geographic distinctions reminiscent of Allen's, and includes a statement on poetics section like Allen's anthology. And, as the text on the back cover of the anthology states: "*In the American Tree* does for a new generation of American poets what Don Allen's *The New American Poetry* did for an earlier generation." Even as language poetry sought to move beyond the achievements of the poets in Allen's anthology, the organization and presentation of *In the American Tree* reiterated Allen's vision of American poetry. This would remain true of many anthologies published in the following decades.

Douglas Messerli's *From the Other Side of the Century* (1994) organizes 35 poets Messerli labels "innovators and outsiders" into four "gatherings": Cultural-mythic poets, Urban poets, Language poets and Performance poets, categories that update Allen's. Several other anthologies that appeared at this time, including Eliot Weinberger's *American Poetry Since 1950* (1993) and Paul Hoover's *Postmodern American Poetry* (1994), explicitly attempt to align themselves with Allen's anthology and its legacy. As Weinberger writes: "For decades, American poetry has been divided into two camps,"[56] a quote later cited by Cole Swenson in her introduction to the anthology *American Hybrid* (2009), edited by Swenson and David St. John. Hoover's *Postmodern American Poetry* (1994) similarly places Allen's anthology at the beginning of a split between academic and avant-garde: "In analyzing American poetry after 1945, it is traditional to point to the so-called battle of the anthologies that occurred with the publication of *New Poets of England and America* (1962)... and *The New American Poetry: 1945–1960.*"[57] That Hoover refers to the 1962 second edition of Hall's anthology rather than the first edition, published in 1957 and titled *The New Poets of England and America*, is just one example of the widespread historical slippage that makes a reexamination of this period necessary. The fact that the primary

---

[55] Allen, xvii, xix.

[56] Eliot Weinberger, *American Poetry Since 1950* (New York: Marsilio Publishers, 1993), xi.

[57] Paul Hoover, *Postmodern American Poetry* (New York: W.W. Norton, 1994), xxxv.

documents of such a key moment in literary history could be mislabeled points to a complexity that goes beyond mere definite articles.

Referring directly to *The New American Poetry* and *The New Poets of England and America* in her preface to *American Hybrid*, Swenson suggests that the poets included in *American Hybrid* show "hybrid" characteristics, combining elements of the poetry in Allen's anthology with the formal poetry in Hall's anthology, thus apparently rendering the two-camp model outdated. Swenson writes, "the notion of a fundamental division in American poetry has become so ingrained that we take it for granted."[58] It bears repeating that this "fundamental division" was first promoted internationally with the publication of Allen's anthology. The desire for a poetry that would bridge that division goes back to the same period. As early as 1964, critic Chad Walsh wrote:

> One can dream, of course, about some... synthesis of the two strands, retaining the formal perfection of the Academics... and retaining also the bardic scope and dionysian outcry of the Wild Men... Perhaps such a synthesis would produce the phenomenon of 'hybrid vigor,' which has been observed by producers of seed corn...[59]

It is a testament to the influence of the bifurcated model of American poetry that Allen's anthology promoted that it took so long for poets and anthologists to take up this suggestion.

While *American Hybrid* purports to show that American poetry is surmounting the division between cooked and raw, it also helps strengthen the assumption of such a split. The editors take the fundamental division for granted as much as they claim readers do. And while a handful of anthologies does not account for more than a half-century of American poetry subsequent to *The New American Poetry*, it indicates that Allen's concepts were adopted uncritically by subsequent editors of anthologies, which are often used as teaching tools and thus influence the way generations of readers think about American poetry. With each subsequent mention of a formal division, and with each further suggestion that it is useful to arrange poems along geographic lines or with vague group names, those concepts—limiting though they may be—become further engrained

---

[58] Cole Swensen and Robert St. John, *American Hybrid* (New York: W.W. Norton, 2009), xii.

[59] Chad Walsh, "The war between Iambs and Ids," *Book Week*, July 26, 1964, 9.

in the minds of readers, editors and poets, obscuring both the similarities among poets of each "camp" and the deeper, sometimes more significant, divisions that go beyond form.

Allen's influence hasn't been confined to anthologies. Another development that suggests the continued impact of *The New American Poetry* is the fact that "New American" has emerged as a name of a movement, a style of poetry that is considered definitive and categorical. This began several decades ago, as a letter from Marjorie Perloff to Donald Allen in 1998 suggests:

> In England, they call the New York School and Beats, the New Americans. All because of your book. There's much talk of the New Americans versus the language poets etc. New Americans includes Ginsberg, Creeley, Dorn along with O'Hara and Ashbery and Koch and it's not a bad term.[60]

This did not only happen in England, nor did it cease in the 1990s. In John Wieners's *Selected Poems* (2015), for example, the poet is referred to as "a founding member of the 'New American' poetry that flourished in America after the Second World War."[61] A review of the same book published in the *Boston Globe* refers to "that insta-canonized cadre of Donald Allen's landmark 1960 anthology, 'The New American Poets, [*sic*]'" and calls Wieners' contemporaries "his fellow News."[62] And, as the curatorial text in an exhibition at Boston's Institute for Contemporary Art, *Leap Before You Look: Black Mountain College 1933–1957* (2015), suggested: "The college played a critical role in shaping many major concepts in post-war art and education, including assemblage, new American poetry, modern dance and music." Thus Allen's book, a subjective conception of post-war Anglophone poetry, has become a model that defines poets who continued to develop for decades after the anthology was published. *The New American Poetry* has not only framed American poetry as a concept, it has also provided the lens through which we read many of our most beloved Anglophone poets, and do not read others.

---

[60] Marjorie Perloff to Donald Allen, October 12, 1998, Box 57, Folder 12, Donald Allen Collection, MSS 3, Special Collections & Archives, UC San Diego Library.

[61] Robert Dewhurst, et al., eds., *Supplication: Selected Poems of John Wieners* (Seattle: Wave Books, 2015), 313.

[62] Michael Andor Brodeur, "For a Singular Poet, an Overdue Fresh Look," *Boston Globe*, October 18, 2015, N25.

The lineage of influence from *The New American Poetry* to later anthologies is clear. Since 1960, Allen's anthology has affected the way that American poetry has been editorialized and anthologized. The most significant poetry anthologies of these decades have either perpetuated Allen's model or reacted against it. While influencing later anthologists, Allen's anthology has also helped entrench the concept of "New American" as a defining characteristic for poets and has promoted the perception of American poetry as split irreversibly between academic and avant-garde.

2.3 THE NEW POETS VERSUS THE NEW POETRY: THE BINARY OF ACADEMIC AND AVANT-GARDE

Robert Lowell's famous binary of cooked and raw was immediately utilized by critics,[63] because it seemed to deftly capture the perceived distance between academic and avant-garde poetry in the 1950s and get to the heart of one of the age's chief anxieties for American poets: the issue of poets in the academy. This topic had caused nervous discussion since the mid-1940s, when the GI Bill and the founding of literary studies programs altered the relationship between poets and universities. This was exacerbated by the anti-academic bias of Allen's anthology and by the interpretation of *The New American Poetry* and *The New Poets of England and America* as adversarial anthologies and a complete picture of the poetry being written at the time. But the binary of academic and avant-garde ignores the stylistic overlaps and personal relationships among supposedly antagonistic poets during the post-war period and has had a detrimental effect on the way Anglophone poetry is perceived on both sides of the Atlantic. Examining the way that Allen developed this anti-academic bias out of a complex social and literary landscape complicates what now seems to be a clear-cut difference, thanks to the overwhelming success of Allen's anthology.

In the early stages of developing *The New American Poetry*, Allen wrote to Charles Olson describing the project in September 1958: "The academic poets of the decade are well enough represented in the Meridian Books anthology edited by Donald Hall, and others, and I do not plan to

---

[63] See, for example, Harvey Shapiro, writing in *The New York Times Book Review* just after the anthology's publication: "The anthology before us is the first extensive collection... of the 'raw' poetry." Harvey Shapiro, "Rebellious Mythmakers," *The New York Times Book Review*, August 28, 1960, 6.

28   S. DELBOS

include their work in the anthology I am compiling."[64] But even earlier, in May 1958, Ginsberg had written to Donald Allen, citing recent poems by Robert Lowell, Louis Simpson and John Hollander and concluding: "I don't know if you're including any 'academic' poetry, but I mention those in case you do intend to. But still it would be great to have a pure new type poetry anthology & leave the formal stance where it belongs in madison ave anthologies."[65] It is interesting that at this point even Ginsberg, a central poet of the anthology and an anti-academic poet if there ever was one, considered it possible that Allen would include academic poets. That was not to be, of course. In July 1958, the editor wrote to Duncan describing his "tentative decisions: to exclude all academic poets, to omit translation, to omit prose poems."[66] The choice of the verb "exclude" here in contrast to "omit" is revealing of Allen's attitude toward what he called academic poets. The main representative of these poets, and the book to which Allen was referring in his letter to Olson, was *The New Poets of England and America*. Taken together, these anthologies would have a significant effect on Anglophone poetry, as suggested above. But the two books that would set off the anthology wars did not only represent a formal division in American poetry, they represented two sides of an argument about what American poetry was and what it should be.

These two anthologies were immediately recognized as opposite poles, with several reviewers noting that no poet was included in both. But more important than their clear differences was the fact that these two anthologies were understood to include between them the whole of Anglophone poetry. In this regard, Thomas Parkinson's review of Allen's anthology in the *San Francisco Examiner* is representative:

> [*The New American Poetry*] fills an obvious gap in anthologies of current poetry, and along with the Meridian *New Poets of England and America*, this book gives a comprehensive image of poetry since 1945. The Meridian

---

[64] Maud, 47.

[65] Allen Ginsberg to Donald Allen, May, 1958, Box 10, Folder 15, Donald Allen Collection, MSS 3, Special Collections & Archives, UC San Diego Library.

[66] Donald Allen to Robert Duncan, July 8, 1958, Box 9, Folder 9, Donald Allen Collection, MSS 3, Special Collections & Archives, UC San Diego Library. There isn't space here to explore the way the landscape of Anglophone poetry might look significantly different if Allen had welcomed translations and prose poems. Does the wide utilization of the prose poem among language poets stem in part from the form's absence in *The New American Poetry* and thus its seeming freshness for later generations?

book is made up of academic poets, and the two books together show clearly the split in American culture between the formalistic academic and the experimental.[67]

Parkinson wasn't alone in believing that reading both anthologies would provide a "comprehensive image" of post-war poetry in English. That image mostly included white men, of whom the academic poets were more uptight and formal and the non-academic poets were more spontaneous and liberated. The belief that two anthologies could be comprehensive of all of this period's poetry was probably due largely to the obvious differences between the two collections. Wright, who was included in *The New Poets of England and America*, was an exception in that he wrote bitterly about the poverty of American poetry as represented by both anthologies. In a review wittily titled "The Few Poets of England and America," he wrote:

> Two signs of the time are those two anthologies, *The New Poets of England and America*, and *The New American Poetry*. In spite of certain ostensible differences concerning which sympathetic critics of each anthology have been rather more than sufficiently vocal, the two books are astonishingly similar in their vanity, in the general effect of dullness which they produce, and in their depressing clutter of anxious poetasters shrieking their immortality into the void.[68]

But Wright is a notable exception that proves the rule. By looking at opposite corners represented by the two anthologies, most editors and critics missed much of the middle ground, which, without much attention given to it after 1960, dwindled to invisibility. Golding has termed this "the 'negative mirror' critique,"[69] whereby critics seemed unable to define *The New American Poetry* on its own terms and instead contrasted it with *The New Poets of England and America* and other existing publications. Golding argues that this had the effect of "underplaying the genuine differences between the traditions upon which Allen and Hall, Pack, and

---

[67] Thomas Parkinson, "A Look at American Poetry since 1945: Some Funny, Some Satiric and Many from San Francisco," *San Francisco Examiner*, July 10, 1960, 7.

[68] James Wright, "The Few Poets of England and America," *The Minnesota Review*, 1/2 (Winter, 1961): 248.

[69] Golding, 206.

30   S. DELBOS

Simpson drew; and overlooking... internal difference."[70] I would argue that this type of critique has also underplayed, if not completely obscured, the genuine *similarities* among post-war American poets who were supposedly so diametrically opposed. It is also crucial to point out that Allen and many of the poets in the anthology themselves promoted this type of critique. Allen cited it in his preface to *The New American Poetry*, his co-editor Warren Tallman cited it again in his preface to *The Poetics of the New American Poetry*,[71] and the vehemently anti-academic writing and correspondence of many of these poets support exactly this type of reading.

Whether termed raw and cooked, hip and square, or academic and avant-garde, division has become central to the identity of American poetry since 1960. By excluding all of the poets in *The New Poets of England and America*, Allen's anthology reinforced a sense of division between tradition and innovation. After 1960, the poets in *The New Poets of England and America* appeared more academic than innovative and more uptight than ever before. But a glance at the rhyming ballads of Robert Creeley and Helen Adam, or the rhymes of Brother Antoninus and Bruce Boyd in Allen's anthology, or the non-rhyming, colloquial poetry of W. S. Graham and May Swenson[72] in the Hall, Pack and Simpson anthology shows just how limited this perception is. Creeley himself "was like [Wilbur, Lowell, and Berryman] a formalist of the sort that New Critics celebrated in the 1940s and 1950s, when he began writing."[73] And further, Swenson's poem "The Key to Everything," included in *The New Poets of England and America*, would not feel out of place in *The New American Poetry*:

> Is there anything I can do
> or has everything been done
> or do
> you prefer somebody else to do
> it or don't
> you trust me to do

---

[70] Golding, 207.

[71] Warren Tallman, "Preface," *The Poetics of the New American Poetry* (New York: Grove, 1973), ix.

[72] Edward Field, included in *The New American Poetry*, specifically mentions Swenson as a poet he felt affinity toward. Edward Field, Interview, Email, January 14, 2014.

[73] Edward Halsey Foster, *Understanding the Black Mountain Poets* (Columbia: University of South Carolina Press, 1995), 104.

it right or is it hopeless and no one can do
a thing...[74]

The publication of *The New American Poetry* would obscure these similarities and stylistic overlaps, alienating even some poets in Allen's anthology, like Brother Antoninus, who wrote to the editor upon reading the anthology:

> Actually I guess my problem is that I fall between the two camps. After the Hall-Pack-Simpson anthology I was all for a general opening out of the line, but with your anthology, seeing how far many of them are willing to go, and have gone, then I find myself cutting back to a more conservative structure, more traditional formal values. I guess it seems to me the poor Muse is being rent between the extremes of academicism and beat. It looks like I will be 'beat to the square and square to the beat' as long as I live.[75]

When somewhat arbitrary divisions are drawn so emphatically, they will inevitably mischaracterize some poets and leave others out of the discourse entirely. What Allen's framework possessed in terms of drama and novelty it was missing in terms of accuracy and sensitivity.

Allen's anti-academic bias is clearly expressed in his introduction to the anthology, where he writes that the shared characteristic of the poets therein is their "total rejection of all those qualities typical of academic verse."[76] What those qualities actually were is not established, causing critics such as David Herd to note that this claim is "slackly formulated"[77] and Katherine Chapman Harrison to call "academic... a wide term."[78] Golding has gone farther, arguing that "rather than an external and easily located 'enemy,' the academy stands metonymically for an internalized set of constraints operating on all New American poets."[79] This harmonizes with what Donald Hall has said: "Remember that 'academic' had nothing to do with teaching at colleges. It was like the Royal Academy of Art in England, and that meant academic in a kind of conventional sense of belonging to

---

[74] Hall, Pack and Simpson, 301–302.

[75] Brother Antoninus to Donald Allen, July 10, 1960, Box 10, Folder 2, Donald Allen Collection, MSS 3, Special Collections & Archives, UC San Diego Library.

[76] Allen, xi.

[77] Woznicki, 156.

[78] Katherine Garrison Chapin, "Fifteen Years of New Writing," *The New Republic*, January 9, 1961, 25.

[79] Golding, 204.

32   S. DELBOS

an established group."[80] But it's important to note that not all of the poets in Allen's anthology felt such enmity toward the academy, although many critics and reviewers of the anthology have assumed that Allen spoke for the poets in his introduction. It is not simply that all the poets "align[ed] themselves with abstract painting, experimental music and jazz," as Allen claimed, or that they had "reject[ed] whatever they feel is 'academic,'"[81] but rather that Allen did that for them.

Allen's anthology waded into an anxious debate about the writer as professor which reached its apogee in the late 1950s and which did indeed make the academy, contrary to Golding, an external force. There are at least three incontrovertible aspects of *The New Poets of England and America*: all of its editors held teaching jobs, it insisted on the shared tradition of British and American poetry and most of the poems therein utilize traditional rhyme and meter. The remainder of this section will examine the distinction between avant-garde and academic poetry, somewhat controversial terms that were widespread in post-war America despite their imprecision.

The pages of literary journals after World War II were strewn with intellectual hand-wringing regarding the effect that the increasing number of poets and writers in the academy would have on American literature. As Charles A. Fenton wrote in his essay "The Writer as Professor" in 1955, "As a subject for debate and invective... this phenomenon of the writer as professor is now a fixed and recurrent one. It is, indeed, no longer a phenomenon; it is a fact."[82] Similarly, in 1958, Louise Bogan would review *The New Poets of England and America*, citing "a widespread belief that close contact with academic life is dangerous for the artist."

> In spite of such warnings, poets of the younger generation have taken to the teaching profession in numbers, and some of the results of this association are coming to light. A recent anthology, *New Poets of England and America*... is edited by three young men who have themselves received fellowships, grants and other honors and who now teach... Although their

---

[80] Donald Hall, Personal Interview, Email, February 11, 2014.

[81] Katherine Garrison Chapin, "Fifteen Years of New Writing," *The New Republic*, January 9, 1961, 25.

[82] James A. Fenton, "The Writer as Professor," *New World Writing 7* (New York City: The New American Library of World Literature, Inc., 1955), 164.

2 RAW AMERICANS: THE PERSISTENCE OF *THE NEW AMERICAN...*   33

work seems to have escaped excessive conventional pressures, academic or otherwise, they all... write in form.[83]

Bogan elaborates on this idea in a later review of Auden, writing: "a teaching poet's followers, by the weight of their numbers and the intensity of their attention, can exhaust the very powers they admire."[84] By 1964, the academic poet had become a cliché. As Chad Walsh wrote laconically that year:

> For the last 20 years the typical life story of the up-and-coming young poet has been a B.A. (probably in English), a fellowship to a summer writers' workshop, an M.A., possibly a Ph.D., an instructorship on some campus that wants a live poet. He burrows in and achieves status and tenure; he creates a widening network with similar poets on other campuses; perhaps he founds a literary quarterly in which he publishes the work of his colleagues at neighboring schools; he gives readings on their campuses...[85]

While this seems very straightforward, the term "academic" as applied to poetry had multiple meanings in the 1950s. Obviously, the growing number of poets who taught at colleges and universities were considered academic. This phenomenon can be traced to three sources: the establishment by the New Critics of the study of literature as a viable topic for higher education; the founding of the nation's first creative writing program in Iowa by Wilbur Schramm in 1936; and the GI Bill, ratified after World War II in part to ease the strain on the American economy and job market of the millions of American soldiers returning from the war.

By funding university education for demobilized soldiers, the government not only improved the skills of the workforce as the American economy expanded in the years following the war, it also staggered the return of these soldiers to work.[86] The result, for poets, was not just that many were able to afford a first-class education, which is exemplified by the fact that Donald Hall, Frank O'Hara, Robert Creeley, John Ashbery, James Schuyler and Kenneth Koch were contemporaries at Harvard and Galway Kinnell and W. S. Merwin were contemporaries at Princeton. The GI Bill also gave these poets and others the necessary credentials to teach. Writing

---

[83] Louise Bogan, "Verse," *The New Yorker*, March 29, 1958, 122–124.

[84] Louise Bogan, "Verse," *The New Yorker*, October 8, 1960, 198.

[85] Chad Walsh, "The war between Iambs and Ids," *Book Week*, July 26, 1964, 2.

[86] Marc Myers, *Why Jazz Happened* (Berkeley: University of California Press, 2013), 57.

34   S. DELBOS

in 1961, Robert Duncan cited "a new class… of university instructors in the arts… and a particular academic culture:"

> In music the twelve-tone system, in painting at the present time hand-me-downs from the abstract expressionism of the 40s and early 50s, and in poetry the urbane conventional poetry of Auden or more recently Wilbur. For this whole professional class, setting standards of taste and moderating the imagination are their historical destinies.[87]

This is one of many commentaries on the disparities among American poets during the post-war years. Edward Brunner is also insightful on the uneasy relationship between the poet and the American academy during this period:

> A wide range of different circumstances made issues of discipline important in the 1950s, including the new and still somewhat uncertain alliance between the university and the practicing poet (what would be the grounds for winning tenure?); the increased social mobility that brought to the campus large numbers of first-generation college students unclear about the protocols of the educational establishment; and for male poets, a nagging defensiveness that emerged when the vocation of writing poetry, which was widely associated with emotional expressiveness, was extended professional status.[88]

Here Brunner suggests why poets who were teachers might strive for formal perfection in their verse, as the writing of poetry became part of their professional resume.[89] Clearly, the above quotes suggest the discomfort felt about poets becoming professors during this period. Take Robert Lowell, citing Randall Jarrell, in his famous cooked and raw speech: "the modern world has destroyed the intelligent poet's audience and given him students,"[90] a quote which also suggests that poets without students are not intelligent. Thanks to slights like this, and because many of the leading

[87] Robert Duncan, January 8, 1961, Notebooks, 1940–1984, Robert Duncan Collection, PCMS-0110, The Poetry Collection of the University Libraries, University at Buffalo, The State University of New York.

[88] Edward Brunner, *Cold War Poetry* (Chicago: University of Illinois Press, 2004), 94.

[89] This also had important implications for what these poets would write about, which will be discussed in Chap. 4.

[90] Robert Lowell, "1960 National Book Award Acceptance Speech," http://www.nationalbook.org/nbaacceptspeech_rlowell.html, May 1, 2015.

mainstream journals of the time were associated with universities, receiving funding and grants through them, poets outside the academy began to perceive that a reigning orthodoxy was standardizing American poetry without consulting them. This led, in many cases, to anger as opposed to the anxiety that many academic poets felt.

In the late 1950s, the language that avant-garde poets used to talk about the academy turned particularly vehement. In contrast to his earlier letter to Allen, in which Ginsberg suggested that the editor might include some academic poets in his anthology, the poet wrote in a letter to Allen in 1960: "A word on the Academics: poetry has been attacked by an ignorant & frightened bunch of bores who don't understand how it's made, & the trouble with these creeps is they wouldn't know poetry if it came up and buggered them in broad daylight."[91] This was a sentiment echoed by Cid Corman, who gave Allen some vivid advice on designing the anthology, writing in 1958: "I would advise keeping the academic crappers out: I mean Hall and the Yale series."[92] Thus while intellectuals wondered how writers in the academy would affect the style of American literature, a deep undercurrent of resentment was welling up among poets who felt they were disadvantaged by a disinterest in or a lack of academic credentials, as well as their unwillingness to write and live in the middle-class, middle-of-the-road style of the academies.

From one point of view these distinctions are simple to draw. If a poet teaches at a university, edits an academic journal or publishes in them exclusively, he or she is academic. But did Olson, Ginsberg and Creeley become academic poets when they took teaching positions? And weren't all of them highly educated themselves? As Bogan wrote in her review of *The New American Poetry*: "the proportion of intelligence and of regular academic training in all these groups is large, and a feeling for language, plain and fancy, appears more often than not."[93] As a critical category, academic is permeable at best. Hall illuminates this by revealing that John Ashbery was originally to be published in *The New Poets of England and America* but was the last poet excluded, for lack of space:

---

[91] Allen Ginsberg to Donald Allen, 1960, Box 10, Folder 15, Donald Allen Collection, MSS 3, Special Collections & Archives, UC San Diego Library.

[92] Cid Corman to Donald Allen, April 16, 1958, Box 11, Folder 12, Donald Allen Collection, MSS 3, Special Collections & Archives, UC San Diego Library.

[93] Louise Bogan, "Verse," *The New Yorker*, October 8, 1960, 200.

36   S. DELBOS

> Therefore John Ashbery got picked for the Donald Allen book, and thus (as
> it were) became a Beat poet. Don Allen's book printed all sorts of different
> poets, many totally un-Beat. Pretty much our bunch was called "academic"
> and a lot of them, including more conventional, "Beat."[94]

The landscape of American poetry would appear different today if Ashbery had been included in Hall, Pack and Simpson's anthology rather than *The New American Poetry*. What at the time seemed a simple editorial decision has had profound effects, as did Allen's insistence on excluding academic poets. And it seems easy to understand Allen's motivations: for an editor who was partial to non-mainstream verse in the late 1950s, universities, with their rigid hierarchies, seemed a breeding ground of stultifying conservatism. The debate about poet-teachers was old news by then, at least for poets who were not teachers, and from Allen's point of view it would have seemed impossible for a poet to be both "new" and associated with the academy.

Wright provides an alternative point of view on the apparent conservatism of poets writing in received form in the 1950s. Citing the fact that he had "helplessly and nauseously swung back and forth terrified" between the poetic styles of Walt Whitman and Edwin Arlington Robinson, he continues:

> there was a time for me – as there was, inevitably, for every young poet writing in America right now – to commit himself to the traditional syntax and the traditional meters of English verse; for many of the writers who preceded us were so sloppy that we had to begin not by revolting against competence and restriction, because except for a few writers there was no competence, but rather to begin by creating *our own* competence.[95]

Here Wright complicates the common notion that American poets writing in rhyme and meter in the 1950s were happy slaves to the academy and tradition. Instead, what Wright describes is a contentious relationship with tradition and one that depended on pushing against predecessors as strongly as the poets of Allen's anthology did, even if those acts of poetic rebellion were not completely evident to the average reader in terms of form. So academic versus avant-garde as a critical division in post-war American poetry is neither as simple nor as accurate as it sounds. And yet,

---

[94] Hall, Interview, February 11, 2014.
[95] Wright and Maley, 131–132.

in many respects our critical understanding of Anglophone poetry in the mid-twentieth century and beyond continues to rely upon these terms.

If there is a division among these poets that can be located in their poems, it is what Wright terms the "competence" with form and meter that distinguished his work and that of his contemporaries in *The New Poets of England and America* from what Silliman has termed "a general emphasis on the materiality of language" which allows the poetry in *The New American Poetry* to come alive "precisely because it resists the conception of a transparent referential language."[96] This is an interesting formulation but one that ignores the complex relationships to tradition that poets on both sides of the divide felt during the mid-twentieth century, a time of renewal and reconsideration for all aspects of American life. Clearly, what Duncan termed a "common concern with the language, with new possibilities in form,"[97] among poets in Allen's anthology would have applied to many poets writing in received form and meter as well. Douglas M. Davis identified these overlaps in 1966, writing:

> The New Poetry is far more diverse than the anthologists and commentators have yet allowed. The stylistic difference between Allen Ginsberg and Gary Snyder, for example, is as wide as the difference between either and a safely neoclassic academic like Richard Wilbur... Indeed, the best of the New Poets – the Olsons, Duncans and Creeleys – are now no strangers to the lecture circuit, to foundation grants, and to some of the mainstream poetry magazines... As bardic as all this sounds, it is in fact a highly sophisticated approach to the mystery of language rhythm – and thoroughly in accord with the latest scholarly studies in metrics.[98]

Such balanced accounts of the post-war poetry scene have not been as influential as those that dramatized a split. But for poets who were teachers, turning away from received forms meant turning away from tradition. Since teaching this tradition was the bedrock of employment, there was a great deal at stake in these debates. So it isn't surprising that they came to a head in the late 1950s: inescapable social and professional conditions helped formulate each poet's relationship with literary tradition and with

---

[96] Ron Silliman, "Four Contexts for Three Poems," *Conjunctions* 49 (2007): 298.

[97] Robert Duncan to William Hogan, June 12, 1960, Box 9, Folder 9, Donald Allen Collection, MSS 3, Special Collections & Archives, UC San Diego Library.

[98] Douglas M. Davis, "Where the Poet Finds Fertile Ground," *The National Observer*, July 11, 1966, 24.

38   S. DELBOS

language itself at a moment when it was more important, professionally, than ever before. And all of this was taking place at a time when every division in American life was emphasized, analyzed and politicized.

In hindsight it is easy to see *The New American Poetry* as the triumph of the outsiders, many of whom would soon enter the academy themselves, as well as the triumph of free verse: the simplified formal breakthrough narrative.[99] Despite this success, Allen never abandoned his anti-academic bias. Instead, he would further entrench his position in several future publications that picked up where *The New American Poetry* left off. Warren Tallman, who edited *The Poetics of The New American Poetry* (1973) with Allen, wrote to Allen in 1972 with thoughts about the book they were preparing, citing the way that the discourse had changed, but also calling for a reemphasis of the success of *The New American Poetry* and its opposition to the academy:

> A great many younger university teachers, guys in their 30's, are now increasingly aware that the age of the University Poets is not only over, but that it was a sell. Your book won that battle, or is winning it, and the fact that it was a battle needs to be pointed out. That's one reason that I cite Robert's "Ideas of the Meaning of Form" since it spells the battle out. Another reason, equally important to my mind, is Britain and Europe, where there is a need for clarity, for them to realize that our guys actually do stem from Whitman by way of Pound and Williams. I feel that too many Englishmen and Europeans still look at America assuming that its [*sic*] all one show and very much need to have the lines drawn since much of the reputation of our book will depend finally on how it is received in England and Europe.[100]

Of course, sticking to the anti-academic line was a necessity for Allen and his co-editor, lest the authority of *The New American Poetry* be challenged. Allen's insistence on the division between academic and avant-garde would have a dramatic impact in both the United States and in Britain, where after 1960 "the gap between academic verse and its opposite... became a permanent feature of the landscape, to the consequent

---

[99] James Longenbach, *Modern Poetry After Modernism* (Oxford: Oxford University Press, 1997), vii.

[100] Warren Tallman to Donald Allen, November 26, 1972, Box 14, Folder 1, Donald Allen Collection, MSS 3, Special Collections & Archives, UC San Diego Library.

impoverishment of both."[101] Born out of the professional literary anxiety of the 1950s as well as feelings of resentment against mainstream poets and publications, Allen's insistence on the binary between academic and avant-garde has permanently impoverished the way we conceive of both British and American poetry, smoothing over the complexity of the post-war moment while unhelpfully highlighting formal divisions and erasing underlying similarities. Instead of a single group of stylistically diverse poets confronting their poetic heritage and the lifestyle and policies of their nation at a crucial turning point in its history, Allen's anthology—along with the discourse surrounding it from passive critics who insist on rehashing timeworn debates—presents us with a group of stereotypically adversarial poets strictly divided by style. This has been perpetuated by subsequent anthologies and internalized by whole generations of poets.

Divisions divide, but they also help to classify, which was another central characteristic of the post-war era in the United States. This was the time when Russell Lynes split hairs to define the characteristics of highbrow, lowbrow and middlebrow culture in terms of everything from entertainment to salads in his famous 1949 essay,[102] which was updated by Dwight Macdonald in 1960;[103] when many a literary cocktail party was broken up by discussions of Dalton Trumbo or Alger Hiss;[104] and when Ornette Coleman was physically attacked for playing free jazz.[105] People took sides on every side during the Cold War; poetry was just one of them. Culture and politics were tightly intertwined during this period, and the style of poem one preferred also seemed to indicate one's relative level of conservatism or liberalism, a division that *The New American Poetry* codified on both sides of the Atlantic. After the publication of Allen's anthology, formal poetry not only seemed more conservative, it also seemed more British.

[101] Woznicki, 100.

[102] Russell Lynes, "Highbrow, Lowbrow, Middlebrow" *Harper's*, http://harpers.org/archive/1949/02/highbrow-lowbrow-middlebrow/, May 1, 2015.

[103] Dwight Macdonald, "Masscult and Midcult," *The Partisan Review* 27, no. 4 (1960): 203–233.

[104] Micki McGee, *Yaddo: Making American Culture* (New York: Columbia University Press, 2008), 80.

[105] John Litweiler, *Ornette Coleman: A Harmolodic Life* (New York: William Morrow and Company, Inc.), 83.

2.4 Our Avant-Garde: *The New American Poetry* and the Deconstruction of Transatlantic Anglophone Poetry

The New American Poetry deepened the split between so-called academic and avant-garde poetries and permanently deconstructed the idea of transatlantic Anglophone poetry, especially when critics juxtaposed it with *The New Poets of England and America*, interpreting them as adversarial anthologies that together provided a complete picture of the poetry being written at the time. Allen's anthology made official the association of American poetry with innovation and British poetry with tradition, a sentiment that had been developing among American poets outside of the mainstream for some time. This fit *The New American Poetry* into the rhetoric and reactionary thinking of American Cold War nationalism, as well as an age-old debate about the independence of American poetry from the British.

Allen's anthology was certainly not the first to collect American poetry to the exclusion of British poetry, although in the 1950s transatlantic anthologies like *The New Poets of England and America*, which promoted the shared tradition of American and British poetry, were the norm. Most anthologists at that time would have agreed with editor Robert Pack, who stated, "I've always felt that British and American poetry was a single tradition."[106] *Modern Verse in English 1900–1950* (1958), edited by David Cecil and Allen Tate, is another representative transatlantic poetry anthology, insisting on the complementary traditions of American and British poetry by including T. S. Eliot in the introduction to the American poetry as well as the British. This underscores the fluidity of national affiliation, as does Tate's introduction to the anthology's American poetry, which claims that "Anglo-American… only by convention can be separated."[107] Similarly, the vastly influential New Critical textbook *Understanding Poetry* included poets from both sides of the Atlantic and drew no contrast between American and British poetry. It was precisely this inclusive transatlantic model that Allen sought to disrupt, and did.

Two of the key distinguishing traits of *The New American Poetry* are that it gathered poets from a short period of time and sought to present a

---

[106] Robert Pack, Personal Interview, Phone, February 23, 2014.
[107] David Cecil and Allen Tate, *Modern Verse in English 1900–1950* (New York: Macmillan, 1958), 40.

2 RAW AMERICANS: THE PERSISTENCE OF *THE NEW AMERICAN...* 41

new development in English-language poetry as specifically American. As Corso wrote to Allen in 1959: "there is no real modern American anthology, anthologies usually consist of history or centuries – you've got a decade anthology; not many decades can boast an anthology."[108] That the publication of Allen's anthology roughly coincided with *The New Poets of England and America* meant that the contrasts between the two were heightened, taking on a significance they might not have otherwise. The Hall, Pack and Simpson anthology became a representative of academic verse and also contained British poetry, in contrast to the pure products of America that Allen's anthology promoted. This helped conflate British poetry with tradition and American poetry with newness, spontaneity and originality.

Allen didn't invent this division out of thin air; it was part of the particular way that many of the most significant poets in his anthology thought about the post-war landscape of American poetry. Poets like Charles Olson "did think in terms of rival schools and aesthetics,"[109] and Allen's anthology gave voice to poets who were discontented with the post-war status quo in American poetry. This dissatisfaction, along with the equality of the American academy with British formal tradition in the minds of many poets, is summed up by LeRoi Jones in the "Statements on Poetics" section in Allen's anthology: "We can get nothing from England. And the diluted formalism of the academy (the formal culture of the U.S.) is anaemic & fraught with incompetence and unreality."[110] England and the academy were equal, and equally undesirable. It is a conflation as misleading as that of two anthologies for all of Anglophone poetry and one that was rooted in stereotypical thinking.

Robert Creeley, writing to William Carlos Williams in 1960, suggested that there was a difference between English and American poems and that it came down to temperament: "It is that American poems are often such a close instance of the environment they spring from, are shots from the hip in that way. There's no time for English brooding, etc."[111] Creeley's use of American cowboy imagery is as much a stereotype as his belief that the English were naturally prone to brooding and indicates the shaky

---

[108] Gregory Corso to Donald Allen, December 8, 1959, Donald Allen Collection, MSS 3, Special Collections & Archives, UC San Diego Library.

[109] Clark, 290.

[110] Allen, 425.

[111] Rod Smith, Peter Baker, and Kaplan Harris, *The Selected Letters of Robert Creeley* (Berkeley: University of California Press, 2014), 224.

42   S. DELBOS

foundations of this division. The distinction between shooting and brooding also illustrates how Allen and others including Creeley, Williams and Charles Olson, who insisted that by the mid-century, American verse had established itself as distinct from the British,[112] saw American poets as fast-thinking, innovative, risk-taking and bold. This was in contrast with what they believed British poetry was, namely caught in a stultifying tradition and the academic models taught in school. Playing into these stereotypes, *The New American Poetry* assimilated and nationalized formally experimental Anglophone poetry, which in the post-war years was being written in Canada, Britain, Ireland and Australia as well as in the United States. Chapter 5 will examine the nationalist aspects of Allen's anthology in depth, but now it is helpful to suggest how this topic should frame the discourse on *The New American Poetry*.

The possibility of—and the argument over—a specifically American poetry goes back at least to 1793, when Elihu Hubbard Smith edited *American Poems, Selected and Original*, an anthology that did little to end the debate. As the British essayist Sydney Smith wrote in 1820, Americans should "make it their chief boast... that they are sprung from the same race with Bacon and Shakespeare and Newton."[113] Ralph Waldo Emerson would famously declare the necessity of a distinctly American literature as early as "The American Scholar" in 1837,[114] a call that Walt Whitman heeded, so that in 1917 Harriet Monroe would write: "Probably never, since this country was a nation, need she fear less than now such comparison between her rising and newly risen poets and those of Great Britain." Yet Monroe noted "a deprecatory, apologetic attitude toward American art,"[115] making her statement more of an appeal for support than a declaration of independence. Two years later Louis Untermeyer would note that American poets were marking their singularity by using "language, that used to be borrowed almost exclusively from literature, [but] comes now almost entirely out of life... The intricate versification has given way to lines that reflect and suggest the tones of direct talk, even of ordinary

---

[112] Ralph Maud, *Poet to Publisher: Charles Olson's Correspondence with Donald Allen* (Vancouver: Talonbooks, 2003), 61.

[113] Sydney Smith, *Edinburgh Review*, XXXIII (January 1820), 79–80. Cited in Alexander C. Charles, *Here the Country Lies: Nationalism and the Arts in Twentieth-Century America*, (Bloomington: Indiana University Press, 1980), 3.

[114] Ralph Waldo Emerson, *Essays and Lectures* (New York: Viking Press, 1983), 51.

[115] Harriet Monroe, "Colonialism Again," *Poetry*, X, (May 1917), 94. Accessible at: http://www.poetryfoundation.org/poetrymagazine/browse/10/2#!/20571230/2

conversation..."[116] Crucially, Untermeyer is referring specifically to *American* conversation as distinct from British.

In his introduction to *The New American Poetry*, Allen mentions William Carlos Williams's *Paterson* (1946), *The Desert Music and Other Poems* (1954) and *Journey to Love* (1955) as "the finest achievements of the older generation" that had been published since World War II.[117] Williams was a touchstone of the anthology from the earliest stages, and Allen even asked the older poet for a blurb for the dust jacket.[118] Williams's insistence on the American idiom is well known. Two years before the publication of Olson's "Projective Verse," Williams wrote "The Poem as a Field of Action," which showed how Williams's concept of measure was bound up with his distinction between American and British English: "Where else can what we are seeking arise from but speech? From speech, from American speech as distinct from English speech... from what we *hear* in America."[119]

The New American Poetry completed a debate that had been going on since the earliest days of publication in the United States, and it also seemed to prove that Williams was correct in his insistence on the existence of the American idiom and its worthiness for poetry, a fact not lost on the older poet. Writing to Allen after receiving the anthology, Williams stated: "one thing the present generation has done, established the American idiom and the variable foot in its poetry."[120] And as he phrased it in 1962: "It's all right if you are not intent on being national... The American idiom has much to offer us that the English language has never heard of."[121] Williams here reveals how much the question of American poetry's independence from British tradition was bound up in nationalism.

---

[116] Louis Untermeyer, *Modern American Poetry* (1919). Accessible at: http://www.bartleby.com/104/1000.html

[117] Allen, xi.

[118] Donald Allen to William Carlos Williams, December 23, 1959, Box 93, Folder 27, Donald Allen Collection, MSS 3, Special Collections & Archives, UC San Diego Library.

[119] William Carlos Williams, "The Poem as a Field of Action," *The Poetry Foundation*, http://www.poetryfoundation.org/learning/essay/237854?page=5, May 15, 2019.

[120] William Carlos Williams to Donald Allen, January 7 1960, Donald Allen Collection, MSS 3, Special Collections & Archives, UC San Diego Library.

[121] William Carlos Williams, Interview with Stanley Koehler, *The Paris Review*, 1962. Accessible at: http://www.theparisreview.org/interviews/4486/the-art-of-poetry-no-6-william-carlos-williams

George Orwell suggests that nationalism is "inseparable from the desire for power,"[122] and certainly the efforts of poets like Williams to claim their own independent tradition was something of a power grab. Transnational criticism has begun to challenge nation-based interpretations of literature, but they remain entrenched, in part because they focus power in the hands of both the critics and the poets of a particular country. Allen, by turning away from the dominant model of the transatlantic poetry anthology, was arguing that the innovative poetry being written in the United States during the post-war period was of a separate category from what was being written in Britain, Canada and elsewhere. Perhaps *The New American Poetry* was "anglophobic,"[123] as some have claimed, and it was certainly pro-American. *The New American Poetry* was both influenced by and helped perpetuate the insistence on American nationalism that was commonplace during the Cold War. That Allen's recontextualization of Anglophone poetry should appear in 1960 is significant, given that the following year saw the publication of *The Continuity of American Poetry* by Roy Harvey Pearce. In this study, Pearce argues for the existence of an unbroken line of tradition from the Puritan poets to those of the mid-twentieth century, a tradition that was independent from Britain. Pearce does not mention *The New American Poetry*, but Allen's anthology could easily be interpreted as continuing this tradition.

Despite the detail and erudition of Pearce's work, he does not account for any of the poets included in Allen's anthology, being concerned instead with their predecessors. Pearce's insistence that the strongest characteristic of American poetry is "the dignity of man,"[124] as well as his claim that "American poets have always been conservatives,"[125] does not seem to do justice to the most innovative poetry written in the United States during the post-war years. Yet Pearce does look forward to new possibilities. He predicts that "American poetry, and thus American culture, is moving into a series of new, perhaps radically new, forms."[126] Allen's description of the poets in his anthology as "a strong third generation"[127] of modernist

---

[122] George Orwell, "Notes on Nationalism," *Orwell.ru*, http://orwell.ru/library/essays/nationalism/english/e_nat, May 1, 2015.

[123] Woznicki, 87.

[124] Roy Harvey Pearce, *The Continuity of American Poetry* (Princeton: Princeton University Press, 1961), 4.

[125] Pearce, 4.

[126] Pearce, 6.

[127] Allen, xi.

innovators also suggests a continuity of American poetry. Despite their seeming differences, Allen's and Pearce's national-focused approaches both grew out of the same cultural moment.

Today it is easy to see Pearce's study—which he developed while teaching at The Salzburg Seminar, which was set up to promote American cultural values just a few kilometers from the Iron Curtain—as a product of Cold War cultural warfare and American exceptionalism. And yet, despite the similarities between Allen's and Pearce's interpretations of American poetry during the Cold War, *The New American Poetry* has remained untarnished in this regard. While Allen's anthology is typically considered a definitive break from the past and one that was prescient in its predictions of the way that American poetry would develop from 1960 on, its framework is conventional and its nationalism is anachronistic. By the late 1950s, the vanguard of political theory was already arguing that "the nation and the nation-state are anachronisms in the atomic age."[128]

The New American Poetry was also anachronistic in the sense that it was engaging in a very old argument about the independence of American poetry from British tradition. The anthology effectively put an end to that debate, definitively establishing American poetry as a concept in the minds of readers on both sides of the Atlantic. There is no greater proof of the effects of *The New American Poetry* in this regard than the evolution of opinion exemplified by Donald Hall, who seems to have immediately sensed the significance of Allen's anthology. In his introduction to an anthology of American poetry published in 1969, Hall wrote, "until very recently, American poetry has functioned as part of the English tradition."[129] And, in 1988, when it was even clearer that the effects of Allen's anthology were permanent, Hall wrote: "twenty-six years ago, three American poets – I was one of them – put together *The New Poets of England and America*... as if 'England and America' shared a common enterprise. No longer would anthologists suggest such a thing."[130] This perception was not limited to American poets. Ben Hickman writes insightfully about the impact of Allen's anthology in England and how it inspired efforts in "de-Anglicizing England"[131] by avant-garde British poets who believed that

---

[128] Robert H. Wiebe, *Who We Are: A History of Popular Nationalism* (Princeton: Princeton University Press, 2002), 2

[129] Donald Hall, *American Poetry* (London: Faber and Faber, 1969), 19.

[130] Donald Hall, "Another Island," *Poetry and Ambition: Essays 1982–88* (Ann Arbor: University of Michigan Press, 1988), 85.

[131] Woznicki, 89.

"the American writer seems open to everything that happens in his country"[132] as opposed to British writers who were limited by tradition and class. Allen's anthology clearly achieved the goal of uncoupling American poetry from the British tradition, but it did so at the cost of impoverishing and nationalizing a rich transnational literary moment, an influential impact that is only beginning to be questioned. At the same time, the anthology whitewashed and masculinized a diverse post-war avant-garde in ways that make it seem startlingly out of touch today.

2.5 Bards of the White Citizens' Councils: Gender and Race in *The New American Poetry*

Forty-four poets are published in *The New American Poetry*, only four of whom are women: Helen Adam, Madeline Gleason, Barbara Guest and Denise Levertov.[133] LeRoi Jones is the sole poet of color. This calls to mind a quip by Walter Lowenfels, who described the mainstream poets of the 1950s as "Bards of the White Citizens' Councils."[134] These imaginary councils would look very similar to one made up of the poets included in Allen's anthology. *The New American Poetry* is considered a liberal force in opposition to the conservatism of the academy, yet it fits neatly into the misogynistic, racist tendencies of conservative Cold War America, a realization that must affect our understanding of the anthology as a revolutionary voice in mid-century American culture. Given the continued influence of the anthology, dealing with its shortcomings also prompts us to question our current conceptions of the avant-garde. This topic first piqued the interest of critics in the 1990s, but while many have noted the anthology's imbalances, few have looked into Allen's archives to reveal the reasoning behind the makeup of the anthology and fewer still have placed the anthology into the Cold War framework, which can tell us something about why Allen made the choices he did.

Poet Joanne Kyger was one of the women who submitted poetry to Allen but was rejected. Speaking recently, Kyger was sanguine about this and the lack of African American poets in the anthology:

---

[132] Woznicki, 91.

[133] Out of 52 poets in *The New Poets of England and America*, seven are women.

[134] Walter Lowenfels, "Poetry and Politics," *Liberation*, June 1959, 12.

2 RAW AMERICANS: THE PERSISTENCE OF *THE NEW AMERICAN...*   47

He did include Denise Levertov, Madeline Gleason, from Mill Valley, and Barbara Guest, a friend of his. I'm not sure where else his tastes would have taken him... I submitted some poems for the anthology, but really hadn't written anything as yet that had any cohesive strength... I don't think African American poetry was recognized as such at that time, something that LeRoi Jones was able to guide to more prominence, as Amiri Baraka.[135]

The resigned nature of this statement contradicts a letter that Kyger sent to Allen in 1959, in which she wrote: "Don't you like *my* poetry? Frankly, I think it's more interesting tha[n] Kirby Doyle's and at least three other people I know. However, perhaps you aren't interested in interesting poetry."[136] Allen responded with essentially the same form of rejection letter he sent to every poet who was excluded from the anthology.[137] In her more recent comments, Kyger suggests that Allen was simply following the status quo when including few women and people of color. This harmonizes with the critical consensus of the era, as more than one study has been written on the dominant masculinity and sexism of post-war American poetry and society.[138] But given *The New American Poetry*'s outsized reputation as a liberating force and Allen's reputation as a canny editor, we should expect more from the anthology than a simple representation of the times.

After 1945, American women were expected to leave the jobs many of them had filled for men during the war and go back into the kitchen, where they would play the role of matriarch and homemaker as the nuclear family became the model for conservatism, economic responsibility and the pursuit of the American Dream. As Sara Lennox has written, "Women after 1945, in their specifically female way as wives, mothers, and household managers in a newly configured domestic unit, took on a role of central importance to postwar economic expansion, progress, and the

---

[135] Joanne Kyger, Personal Interview, Email, January 13, 2014.

[136] Quoted in Alan Golding, "*The New American Poetry* Revisited, Again," *Contemporary Literature* 39.2 (1998): 198.

[137] Allen wrote: "Dear Miss Kyger... I do like your poetry but the limits I had to set to the anthology finally made it impossible for me to include any of your work. I regret this very much." Donald Allen to Joanne Kyger, December 28, 1959, Box 11, Folder 12, Donald Allen Collection, MSS 3, Special Collections & Archives, UC San Diego Library.

[138] See Michael Davidson, *Guys Like Us: Citing Masculinity in Cold War Poetics* (Chicago: University of Chicago Press, 2004), and Andrew Mossin, *Male Subjectivity and Poetic Form in "New American" Poetry* (New York: Palgrave Macmillan, 2010).

48   S. DELBOS

triumph of the American Way."[139] The role of the American woman in the early Cold War was irreplaceable, but it gave women little independence or freedom of expression. Elaine Tyler May argues that the model of the post-war home and family, which has generally been considered a throwback to a more nostalgic era of American life, was actually "the first wholehearted effort to create a home that would fulfill virtually all members' personal needs through an energized and expressive personal life."[140] The woman, in the role of mother, wife and caretaker, was crucial to this new conception of the household. This was a time when the freedom and creative choices of women were largely limited to what they would serve for dinner and what brand of appliance they used. As Nixon told Khrushchev in their infamous "kitchen debate" in 1959, "To us, diversity, the right to choose... is the most important thing... We have many different manufacturers and many different kinds of washing machines so that housewives have a choice."[141] In an era when people of color and women were at times actively discriminated against, Nixon's espousal of diversity is laughable. Yet *The New American Poetry* did little to rethink the status quo.

There were many women who were willing to do more than work in the kitchen during this period, and the early Cold War produced a number of notable female poets. Of all the women writing innovative poetry in the post-war years, three are especially relevant to this discussion, because Allen was aware of them. The first is Daisy Aldan, a poet and anthologist from New York City, with whom Allen was in contact and whose anthology *A New Folder* was something of a touchstone for Allen's conception of his anthology.[142] At least two other prominent female poets, Jeanne McGahey and Rosalie Moore, were familiar to Allen, if not from his own

---

[139] Sara Lennox, "Constructing Femininity in the Early Cold War Era," The University of Michigan Press, https://www.press.umich.edu/pdf/0472113844-ch4.pdf, March 20, 2018.

[140] Elaine Tyler May, *Homeward Bound: American Families in the Cold War Era* (New York: Basic Books, 1988), 11.

[141] Sara Lennox, "Constructing Femininity in the Early Cold War Era," The University of Michigan Press, https://www.press.umich.edu/pdf/0472113844-ch4.pdf, March 20, 2018.

[142] Aldan's anthology was inspired at least in part by the appearance of *The New Poets of England and America*. As she wrote to Allen on October 17, 1960: "I have been told about Louise Bogan's [negative] review [of *The New American Poetry*] in *The New Yorker*, and someone is sending it to me today. If you remember, it was she who so highly praised Donald Hall's dull book, and it was that very book which sparked me to go ahead with my plan to publish *A New Folder*, so this shouldn't bother you at all." Daisy Aldan to Donald Allen, October 17, 1960, Box 57, Folder 19, Donald Allen Collection, MSS 3, Special Collections & Archives, UC San Diego Library.

2 RAW AMERICANS: THE PERSISTENCE OF *THE NEW AMERICAN...*   49

reading then from a 1956 letter from Robert Duncan in which Duncan names these poets, members of a California-based movement of post-war poetry known as the Activist Group, as individuals who "would be necessary if the collection were to convey all the lively" movements in post-war American poetry.[143] If Allen was trying to present a complete picture of the innovative new poetry being written in the United States after World War II, these lacunae are important. The work of these female poets is now virtually unknown, whereas their inclusion in *The New American Poetry* would have brought them to a wider audience. Their inclusion would also have crucially altered our perception of the diversity of American poetry. A similar case can be made for poets of color.

By 1960, the Civil Rights Movement had already gained significant ground. After the Supreme Court declared that school segregation was unconstitutional in 1954, a Civil Rights Commission was established in 1957, and in 1960 the nation's fifth Civil Rights Act was passed, which permitted federal inspection of voting records in an attempt to enforce the voting rights of African Americans. Of course, the backdrop to this progress was racism and the harassment of African Americans, which continued even after the Civil Rights Acts of 1964 and 1968. Many critics have pointed out that the Cold War played an important role in the passage of civil rights legislation in the 1950s and 1960s, because racism and segregation were key pieces of Soviet propaganda against the United States:

> During the Cold War, the Soviet Union frequently pointed to segregation and civil unrest as proof of American hypocrisy. This propaganda was sufficiently widespread, and contained enough truth, that leaders of both parties began arguing that segregation undermined the United States' position in the Cold War, helping to ease the passage of civil rights legislation in the 1950s and 1960s.[144]

Given the numerous ways that Allen's anthology harmonizes with the social and artistic atmosphere of Cold War America, it is curious that he

[143] Robert Duncan to Donald Allen, December 15, 1956, Box 63, Folder 5, Donald Allen Collection, MSS 3, Special Collections & Archives, UC San Diego Library.

[144] Sherrilyn Ifill, "It's time to face the facts: Racism is a national security issue," *The Washington Post*, December 18, 2018, https://www.washingtonpost.com/opinions/its-time-to-face-the-facts-racism-is-a-national-security-issue/2018/12/18/f9746466-02e8-11e9-b5df-5d3874f1ac36_story.html?utm_term=.839176a9259b, March 21, 2018.

50 S. DELBOS

chose not to emphasize this issue more in the composition of his anthology. Instead, *The New American Poetry* reflects the worst tendencies of the time.

There were several important avant-garde African American poets in the late 1950s whose work was eligible for publication by Allen. Some of the most prominent were Bob Kaufman, a stand-out on the San Francisco scene; Ted Joans, a Beat and surrealist poet who was an important early voice in jazz poetry; Clarence Major, an innovative midwestern poet; Steven Jonas, who lived and worked in Cambridge, Massachusetts, and knew Jack Spicer when the California poet was in Massachusetts in the mid-1950s;[145] and Norman Pritchard, an African American poet living in New York City. As Golding writes, "at the very least it would be surprising if Allen did not know of Steven Jonas, Bob Kaufman, and Clarence Major, and perhaps Ted Joans."[146] Indeed, Allen's correspondence shows that he was aware of most, if not all, of these poets, and his papers show that Jonas submitted poems to *The Evergreen Review* in 1958 and was rejected.[147] The exclusion of Jonas is particularly important, given that John Wieners insisted on his primacy both in the Boston poetry scene and in innovative American poetry in the 1950s.[148] His inclusion in the anthology would have had a significant effect on his reputation as well as our conception of the post-war avant-garde. Allen's correspondence with Marjorie Perloff from the late 1990s suggests that he excluded Jonas for aesthetic rather than personal reasons.[149] The editor similarly described Kaufman's work, writing to Lawrence Ferlinghetti, "Kaufman I dig very much as a prose writer, haven't got any focus on his verse."[150]

Contrary to its innovative, liberating reputation, *The New American Poetry* was deeply influenced by some of the worst characteristics of conservative post-war America, when racial and gender imbalances were

---

[145] Lewis Ellingham and Kevin Killian, *Poet Be like God: Jack Spicer and the San Francisco Renaissance* (Hanover, NH: Wesleyan University Press, 1998), 70.

[146] Golding, 197.

[147] Donald Allen, Box 65, Folder 14, Donald Allen Collection, MSS 3, Special Collections & Archives, UC San Diego Library.

[148] Michael Seth Stewart, ed., *Stars Seen in Person: The Selected Journals of John Wieners* (San Francisco: City Lights Books, 2015), 124–129.

[149] Donald Allen to Marjorie Perloff, June 10, 1998, and June 19, 1999, Box 57, Folder 12, Donald Allen Collection, MSS 3, Special Collections & Archives, UC San Diego Library.

[150] Donald Allen to Lawrence Ferlinghetti, June 10, 1960, Box 63, Folder 25, Donald Allen Collection, MSS 3, Special Collections & Archives, UC San Diego Library.

ubiquitous. The success and continued influence of Allen's anthology, as established above, mean that the anthology's lack of representation of female poets and poets of color continues to affect the way we think about innovative American poetry today. Inasmuch as *The New American Poetry* freed American poetry from its dominant formal constraints, it also codified a racial and gender imbalance that, like other aspects of the anthology, continues to persist. Recent controversies in American poetry—including Kenneth Goldsmith's use of Michael Brown's autopsy report and his subsequent profile in *The New Yorker*,[151] which incited a debate focusing on white males' continued dominance in avant-garde American poetry—suggest that these issues remain painfully unsettled.[152] That pain should not preclude an accurate reconsideration of the anthology's development and ramifications.

If there is any upside to the racial and gender exclusions of *The New American Poetry*, it is that they had a generative effect. Just as the avant-garde's lack of a voice in mainstream poetry would lead these poets to establish their own places of literary production in little magazines and independent presses which Allen brought together for the first time in a handsome publication from a prominent press, the feeling among poets of color and female poets that they were being excluded from the mainstream of American poetry—which in 1960 began to include the avant-garde, thanks to Allen's anthology—would help inspire the establishment of the Black Arts Movement and the Nuyorican and feminist poetics of the upcoming decades. In that sense, at least, the inequality of *The New American Poetry* was a catalyst for positive change, although those changes have not been dramatic enough. More than 60 years after its publication, Allen's anthology remains an active presence in American poetry, influential for poets and referenced by contemporary editors and critics. Reexamining the inequality of the anthology forces us to take a closer look at the important role that women and people of color have played in poetic innovation. The fact that we must attend to these missing figures of

---

[151] Alec Wilkinson, "Something Borrowed," *The New Yorker*, October 5, 2015, http://www.newyorker.com/magazine/2015/10/05/something-borrowed-wilkinson, May 1, 2016.

[152] The contemporary implications of the racial and gender imbalance of Allen's anthology will be taken up at length in Chap. 6. These paragraphs serve as an introduction to this topic, which is crucial for any reconsideration of *The New American Poetry* and its legacy for the post-war avant-garde.

the Anglophone avant-garde shows just how influential Allen's presentation of a predominantly white, male avant-garde has been.

The New American Poetry is a Cold War anthology. To imagine this groundbreaking American poetry anthology as rooted within and decisively influenced by that politicized, paranoid, problematic period—when nationalism was at a fever pitch, when racism and misogyny were everyday occurrences and when widespread societal fears about communism "were to distort and enfeeble American culture"[153]—has disrupting and stimulating effects on the way we read all of Anglophone poetry. It is rare for a single anthology to have such a lasting effect and to be so influential, both positively and negatively. For this reason, two questions frame the following chapters: why was Allen's model of American poetry so effective, and are the anthology's divisions and conflations still useful for critics today?

---

[153] Stephen J. Whitfield, *The Culture of the Cold War* (Baltimore: Johns Hopkins University Press, 1996), 2.

CHAPTER 3

Behind Enemy Lines: *The New American Poetry* as a Cold War Anthology

Allen's anthology has been examined from numerous angles by literary critics,[1] but one important context remains generally unexamined: *The New American Poetry* is, perhaps above all, a Cold War anthology. The model of American poetry we have inherited from Allen's book reflects the nationalist mindset of this period and created the framework we still use to think about poetry written in English since World War II. While other aspects of Cold War culture have been reconsidered in recent years, *The New American Poetry* remains untouched by this growing body of criticism. Some of the most significant works of American arts and culture during the post-war period were entangled with Cold War politics, and *The New American Poetry* is no exception. Through the influence of Allen's anthology, Cold War patterns continue to inform contemporary Anglophone poetry.

This chapter returns Allen's anthology to its original context, considering how the Cold War helped create the literary tensions from which the book emerged and through which it was read. The first section examines the political and cultural atmosphere in the United States in the 1950s to

---

[1] These include anthologies and canonization in Alan Golding's *From Outlaw to Classic: Canons in American Poetry;* sexuality and gender politics in Andrew Mossin's *Male Subjectivity and Poetic Form in "New American" Poetry* and the anthology's lasting influence on poets in John Woznicki's *The New American Poetry: Fifty Years Later*, among others.

© The Author(s), under exclusive license to Springer Nature   53
Switzerland AG 2021
S. Delbos, *The New American Poetry and Cold War Nationalism*,
Modern and Contemporary Poetry and Poetics,
https://doi.org/10.1007/978-3-030-77352-6_3

illuminate the conditions that affected literary life and influenced the thinking of Allen and many poets. Next the chapter examines the prevailing myopia of many critics regarding experimental poetry after World War II, uncovering the conditions that made the poets in Allen's anthology feel like outsiders, influencing not only how they thought about their place in American poetry but the way that Allen presented them. The third section examines how Allen's designs for the anthology were inspired in part by an exhibition of abstract expressionist painting, which was itself an instrument of Cold War cultural warfare sponsored by the CIA. Reassessing the Cold War roots of Allen's anthology forces us to reconsider its persistent application as a model for American poetry even into the twenty-first century.

3.1   DIVIDED TOGETHER: LITERARY LIFE IN COLD WAR AMERICA

For such a divisive, politicized and violent era, the Cold War got off to a strong start for the United States. There was a pervasive sense of optimism after World War II, as it became clear that the country was the undisputed victor, and this would have consequences for every aspect of American life. But the emergence of America as a global superpower began even before the war ended. As early as 1941 Henry Luce, owner of the *Time* magazine publishing empire, had written of "The American century," encouraging Americans to recognize "our opportunity as the most powerful and vital nation in the world... to exert upon the world the full impact of our influence, for such purposes as we see fit and by such means as we see fit."[2] With the end of the war, this belief would become only more engrained and more visible in the country's economic, political and cultural hegemony.

After World War II, and after 1950 specifically, there was a widespread sense that American culture needed to be renewed, reconsidered and reconfigured for the second half of the century, a process Lary May has called "recasting America."[3] The country had experienced a turning point and many artists and intellectuals felt its creative culture should reflect this. It is a trend that is evident, for example, in Charles Olson's reply to

[2] Henry Luce, *The American Century* (New York: Farrar and Rinehart, 1941), 30.
[3] Lary May, *Recasting America: Culture and Politics in the Age of Cold War* (Chicago: University of Chicago Press, 1989).

3 BEHIND ENEMY LINES: *THE NEW AMERICAN POETRY* AS A COLD...   55

Allen in 1959, after the editor had written to the poet, proposing a section in *The New American Poetry* devoted to influential Modernists. Olson wrote: "I wldn't myself add either of those two units: either the 'aunties' or the grandpas… In fact those connections strike me as smudging the point: 1950 on."[4] In fact, only two of the dated poems in the anthology were written before 1950.[5]

There is an element of self-promotion in Olson's insistence on newness.[6] Yet placed within the sociohistorical context of Cold War America, the anthology's promotion of what was "new" in American poetry seems part of a larger trend of innovation and invention to prove that American culture was vibrant and developed enough to win the future, so that by 1959 art critic Harold Rosenberg could write about *The Tradition of the New* in American creative culture. Allen's description of "the new American poetry" as "the second phase of our twentieth-century literature"[7] in his introduction to the anthology expresses a sense of mid-century renewal that was felt across all of the arts. Describing the New Year's Eve party ringing in 1950 at The Club, where the most prominent New York abstract expressionists gathered, Mark Stevens and Annalyn Swan write:

> Sometime during the marathon [party] Philip Pavia stood up and delivered a ringing proclamation. "This is the beginning of the new half century," he announced. "The first half of the century belonged to Paris. The next half century will be ours." De Kooning echoed the thought. "This is 1950," he said. "This is when it's going to happen."[8]

For many, the early 1950s seemed a golden era in which the country and those in it—even if, like de Kooning, they were immigrants—would prosper. Of course, behind this was the specter of nuclear annihilation, and it was this dramatic juxtaposition of optimism, status quo and doom that the Beats in particular would confront. Furthermore, the American sense of optimism brushed shoulders with a more conservative national outlook

---

[4] Maud, 59–60.

[5] These are "Advent" by Brother Antoninus (1949) and "The Shrouded Stranger" by Allen Ginsberg (1949).

[6] In fact Olson dated his own mature writing to the year 1950. Tom Clark, *Charles Olson: The Allegory of a Poet's Life* (Berkeley: North Atlantic Books, 2000), 153.

[7] Allen, xii.

[8] Mark Stevens and Annalyn Swan, *De Kooning: An American Master* (New York: Alfred A. Knopf, 2004), 292.

and a view of the world in which you were either with or against the United States. These conditions would influence Allen and his poets, and they would also have an effect on critical discussions of the era's art and culture.

That the Cold War was a time of divisions in American poetry as much as in politics is summed up most famously by Robert Lowell's 1960 speech accepting a National Book Award for *Life Studies*. While mentioned earlier, Lowell's statement deserves further explication here. The poet observed: "two poetries are now competing, a cooked and a raw":

> The cooked, marvelously expert, often seems laboriously concocted to be tasted and digested by a graduate seminar. The raw, huge blood-dripping gobbets of unseasoned experience are dished up for midnight listeners. There is a poetry that can only be studied, and a poetry that can only be declaimed, a poetry of pedantry, and a poetry of scandal. I exaggerate, of course.[9]

The ways this now-famous exaggeration played out in the era's poetry and criticism are complex. For Lowell was at once correct and misleading. While conflict was endemic to the Cold War, it was also an era of unity. To suggest that the period's most important characteristic was division is a simplification. The 1950s was one of the richest periods in American history for collaborative artistic projects that crossed boundaries of genre. Jazz musicians, painters and poets worked together, socialized, collaborated and influenced one another at this time, almost as a matter of course. Examples of this include Grace Hartigan and Frank O'Hara's series *Oranges* (1952); O'Hara's series with Larry Rivers, *Stones* (1960); James Merrill's deep interest in and support of numerous modern painters; the multi-disciplinary artistic community at Black Mountain College and The Five Spot in New York City;[10] and dozens of other creative collaborations on both coasts and in midwestern cities like Chicago, many of which were documented in magazines that combined art and poetry, including *The Tiger's Eye* and *Folder*. In addition, bassist Charles Mingus released a number of recordings of jazz and spoken word in the 1950s; poets including

---

[9] Robert Lowell, "1960 National Book Award Acceptance Speech," http://www.nationalbook.org/nbaacceptspeech_rlowell.html, May 1, 2015.

[10] For an excellent consideration of The Five Spot with respect to Pierre Bourdieu's concept of the field of cultural production, see: David Neil Lee, *The Battle of the Five Spot: Ornette Coleman and the New York Jazz Field* (Hamilton: Wolsack and Wynn, 2014).

Kenneth Patchen, Kenneth Rexroth and Lawrence Ferlinghetti performed poetry with jazz throughout the decade; and in 1958 the album *Jazz Canto Vol. 1* featured poems from William Carlos Williams, Walt Whitman and Lawrence Lipton, among others, read to live jazz accompaniment. The leading jazz critics of the period, Whitney Balliett and Nat Hentoff, make near-constant reference to literature in their reviews.

Artist and writer Basil King has described this period as particularly fruitful for collaboration, especially in New York City:

> We were just people with the same interest. With LeRoi and *Yugen*, we'd get together and have coffee and a couple of joints and staple the thing together. We didn't have money. Then with something like The New York Poet's Theatre, people would pitch in not because they were going to take it to Broadway, but because it was fun and interesting and there was an energy there… That sort of intimacy bred a lot of exchanges among artists and writers. There was cooperation and collaboration, and life was a lot more communal… So yes, there was collaboration. In New York, Frank O'Hara was the catalyst. He had his hands on the first generation and the second generation abstractionists. He was quite marvelous the way he could bring people together.[11]

King is not the only one to suggest that the period was one of collaboration. Other important figures from the period also suggest that the concept of two rival poetry camps was never completely accurate.

Robert Pack has said that he was surprised by the way readers and critics interpreted Allen's anthology as a rejoinder to *The New Poets of England and America*:

> At that time, my sense of the tradition… was poets who wrote in recognizable forms. But attention to perceived forms only wasn't a conscious intention with the anthology… I never did and still don't really think of them as warring camps. That was I think a publicity response that kind of stuck when the Allen anthology came out.[12]

Donald Hall agreed with his co-editor, saying: "people who were not poets tried to keep the 'battle' alive. I suppose it was amusing to take sides. The poets were ecumenical… Snyder and Creeley and I became close

---

[11] Basil King, Personal Interview, Telephone, April 7, 2018.
[12] Robert Pack, Personal Interview, Telephone, March 23, 2014.

58   S. DELBOS

friends."[13] Hall's correspondence with Allen bears this out. As he wrote in September 1960:

> I'm doing a review of American poetry in 1960 for the BBC, a half hour on the Third, and I'd like to have copies [of *The New American Poetry*]. Could you ask to have them sent? I wrote Grove but nothing happened. I've seen the book, but just glanced at it. I have come around to Creeley like mad, by the way. And I like Levertov, Duncan and Snyder. Many of the rest I haven't read. I don't always like Duncan. (You told me about him seven years ago.) I didn't like The Field, but there's a lot in the Selected Poems. I think Levertov and Creeley have both improved enormously in the last three years. Corso seems to me to foul up the ends of his poems. That Marriage one is great until the end, and Bomb fails in the same place. Or so I feel.[14]

This is diplomatic praise indeed from the front lines of the so-called "anthology wars," when, as early as 1961, Robert Creeley wrote to Donald Allen: "There seems a great shift of some kind in progress, as witness Hall and, for example, his excellent review of Maximus in the Nation etc."[15]

To cite other examples of poets reaching across the assumed divide in American post-war poetry, Louis Simpson wrote to John Logan in 1965 upon hearing Gary Snyder read in San Francisco, commenting, "He is very good, indeed."[16] Robert Duncan often expressed admiration for the work of Robert Lowell, who wrote to Duncan in 1962 regarding his own formal and free verse experimentation in *Life Studies* and other recent poems, signing off: "you are an older more experienced hand at these experiments. I like to think we swim in the same water."[17] Duncan himself had suggested a similar sentiment to Allen in 1958, writing: "There have been recently intimations of an unconventional perspective that appears [in] work by Lowell (like the beautiful group of poems that appeared in

---

[13] Donald Hall, Personal Interview, Email, February 11, 2014.

[14] Donald Hall to Donald Allen, September 22, 1960, Box 64, Folder 24, Donald Allen Collection, MSS 3, Special Collections & Archives, UC San Diego Library.

[15] Robert Creeley to Donald Allen, August 30, 1961, Box 62, Folder 5, Donald Allen Collection, MSS 3, Special Collections & Archives, UC San Diego Library.

[16] Louis Simpson to John Logan, February 21, 1965, John Logan Collection, The Poetry Collection of the University Libraries, University at Buffalo, The State University of New York.

[17] Robert Lowell to Robert Duncan, February 2, 1962, Box: 53, Robert Duncan Collection, PCMS-0110, The Poetry Collection of the University Libraries, University at Buffalo, The State University of New York.

Partisan last), Roethke (see the poem in the current Botteghe Oscura) and Elizabeth Bishop..."[18] Allen Ginsberg also mentioned to Donald Allen that he and Gregory Corso had "thought Robert Lowell's new style poems in Partisan were great,"[19] referring to five poems from *Life Studies* Lowell had published in the journal. James Merrill's biography contains numerous anecdotes about him spending time with New York School poets, as he was closely involved with The New York Poet's Theatre. He also gave Gregory Corso money on several occasions.[20] Richard Wilbur speaks in detail about meeting Beat poets at parties in San Francisco.[21] James Wright often enthused about the work of Gary Snyder and Kenneth Rexroth, whom he called "a personal friend of mine (another of my dirty little secrets)" but went on to describe the close-mindedness of academic critics as opposed to the poets of the period: "I swear to God that if I even mention this fact among my academic friends, a really dreadful and powerfully oppressive hush suffocates the whole room – it is exactly as though I had grinned, slapped somebody's grandmother on the back, and shouted, 'Well, Granny, I buggered another stray dog last night!'"[22]

Clearly some professors didn't believe the work of Rexroth and Snyder should be taken seriously. For their part, the Beats were often vocal in their anti-academicism, but this seems to have been more in the service of self-promotion than an attempt to accurately portray the times. Gestures of conciliation appear even in seemingly anti-academic statements like Corso's "The Literary Revolution in America," an essay that attempts to define the "new American poet" who "does not live on a campus":

> The new American poet is not serious... The serious poets are the academic poets, those holders of two jobs, those critic-poets, those good citizens of the community poets, they are serious... because all believe in Capital Punishment, and psychotherapy, and formality, jobs, marriages, careers,

---

[18] Robert Duncan to Donald Allen, July 12, 1958, Box 9, Folder 9, Donald Allen Collection, MSS 3, Special Collections & Archives, UC San Diego Library.

[19] Allen Ginsberg to Donald Allen, May, 1958, Box 10, Folder 15, Donald Allen Collection, MSS 3, Special Collections & Archives, UC San Diego Library.

[20] See Langdon Hammer, *James Merrill: Life and Art* (New York: Knopf, 2015), 268.

[21] William Butts, *Conversations with Richard Wilbur* (Jackson: University Press of Mississippi, 1990), 191.

[22] Wright and Maley, 116–117.

60   S. DELBOS

universities, and money, money, money, they have no alternative but to be serious.[23]

While this seems rather clear cut, the essay, from 1957, then goes on to recommend, curiously, the poetry of John Crowe Ransom, Robert Lowell and "Mr. Jarrell's latest book of verse *The Seven League Crutches* [*sic*]... a must for anyone interested in modern American verse."[24] Despite the appearance in print of straw men in tweed, the deeper relationships and recommendations among supposedly opposed poets indicate how the divided model of post-war American poetry does not comfortably fit the terrain. One significant, if overlooked, anthology that predates Allen's further clarifies what Donald Hall called the ecumenical nature of poets during this period.

One of the most interesting poetry publications of the 1950s was *A New Folder, Americans: Poems and Drawings*, edited by Daisy Aldan and published in 1959. It is a remarkable book that was, according to Edward Field, "more inclusive of the poets in New York than Donald Allen's was."[25] With its inclusion of prints by Jackson Pollock, Franz Kline, Larry Rivers, Joan Mitchell, Willem de Kooning and other Abstract Expressionists, it prefigures Allen's insistence on the shared affinities between modern poetry and modern painting[26] and achieves a symbiosis between poetry and art that Allen could only hint at. But even more notable is that it acknowledges no separation between academic and avant-garde poets. Included in its pages are LeRoi Jones, Jack Kerouac, Allen Ginsberg, Gregory Corso, Charles Olson, Robert Creeley and others found in Allen's anthology. But it also features poetry by James Merrill, Harold Norse and Richard Eberhart, among other poets who preferred received forms.

As a document that suggests a path not taken, a path that was in fact completely obscured by Allen's anthology, *A New Folder* is fascinating.[27]

---

[23] Gregory Corso, "The Literary Revolution in America," *Litterair Paspoort*, 100, Amsterdam, (November 1957): 193–196. This essay is also curious because it identifies Michael McClure as a "representative of the Black Mountain School."

[24] Corso, "The Literary Revolution in America."

[25] Edward Field, Personal Interview, Email, January 14, 2014.

[26] Allen, xi.

[27] Another interesting path not taken concerns Allen's early "plan to include some quite long poems," as he wrote in a letter to Cid Corman in 1958. His early draft of the anthology's introduction bears out his plan:

3 BEHIND ENEMY LINES: *THE NEW AMERICAN POETRY* AS A COLD... 61

There is no doubt that Allen was aware of its existence, and there are actually three poems included both in *The New American Poetry* and *A New Folder*: Denise Levertov's "The Sharks," Robert Creeley's "If You" and Jack Kerouac's "230th Chorus." In a letter to Daisy Aldan in 1960, Allen noted the overlap, writing: "I had tried to avoid using poems that were in your book, but slipped up in three cases, as you point out, without noticing it."[28] Later Aldan commiserated with Allen on Louise Bogan's negative review of *The New American Poetry* and hinted at the shared affinities between the anthologies:

> I have been told about Louise Bogan's review in *The New Yorker*, and someone is sending it to me today. If you remember, it was she who so highly praised Donald Hall's dull book, and it was that very book which sparked me to go ahead with my plan to publish *A NEW FOLDER*, so this shouldn't bother you at all. We know where HER taste lies.[29]

Bogan's review wasn't all negative, however. She did remark that *The New American Poetry* was "edited in a most neat and orderly fashion, with a preface, by Donald M. Allen."[30] In any case, it is interesting to note that *The New Poets of England and America* was a catalyst to Aldan as well as

> One prominent feature of the period is the recreated long poem. Robert Duncan's <u>The Venice Poem</u> (1948, now happily again in print in his <u>Selected Poems</u>) was the first sustained achievement. The second, Charles Olson's "The Kingfishers" (1949), has profoundly influenced many of his contemporaries and remains one of the starting posts for the course; and Allen Ginsberg's <u>Howl</u> (1955-56) has already assumed the status of <u>The Waste Land</u> for our age. Several other examples assembled here are Robert Duncan's "A Poem Beginning with a Line by Pindar," Jack Spicer's "Imaginary Elegies," Gregory Corso's "Marriage," Frank O'Hara's "Ode to Michael Goldberg ('s Birth and Other Births)," Stuart Perkoff's "Feasts of Death, Feasts of Love," Gary Snyder's <u>Myths & Texts</u> (most of Part II "Burning" is included), Edward Marshall's "Leave the Word Alone," and Michael McClure's "Peyote Poem."

Allen did indeed include these poems in the anthology, but he decided against putting the spotlight on the long poem as a "recreated" form in the framework of post-war American poetry. Donald Allen, "Preface," Box 9, Folder 6, Donald Allen Collection, MSS 3, Special Collections & Archives, UC San Diego Library.

[28] Donald Allen to Daisy Aldan, May 28, 1960, Box 74, Folder 8, Donald Allen Collection, MSS 3, Special Collections & Archives, UC San Diego Library.

[29] Daisy Aldan to Donald Allen, October 17, 1960, Box 74, Folder 8, Donald Allen Collection, MSS 3, Special Collections & Archives, UC San Diego Library.

[30] Louise Bogan, "Verse," *The New Yorker*, October 8, 1960, 199–200.

Allen. In addition, Allen seems to have used Aldan's anthology as a contrastive publication to guide his editorial choices. Writing to Robert Creeley in August 1959 about the "considerable problem" Robert Duncan had posed in deciding whether or not to allow his work to be included, as well as giving Allen long lists of poets whose work he should include, the editor concluded:

> Were I to follow his directives (which change from day to day) I should end up with something close to Daisy Aldan's Folder anthology. In short I have tried to compose the anthology as objectively as possible and continue to oppose those arguments from all sides which seem purely political to me. Each poet would edit his anthology very differently, nor is mine a compromise but rather my view of the center of the present.[31]

A contrast is evident here, between the anthology's iconic influence and Allen's intention of representing "my view." This is one of the key tensions of *The New American Poetry* in terms of its long-term effect: one editor's view of mid-century American poetry became internationally significant as an educational and critical model.

Other poets also broached the topic of Aldan's anthology with Allen. James Broughton wrote to the editor that Aldan "made a point with her *Folder* by cutting across the political barriers and showing the wide sense of poetic excitement going on unsuspected beneath the official approvals."[32] Soon after, Allen responded:

> Yes, I too liked the way Daisy Aldan cut through all the political barriers, as you say, and showed the poetic excitement. Hers is a very individual choice, based on her own experience in editing *Folder* of course, and it has a definite charm I believe. One thinks of it as an album, a pleasant book to have, but I rather wonder what kind of an impression it might make on a reader completely unaware of the new poetry in America.[33]

It is ironic that Allen here belittles Aldan's selection as "a very individual choice" while in his previous letter to Creeley he had declared that *The*

---

[31] Donald Allen to Robert Creeley, August 10, 1959, Box 9, Folder 12, Donald Allen Collection, MSS 3, Special Collections & Archives, UC San Diego Library.

[32] James Broughton to Donald Allen, September 1, 1959, Box 10, Folder 3, Donald Allen Collection, MSS 3, Special Collections & Archives, UC San Diego Library.

[33] Donald Allen to James Broughton, September 4, 1959, Box 10, Folder 3, Donald Allen Collection, MSS 3, Special Collections & Archives, UC San Diego Library.

New American Poetry represented "my view of the center of the present."[34] But more importantly, Aldan's anthology suggests that Allen's exclusion of poets writing in received form was not a foregone conclusion, no matter how many people claimed there was a division in American poetry. This was Allen's conscious decision. Allen here also suggests that some readers may not be aware of the "new poetry in America." The next section of this chapter considers how and why this poetry may have been obscure to the average reader. First, it is important to examine how Cold War political discourse could influence and intersect with the way poets and critics discussed poetry.

As suggested above, Lowell's binary contains some elements of truth. But only some. Divisions were indeed engrained in American culture during the Cold War, from the us-versus-them of democracy and communism to race relations and youth culture's assertion of its independence. That the so-called anthology wars should have their genesis in the Cold War comes as no surprise; cooked and raw are exceptionally problematic as critical categories,[35] but there were indeed differences of opinion among American poets during this period, especially between those who held important institutional positions and those who felt themselves to be stuck in the margins. More intriguing are the factors that made the binary of raw and cooked so comfortable for everyone involved.

Competition or disagreement among poets is nothing new. Divisions between groups of people with opposing opinions may be a sine qua non of artistic history. But what is particularly interesting about discussions of poetry during this period is the use of violent and militaristic rhetoric. One pertinent example is a letter from Robert Creeley to Cid Corman in 1950, which draws attention to the academic and avant-garde split and to the division of old and new in violent terms:

> That's what makes me distrust KENYON, i.e., they aren't interested in the development of individual artists, or in the development of any group. They are interested in the maintenance of a deliberate and perfectly coherent critical method, confined, as it must be, by the ideas of Ransom on everything

[34] Donald Allen to Robert Creeley, August 10, 1959, Box 9, Folder 12, Donald Allen Collection, MSS 3, Special Collections & Archives, UC San Diego Library.

[35] This should be clear to any serious reader of the period's poetry. One further suggestion of how imprecise these terms are is the fact that Ezra Pound, reviewing Robert Frost's first book in 1913, called it "a little raw." Humphrey Carpenter, *A Serious Character: The Life of Ezra Pound* (Boston: Houghton Mifflin, 1988), 201.

64   S. DELBOS

imaginable, to be put together, eventually, with the more rash, and conse-
quently, more overtly stupid, pronunciamentos of Tate. Don't watch a man
when he's judging something 100 years dead, in time; because he may fool
you, having the benefit of the "tradition." Watch what he says on what's at
hand; if he can't come to sense there, or if his method reveals itself as defi-
nitely limited for purposes having nothing to do with its subject, then, dam-
mit, shoot.[36]

Creeley's conclusion is rhetorically violent, and yet such language was not
used only when expressing disagreement among poets of the era. It is
present even in moments of praise, such as this May 1958 letter from
Ginsberg to Allen:

The anthology also sounds like an undreamt of early windfall miracle. It
should be a great bomb & clear the air almost immediately of all the doubting critical bullshit – most of the material will come as a complete surprise to
a place say like the English dept at Columbia – or people like Simpson (silent
gener) & Timbimatu [sic] (ignorant preface to new World Writing poetry
selection... it was just dumb statements about prissy lifeless poetry.)... here
you have this tremendous goldmine to unload all at once – should be a historic piece of publishing. Be as big event as, as weird & hopeful, as K's sud-
den destalinization speech. Maybe save the world. Yow.[37]

Ginsberg's comparison of Allen's anthology, the atomic bomb and
Khrushchev's speech after the death of Stalin shows how deeply Cold War
political rhetoric was ingrained in the American consciousness. This kind
of language influenced the conception of the anthology wars and in turn
continues to influence the critical perception of post-war and contemporary American poetry, even as many of the poets themselves politely socialized in person. For Ginsberg was far from the only poet using such
rhetoric.

James Broughton suggested Allen's anthology "implies some kind of
Manifesto, even Party Line, and a passion for the New at whatever cost."[38]
Chad Walsh wrote "diplomatic relations between the two poetic blocs
resemble the short-wave exchange of compliments that the Soviet Union

[36] Smith, Baker, and Harris, 31.
[37] Allen Ginsberg to Donald Allen, May, 1958, Box 10, Folder 15, Donald Allen Collection,
MSS 3, Special Collections & Archives, UC San Diego Library.
[38] James Broughton to Donald Allen, May 23, 1960, Box 9, Folder 3, Donald Allen
Collection, MSS 3, Special Collections & Archives, UC San Diego Library.

and the United States sponsor."[39] Michael Davidson suggested that the Cold War binary is written into some of the most significant poems of the era, including Olson's "The Kingfishers," which opens *The New American Poetry*.[40] At a time when backyard bomb shelters and air raid drills were a daily reality, apocalyptic political rhetoric crept into both American life and poetry. It was perhaps an unavoidable outcome of the age's demands. These demands and their effects on poets have been mostly passed over by contemporary criticism, however, as a few critics such as Adam Piette have pointed out.[41] But the inflammatory rhetoric of the Cold War seems to have been taken for granted at the time. In this way even Cold War America's most outspoken critics, like Ginsberg, were influenced by the atmosphere of the age.

Numerous cultural critics have written about how the emphasis on spontaneity in American art during this period was a response to the stultifying insistence in mainstream society on conformity and the ideology of consensus.[42] This domestic-oriented status quo is visible most potently and humorously in the infamous "kitchen debates" between US Vice President Richard Nixon and Soviet Premier Nikita Khrushchev at the American National Exhibition at Sokolniki Park in Moscow on July 24, 1959, mentioned above in the context of housewives and diversity.[43] Ensconced in the well-stocked kitchen of a model ranch-style home, Nixon and Khrushchev discussed the relative merits of the communist and democratic systems, with the material wealth of American society serving as the ultimate example of democracy's superiority. For a generation of Americans young enough to question the worth of such materialism, in part because they had not yet become full members of the workforce and taken on middle-class responsibilities, conformist America provided a target to rebel against.[44] American youth culture would focus on the man in

---

[39] Chad Walsh, "The war between Iambs and Ids," *Book Week*, July 26, 1964, 2.

[40] Michael Davidson, *Guys Like Us: Citing Masculinity in Cold War Poetics* (Chicago: University of Chicago Press, 2004), 218.

[41] Adam Piette, *The Literary Cold War: 1945 to Vietnam* (Edinburgh: Edinburgh University Press, 2009).

[42] See Daniel Belgrad, *The Culture of Spontaneity: Improvisation and the Arts in Postwar America* (Chicago: University of Chicago Press, 1998).

[43] "Nixon and Khrushchev Have a 'Kitchen Debate,'" *The History Channel*, http://www.history.com/this-day-in-history/nixon-and-khrushchev-have-a-kitchen-debate, May 15, 2015.

[44] Similarly, Philip Roth suggested that the Communist Party provided writers living under the regime a common enemy and a constant source of inspiration. Ivan Klíma, *The Spirit of Prague* (London: Granta, 1994), 50.

66   S. DELBOS

the white collar and gray flannel suit.[45] For American poets, the conform-ism of American society was metonymized in the "prissy lifeless poetry"[46] of formal, so-called academic, poets, even if those poets proved to be pleasant in person. By attacking this poetry with such rhetorical violence, and by writing in an alternative style, these non-mainstream poets seemed to be attacking mainstream American poetry as well as American values, a fact not lost on conservative critics.

Numerous reviewers of *The New American Poetry* suggested the book had political ramifications. J. R. Goddard's review in *The Village Voice* is representative: "you can be on the right side politically but the wrong side aesthetically. These people are making bad poetry out of a good cause."[47] Other commentaries quickly take a melodramatic turn. In his review of the anthology John Simon moves in the span of two paragraphs from discuss-ing the book to detailing the case of "a young Negro hipster who called himself 'Mau Mau' [who] was arrested in Greenwich Village for living with – and off – an unfortunate minor girl."[48] Such conflations of poetry and politics were not uncommon. John Robert Colombo wrote: "many of these writers sound like a cross between the bible and the Communist Manifesto."[49] N. Scott, writing for *People's World*, complained that the poets in Allen's anthology were "living in a sick limbo."[50] Perhaps the most outrageous assessment of Allen's anthology came from Curtis Zahn, who wrote in his review: "Regrettably, I feel that the reading public is being raped again."[51] James Boatwright also wrote of the poetry in overtly political terms:

> the fight for the kingdom of poetry goes on… what this anthology witnesses is a vigorous new battle, a determined effort to depose the tyrant, to upset the throne… They don't like Eliot, naturally, nor do they like New Critics and New criticism, conventional poetic forms, useful and impersonal poetry,

[45] See Sloan Wilson's novel *The Man in the Grey Flannel Suit* (1955), and C. Wright Mills's *White Collar: The American Middle Classes* (1951).

[46] Allen Ginsberg to Donald Allen, May, 1958, Box 10, Folder 15, Donald Allen Collection, MSS 3, Special Collections & Archives, UC San Diego Library.

[47] J. R. Goddard, "There Are No Schools – Just Kindergartens," *The Village Voice*, May 11, 1961, 9.

[48] John Simon, "Sleight of Foot," *Audit*, 1.6, October 26, (1960): 3.

[49] John Robert Colombo, *Tamarack Review*, Summer (1960): 85–86.

[50] N. Scott, "Poets Living in a Sick Limbo," Box 74, Folder 5, Donald Allen Collection, MSS 3, Special Collections & Archives, UC San Diego Library.

[51] Curtis Zahn, "An Inch of Culture," *Trace*, 39, September–October (1960): 40–44.

3 BEHIND ENEMY LINES: *THE NEW AMERICAN POETRY* AS A COLD...

ex-President Eisenhower, the machine, the Bomb, the Organization Man, Protestantism, middle-class attitudes towards marriage and sex, and the aimlessness and coldness of heart of contemporary man.[52]

One might wonder how something like this could be written with a straight face. But these reviews reveal the temper of the times, when most established critics created a united front against the upsurge of younger, rebellious writers. As Filreis has pointed out, "many poetic traditionalists who had long thought of themselves as apolitical found, especially in the late 1940s, that they were shifting quickly into politicized vocabularies and borrowing analyses from anticommunist colleagues."[53] As we have seen, this shift was also evident among poets of the period who were not traditionalists.

Even reviews of the anthology that were not explicitly political equate the poetry with social entropy while dramatizing the supposed violence and anger of the poets. As Louise Bogan wrote in *The New Yorker*:

History seems to have fallen in a heap upon the minds and sensibilities of many members of the latest American "school" of poetry... their hatred of iambic pentameter is intense... does their violence stem from a deliberate attempt to extend consciousness, or are many of them actually out of control?... what degree of anarchy can be projected in poetry?[54]

Words like "hatred," "violence," "out of control" and "anarchy" are distinctly melodramatic but perhaps not out of place in a poetry column that also included a review of a biography of Robert Frost, whom Bogan calls a "fine lyricist [who] holds conservative views... an extoller of all the middle virtues." Blurring the border between poetry and politics, Bogan continues:

Today, when it has become difficult to hymn any kind of hero, the poet who is able to name over, with conviction, the more ascertainable and definable decent human qualities and who aligns himself with a positive view of man's nature and man's fate may rightly claim the title of bard. And it would be a poor-spirited society that would deny the attraction of such a figure.[55]

---

[52] James Boatright, *Shenandoa* 12.2, Winter, (1961).
[53] Filreis, xi.
[54] Louise Bogan, "Verse," *The New Yorker*, October 8, 1960, 199–200.
[55] Louise Bogan, "Verse," *The New Yorker*, October 8, 1960, 197.

68   S. DELBOS

Bogan does not explicitly compare Frost with the poets of Allen's anthology, but the implications would have been clear for any reader. A conservative bard with an optimistic view of man's nature and man's fate was everything Allen's poets were not. And if a society that fails to laud a poet like Frost is poor-spirited, so too is a society that lauds poets like those in *The New American Poetry*.

For critics like Bogan who had come of age in the 1930s and 1940s, the conflation of radical form and radical politics would have seemed natural. M. L. Rosenthal, editor for *The Nation*, was one of the most vocal critics of what he termed "an esthetic war between conservatives and radicals in poetry"[56] during this period. Rosenthal was also one of the perceptive critics "who connected the New American Poetry with the 1930s."[57] So when John Simon, reviewing the anthology, wrote that the "genealogy" of the poets included "can be traced from Whitman through Sandburg, Fearing and Patchen, (three names almost never mentioned by our poets, lest the show be given away),"[58] it is unclear whether he's talking about the show of originality or the show of being apolitical.

Bogan's evocation of iambic pentameter to tell the reader something about the mental state of the poets in the anthology is representative of a certain type of criticism of the period. This formal framework for interpreting the anthology, which Allen encouraged through his introduction and the "Notes on Poetics" section, foreshadows many later readings of *The New American Poetry* which focus on the form of the poems at the expense of any consideration of what they are advocating. As Walter Kalaidjian has remarked:

> However lodged "against" academic formalism, the confessional, regional, neosurrealist, "deep imagist" and other aesthetic schools and movements were surprisingly reticent about the broader, ideological investments and effects of their own formal choices. Like their academic counterparts, the

---

[56] Filreis, 7.

[57] Filreis, 314.

[58] Simon, 4. Similarly John Robert Colombo, commenting in the *Tamarack Review* in Summer 1960, wrote: "It is unfortunate that Allen had to omit the semibeat ancestors of these younger poets, for where would the beat movement be without Kenneth Rexroth, Kenneth Patchen, and Kenneth Fearing?" Columbo, 85.

"new" poets largely eschewed any overtly political commitments or affiliations in the wider social field.[59]

This discounts the crucial role that critics and editors such as Allen played in the interpretation of these poets. While a poem like Ginsberg's "Howl" does not proclaim the poet as a member of any political movement or party, it certainly makes clear his opposition to conventional politics and situates him in "the wider social field." A poet like Ray Bremser, who wrote "I am a traitor fascist / ... call me a communist,"[60] stands out from the majority of the poets in Allen's anthology who did not make explicit political statements. That doesn't necessarily mean they did not try to.

It is possible that Allen played an active role in making his anthology less political than some of the poets themselves may have wanted. At several points in his correspondence he mentions ignoring the "political" suggestions of poets with whom he consulted,[61] which is something that critics at that time could not have been aware of. A review of the anthology in the *Times Literary Supplement* in 1961 quibbled with the "Statements on Poetics" section of the anthology, remarking, "surprisingly few of the statements deal with what one would have thought was the all-important question of subject-matter, and how far, writing at such a time as this, the poets should be 'committed.'"[62] Allen actually dissuaded at least one poet, Denise Levertov, from including a political statement in this section:

> I'm still bothered by your paragraph on shocking the bourgeois, Denise. Please don't mistake me: one chief purpose of the anthology, that I hope to accomplish through choice of poems and also through the arrangement of the poets, is very much the essence of that paragraph. A chief reason for asking you and Bob, Charles and a few others to give me statements on poetics was to underscore this as well as the other points you make in your statement. My worry over the paragraph is your reference to Hiroshima... Hiroshima is of an entirely different order, surely. And what else has the

[59] Walter Kalaidjian, *Languages of Liberation* (New York: Columbia University Press, 1989), 7.

[60] Allen, 353.

[61] Donald Allen to Robert Creeley, August 10, 1959, Box 9, Folder 12, Donald Allen Collection, MSS 3, Special Collections & Archives, UC San Diego Library.

[62] "Review of *The New American Poetry*," *The Times Literary Supplement*, August 4, 1961, Box 74, Folder 5, Donald Allen Collection, MSS 3, Special Collections & Archives, UC San Diego Library.

middle-class of Europe and America been writing about since 1945? Buchenwald and Hiroshima are still today the constant irritants in middle class attempts to arrive at a comfortable philosophical concept of man. A really profound subterranean shock still vibrates from those catastrophes through all our lives... It is most important to make the point that the role of poetry, its social function, is as you say, to awaken sleepers by other means.[63]

It is intriguing that Allen seems to agree with Levertov's sentiment while refusing to include it in the anthology, suggesting that poets had "other means" than politics to affect the reading public. Considering the way that conservative critics during this period politicized discussions of poems that weren't necessarily political, one can imagine the negative reception the anthology would have received if it had been more explicitly political.

The Cold War was a time of both division and unity, and it was also a time when critics and cultural commentators were primed to discuss all differences of opinion in dramatically political and militaristic terms. Politics were personal, and poems were political. Allen seems to have downplayed political content in his anthology—which could have revealed real, substantive, ideological differences among poets of the period—while emphasizing a formal division between academic and avant-garde, a framework that would be extremely influential in part because it allowed poets to distinguish themselves within accepted limits of differentiation. In the same way, poets like Ginsberg and Corso proclaimed their opposition to academic poetry in gestures of self-promotion that concealed real points of intersection and understanding among many seemingly opposed poets of the period. So Robert Lowell's famous division between raw and cooked was as influenced by the realities of American poetry as by the dualism of the Cold War, a general tendency in American culture to highlight even minute divisions.

Despite cordial relationships among seemingly opposed poets during this period, major literary publications remained in the hands of a few. Not only were avant-garde poets outside the mainstream, they were largely ignored by established critics until the publication of *The New American Poetry*. Since these critics held the most prominent and influential positions in the 1950s, their attention to, or their ignorance of, new poetry would have a significant effect on its reception. The myopia of these

---

[63] Donald Allen to Denise Levertov, August 26, 1959, Box 9, Folder 10, Donald Allen Collection, MSS 3, Special Collections & Archives, UC San Diego Library.

critics, whether premeditated or accidental, inspired a galvanizing sense of alienation in poets outside of the mainstream, creating the environment in which an avant-garde could establish itself.

3.2   Another Bunch: Obscurity and Alienation in Post-war American Poetry

The complexities surrounding *The New American Poetry* and *The New Poets of England and America* and the milieus in which they were published have been too often simplified into capsule summaries of the post-war era that take for granted a split in American poetry while ignoring the many points of intersection among the poets contained in these anthologies. This tendency is exemplified in the following quotation from poet and critic William Corbett, written in the late 1990s:

> [*The New American Poetry*] was the anthology that meant to give the sons and daughters of Pound, Williams, Stein, French surrealism, Pasternak, and the Objectivists, in short, the modernist avant-garde, their platform. These were the days when a fault line split American poetry into the Academic (the Donald Hall, Robert Pack, and Louis Simpson anthology *New Poets of England and America*, [*sic*] 1957, unfurled this banner and published not one of the poets in Allen's anthology) and the Beats/Black Mountain/San Francisco and New York School poets Allen published. Academic poets generally worked in traditional form and meter, as opposed to those lords and ladies of misrule who carried forward the modernist program in all its various energies. Allen's *New American Poets* [*sic*] proved decisive in the history of little magazines because, rejected by, or unwilling to be published in, the mainstream, they started their own magazines.[64]

Corbett here rightfully highlights the international influences of many of the poets in Allen's anthology, influences that were obscured by the editor's insistence on a strictly national presentation. However, his suggestion that *The New Poets of England and America* staked a claim in contrast to Allen's poets or refused to publish them suggests that Hall and his fellow editors had an anti-modern agenda in mind when compiling their anthology. This ignores the fact that *The New Poets of England and America* was published before Allen's anthology and is contradicted by

---

[64] William Corbett, *All Prose: Selected Essays and Reviews* (Brooklyn: Pressed Wafer, 2018), 206–207.

72   S. DELBOS

both Pack and Hall, who suggest, in their recollections of the period, that ignorance has been construed as enmity in hindsight. As Jed Rasula has written, it is past time to "readjust [these] stereotypes."[65]

Due in some cases to genuine ignorance and perhaps in others to political motivations, there was a widespread critical myopia in the post-war years concerning non-traditional poetry published by independent journals and presses. One of Allen's motivations for creating his anthology was that the work of the poets had "appeared, if at all, only in little magazines, many of them very obscure."[66] That obscurity could certainly be the cause of the ignorance of some mainstream critics regarding the work of these poets. Donald Hall, one of the era's most significant and insightful editors and poets, insisted that he, Robert Pack and Louis Simpson weren't consciously excluding the work of the Beats when they compiled *The New Poets of England and America*; they simply had not heard of them:

> Pack and Simpson and I did not edit with any notion of a conflict with another school of poets. Pack and I had never heard the name Allen Ginsberg. Louis had known him at Columbia, where he was writing little Elizabethan ballads – nothing like "Howl." None of us knew anything of Snyder or Robert Duncan. If we had known the work of many of them, probably we would not have put it in anyway. We were more conventional – but we didn't know about them, so we never had a chance to judge.[67]

That one of the period's most astute figures would not have heard of Allen Ginsberg as late as 1957, a year after the publication of *Howl*, is improbable, but it also suggests the hierarchical dissemination of information in mainstream poetry publications of the period. Hall's essay "The New Poetry: Notes on the Past Fifteen Years in America," published in 1955, is also significant in this regard. In it Hall gives a detailed summary of the most important publications, movements and innovations in poetry since 1940. Not a single poet included in *The New American Poetry* is

---

[65] Jed Rasula, *American Poetry Wax Museum: Reality Effects 1940–1990* (Urbana, IL: NCTE, 1996), 227.

[66] Donald Allen to The Rockefeller Foundation, 1960, Box 88, Folder 6, Donald Allen Collection, MSS 3, Special Collections & Archives, UC San Diego Library.

[67] Donald Hall, Personal Interview, Email, February 11, 2014. This contradicts a letter from Hall to Allen in 1960, in which Halls says that Allen had informed him of Robert Duncan "seven years ago." Donald Hall to Donald Allen, September 22, 1960, Box 64, Folder 24, Donald Allen Collection, MSS 3, Special Collections & Archives, UC San Diego Library.

mentioned, despite the fact that many of them had already published collections by the time Hall's essay appeared, including William Everson (Brother Antoninus), John Ashbery, Paul Blackburn, James Broughton, Gregory Corso, Robert Creeley, Robert Duncan, Larry Eigner, Madeline Gleason, Kenneth Koch, Philip Lamantia, Denise Levertov, Frank O'Hara, Charles Olson and Jonathan Williams.[68]

Another example of the absence of the avant-garde in many considerations of post-war poetry is Malcolm Cowley's essay on the post-war poetry scene, "The Time of the Rhetoricians," published in *New World Writing* in 1954. The essay asserted that the post-war era was defined by criticism rather than poetry, which Cowley suggested was exemplified in contemporary journals that published more criticism than creative writing. "The literary quarterlies of the 1950s are mature, solid, academic,"[69] Cowley writes, with seemingly no awareness of the independent literary journals that would be cited by Allen in his anthology, including *The Ark*, which began publication in 1947, *Contact*, published from 1952; Daisy Aldan's *Folder*, published between 1953 and 1956; and *Golden Goose*, published between 1948 and 1954. Cowley's essay suggests the ignorance, whether willed or genuine, of mainstream critics of the 1950s. It was a situation that would shift by 1959, when even popular publications began taking notice of small presses. As Lloyd Zimpel wrote that year in *The Nation*: "These obscure little operations were never so plentiful as they are now – probably because many of the most significant little magazines and quarterlies – traditional outlets for the yeastier, half-baked and wildly-talented – are regrouping around writers of fashion, both academic and beat."[70]

---

[68] Allen, 447.

[69] Malcolm Cowley, "The Time of the Rhetoricians," *New World Writing* 5 (New York City: The New American Library of World Literature, Inc., 1954), 185. Interestingly, Cowley had published an essay almost a decade before in which he longed for the excitement and experimentation of the little magazines of the 1920s and suggested that magazines in the 1940s had fallen victim to "critical inbreeding." As Jeff Weddle points out, this essay, from 1947, seems to prefigure *The New American Poetry* and the mimeograph revolution. Malcolm Cowley, "The Little Magazines Growing Up," *The New York Times*, September 14, 1947, https://www.nytimes.com/1947/09/14/archives/the-little-magazines-growing-up-the-little-magazines.html, April 15, 2018.

[70] Lloyd Zimpel, "They Also Serve Who Only Lie in Wait," *The Nation*, September 26, 1959. See also Louise Bogan's Verse column in *The New Yorker* on April 13, 1957, in which she writes about "a new generation of 'experimentalists' … published almost without exception by small presses." Louise Bogan, "Verse," *The New Yorker*, April 13, 1957, 174.

74   S. DELBOS

Ammiel Alcalay has placed these independent publications within a larger framework of underground presses during the Cold War, which fostered a sense of community and belonging among those who contributed to them and read them. These small presses and magazines were crucial for Allen's project, and they also gave a much-needed outlet to generations of writers and poets who felt that they were outcasts from mainstream publications and academic posts. Alcalay writes:

> Here we can trace an important form of lineage: a direct line leading from an initiative like *The Floating Bear* [published by Diane di Prima and LeRoi Jones in New York City from 1961 to 1971] to the underground press, breaking through the Cold War policy of communication as propaganda to the counterculture's call for communication as empowerment, exploration and kinship.[71]

While *The Floating Bear* did not begin publication until after the appearance of *The New American Poetry*, it came directly out of the lineage of Allen's anthology and his editorial investigations into the literary counterculture, as well as LeRoi Jones's earlier magazine *Yugen*. Other archivists of the so-called mimeograph revolution have explicitly placed Allen and his anthology at the root of this rapidly developing community of writers and publishers that would flourish in the 1960s and 1970s. As Steven Clay and Rodney Phillips write:

> When the Allen anthology came out, several of the featured poets had barely been published. Of necessity, they existed on the margins, outside mainstream publication and distribution channels. Of necessity, they invented their own communities and audiences (typically indistinguishable), with a small press or little magazine often serving as the nucleus of both.[72]

Despite its nationalist focus and its limitations in terms of representation of women and people of color, Allen's anthology was a vital catalyst for alternative writing in the United States, both opening the field to new frameworks of consideration and offering models for other writers and editors to follow. Especially important in this regard was Allen's inclusion of presses and publishers of note in the back of the anthology. As

---

[71] Ammiel Alcalay, *a little history* (Los Angeles: re: public, 2013), 189.
[72] Steven Clay and Rodney Phillips, *A Secret Location on the Lower East Side: Adventures in Writing, 1960–1980* (New York: The New York Public Library, 1998), 13.

anachronistic as a list of mailing addresses may seem in the twenty-first century, its importance and utility—and its ultimate effect on the landscape of American letters—cannot be overstated.

Given the fecundity of non-mainstream publishing in the 1950s, it is difficult to say whether explanations of ignorance such as Hall's of Ginsberg should be taken at face value or whether they are indicative of selective recall. But in many cases the poets Allen published truly were obscure. After all, this was well before the internet, when even those who were interested in poetry would have to make considerable efforts to reach out beyond their own immediate literary community. Poet Edward Field, himself included in *The New American Poetry*, described the enlightening effect the anthology had on him, attesting to the fact that even seemingly large-looming figures such as Olson were not household names:

> A lot of the poets were new to me, but the categories roughly made sense. Before then, I'd only thought of American poetry as divided into the Beats in San Francisco, formalist poets who taught in universities and published in the literary quarterlies, and everybody else… I was surprised to learn about the influence poets like Charles Olson had – I'd known nothing about him before. I confess that I lived in a world of my own.[73]

It may be too dramatic to suggest a willful conspiracy on the part of American critics to ignore the work of younger, more avant-garde American poets who hadn't had the opportunity, or perhaps the motivation, to publish work with large presses and in prestigious journals.[74] In any case, descriptions of the period by Hall, Cowley and Field suggest that a not insignificant sub-community was forming in American poetry, making this an era when it was possible for important poets to be unknown to even interested practitioners in other locations. Furthermore, the presumption of a divide between academic and avant-garde poets obscured the rich complexity of the poetry that was actually being written. What united the poets Allen collected was not a singular method or manifesto,[75] nor is Allen's suggestion that they had rejected all qualities of academic

---

[73] Edward Field, Personal Interview, Email, January 14, 2014.

[74] Filreis refers to this as "a blindness to what would become the innovative New American Poetry – finally consolidated in Donald Allen's *The New American Poetry* (1960) – [that] functioned from emotional projection of aesthetic innocence onto political guilt, a modernist prelapsarianism in its own right." Filreis, 56.

[75] Though it could be argued that Charles Olson's essay "Projective Verse" served as a manifesto for many of the poets included in Allen's anthology, this was certainly not the case for all of them.

verse wholly accurate. One defining quality of the poets in Allen's anthology was their feeling of alienation, caused by the fact that they were not being promoted in academic or mainstream journals.

By the late 1950s there was a general sense of frustration among many of Allen's poets who believed that mainstream poets and critics who were prejudiced against experimentation had fixed the game. This provoked many to start their own publications and to vent their frustrations on their own pages. Nowhere is this more visible than in *Yugen*, edited by LeRoi Jones and his wife Hettie. For example, issue five, published in 1959, was ironically dedicated "FOR THE ACADEME," with two quotations. The first is from Edward Dahlberg: "It is redundant to be temperate if one is already impotent." The second is from Robert Creeley: "A tradition becomes inept when it blocks the necessary conclusion: it says *we* have felt nothing, it implies others have felt more." This is a clear example of taking out frustrations about the academy in print, an ongoing inspiration for independent magazines like *Yugen*.

LeRoi Jones's response to the announcements of the National Book Award and the Pulitzer Prize of 1960, won by Robert Lowell's *Life Studies* and W. D. Snodgrass's *Heart's Needle*, respectively, suggests that a feeling of alienation among the poetic avant-garde had reached the boiling point by 1960:

> To give The National Book Award to Robert Lowell is a simple & representative methodology. A fixture. It is not literary; or, to get at it from another way, it is merely literary. *Life Studies* is a good book... I mean, let me propose that Olson, Creeley and Duncan are better. And I still mean to say Lowell is the best of a bunch. Another bunch. But in giving The Pulitzer Prize for poetry to W. D. Snodgrass, it becomes viciously apparent that the methodology, the fixture, the cookie tournament, is one (if we squint in hopeless paranoia at all the phenomena of our lives) of actual filth.
>
> The NBA was easy to accept (& with only a slight, say, grimace of ironic prehension). But if the prize is Only a gift, i.e., "he got one... let's give ool' Snod the other." It, this "ficture," becomes more than just another example of the simplemindedness &/or immaturity of the official literary hierarchy. It is suddenly an ugly dishonesty, horribly obscene, that shd [*sic*] scare the hell out of anyone unfortunate enough not to be in on it. An ugliness that screams at us to injure it.[76]

---

[76] LeRoi Jones, "Putdown of the Whore of Babylon," *Yugen* 7, 1960, 4.

It is difficult to imagine a starker *crie de coeur* against the American post-war poetry establishment, and it is important to register Jones's sentiment of being "unfortunate enough not to be in on" the fixing of the literary game. This was a perceived injustice—even a perceived conspiracy—that Allen's anthology would go a long way toward correcting, not only by presenting poets whose work was not generally available to a mainstream audience but also by thrusting lesser-known poets into the spotlight where they could no longer be ignored.

That is not to say that all of Allen's contemporaries were enthusiastic or optimistic about the possibility of a specifically avant-garde anthology. Even some of those who were inclined to side with Allen's preferred style of American poetry were skeptical. Robert Creeley thought that Allen's clear opposition to *The New Poets of England and America* could weaken the anthology's impact, since *The New American Poetry* "obviously fronts on the academic, i.e., battles with that tone and manner, etc.," and "it may seem an 'other side of the tracks' collection – which would be a shame."[77] Creeley's initial reservations made his final opinion of the anthology even more significant. As he wrote to Allen in 1959:

> [*The New American Poetry*] is the biggest break any of us have had, in years, and you've done us all a great, great service – by forcing a recognition that something other than Snodgrass is being written... Again and again every damn one of us, in any such anthology, have simply been treated as if we didn't exist – which was of course the simplest way of cutting us out. So, now it can be told, – and that's great.[78]

Other poets in the anthology were equally excited about the way *The New American Poetry* brought their work official recognition. James Broughton wrote to Allen after receiving what he called "the Donald M. Allen Anthology of Great American Poetry," which "delight[ed]" him in its "outrageousness most of all." He expressed pleasure at "having all those miscellaneous persons gathered under some sort of one roof... Even if you are proved crashingly wrong in the long end, it is a stunning beau geste."[79]

---

[77] Robert Creeley to Donald Allen, April 10, 1958, Box 9, Folder 12, Donald Allen Collection, MSS 3, Special Collections & Archives, UC San Diego Library.

[78] Robert Creeley to Donald Allen, December 12, 1959, Box 9, Folder 12, Donald Allen Collection, MSS 3, Special Collections & Archives, UC San Diego Library.

[79] James Broughton to Donald Allen, May 23, 1960, Box 9, Folder 3, Donald Allen Collection, MSS 3, Special Collections & Archives, UC San Diego Library.

78   S. DELBOS

Similarly, Lew Welch praised Allen, writing, "you have solidly established yourself as the editorial genius of the age."[80] This must have been welcome praise after such an arduous editorial process and an early sign of the effect the anthology would have in winning attention if not approval for the poets included.

Whether due to a concerted effort on the part of conservative critics or because of actual ignorance, the coalescing of a community of alienated American poets in the post-war era helped create a sense of urgency for publication. And as the work of these poets began to come to fruition in various independent publications, a sense of momentum and significance took hold and led ultimately to the publication of *The New American Poetry*. Some reviewers would downplay the relevance of Allen's anthology in exactly the way Creeley predicted, but its ultimate effect was staggering. So staggering, in fact, that some of its most troubling characteristics have remained unconsidered, including its ties to the Cold War conception of American culture sponsored by the CIA.

3.3   WEAPONS OF THE COLD WAR: *THE NEW AMERICAN POETRY* AND *THE NEW AMERICAN PAINTING*

On June 3, 1959, approximately five months before he submitted the anthology to Grove Press, Donald Allen wrote to Charles Olson that "The New American Painting show has come back from Europe and is installed in the Modern Museum – yesterday I studied it with care and came away with clearer conceptions of how to handle the anthology."[81] What Allen took from the exhibition was not only the title but a general way of organizing the anthology.[82] By July 20, 1959, he could write to Gary Snyder of "this anthology of the new American poetry I'm struggling with."[83] And by September 4, the phrase had received official capitalization, as

---

[80] Lew Welch to Donald Allen, May 23, 1960, Box 9, Folder 8, Donald Allen Collection, MSS 3, Special Collections & Archives, UC San Diego Library.

[81] Donald Allen to Charles Olson, June 3, 1959, Series II: Correspondence, undated, 1910–1970, the Charles Olson Research Collection, Archives & Special Collections at the Thomas J. Dodd Research Center, University of Connecticut Libraries.

[82] Brad Gooch, in his biography of O'Hara, notes that the title of Allen's anthology "echoed" the title of the exhibition, but does not argue further. Brad Gooch, *City Poet: The Life and Times of Frank O'Hara* (New York: Harper, 2014), 354.

[83] Donald Allen to Gary Snyder, June 20, 1959, Box 10, Folder 27, Donald Allen Collection, MSS 3, Special Collections & Archives, UC San Diego Library.

3 BEHIND ENEMY LINES: *THE NEW AMERICAN POETRY* AS A COLD... 79

Allen wrote to James Broughton, "I propose to call the anthology 'The New American Poetry.'"[84]

The New American Painting, organized by the International Program of The Museum of Modern Art under the auspices of the International Council at The Museum of Modern Art, was put together in 1957 and toured eight European cities in 1958 and 1959: Basel, Milan, Madrid, Berlin, Amsterdam, Brussels, Paris and London. Drawing on a wide spectrum of lenders and assisted by Frank O'Hara,[85] the exhibition was conceived as a way to promote the painting that had been produced in America since World War II, namely, according to the curators, abstract expressionism.[86] It is not difficult to imagine why Allen would have felt inspired by this vibrant exhibition, which featured some of the most original and exciting American painters to have emerged since World War II.

One of the unique aspects of *The New American Painting* is the emphasis it put on each artist's individuality. Alfred H. Barr's introduction to the exhibition describes the artists' "uncompromising" individualism.[87] Barr's opening remarks in the catalogue appear after epigraphs from nine of the artists, expressing their personal beliefs about the newness and significance of their work. Of these, the first, from Clyfford Still, is representative: "We are now committed to an unqualified act, not illustrating outworn myths or contemporary alibi. One must accept total responsibility for what he executes."[88] Each of the artists in the catalogue is represented not only by reproductions of paintings but by a personal statement about his or her art and beliefs on the role and method of the artist. These are similar to the Statements on Poetics included in Allen's anthology, as they are discourses from practitioners rather than critics.

The artist statements in the catalogue of *The New American Painting* weren't exactly an innovation. But what is striking about the exhibition and its catalogue in reference to *The New American Poetry* is the way each artist is given the space to present himself or herself as an individual, and

[84] Donald Allen to James Broughton, September 4, 1959, Box 10, Folder 3, Donald Allen Collection, MSS 3, Special Collections & Archives, UC San Diego Library.

[85] *The New American Painting* (New York: The Museum of Modern Art, 1959), 6.

[86] Seventeen artists were included: William Baziotes, James Brooks, Sam Francis, Arshile Gorky, Adolf Gottlieb, Philip Guston, Grace Hartigan, Franz Kline, Willem de Kooning, Robert Motherwell, Barnett Newman, Jackson Pollock, Mark Rothko, Theodoros Stamos, Clyfford Still, Bradley Walker Tomlin and Jack Tworkov.

[87] *The New American Painting*, 15.

[88] *The New American Painting*, 15.

80   S. DELBOS

yet as a whole these 17 artists are presented as part of a particular tendency in contemporary American painting. Allen would use precisely this method for his anthology, producing a uniquely up-to-date collection of poetry that showcased a group of individuals supposedly united as much by time and place as by a shared set of stylistic and aesthetic beliefs. This style of presentation would allow Allen to foreground chronology and geography, presenting a diverse group of poets in a relatively coherent manner.

The New American Painting was just as polarizing as *The New American Poetry* would prove to be.[89] If that were the whole story, the fact that Allen was directly influenced by this exhibition would be an interesting footnote to the history of the anthology. But this exhibition sits squarely at the center of what has become one of the most intriguing and controversial aspects of the Cold War for humanities scholars: the cultural warfare sponsored by the State Department, the CIA and their umbrella organization, the Congress for Cultural Freedom (CCF), a group that promoted certain strands of American art and culture as counterexamples to that of the Soviet Union. It was revealed in 1966 that the CIA had created and secretly funded the CCF in an effort at Cold War cultural propaganda.[90] In 1974 Eva Cockcrover argued that the CCF's support of abstract expressionism was a "Weapon of the Cold War."[91] More recently, Frances Stonor Saunders has shown that *The New American Painting* was financed by the CCF, making the exhibition more than simply a representation of the most innovative contemporary American art.[92] *The New American Painting* was a cog in America's Cold War machine that influenced *The New American Poetry*.

The success of a propaganda project like *The New American Painting* depended on its ability to not draw attention to itself as anything but an exhibition of painting. By all accounts, this worked. As Basil King said,

[89] For one particularly incendiary review, see Geoffrey Wagner, "The New American Painting," *The Antioch Review*, 14. 1, Spring, 1954: 3–13. JSTOR, http://www.jstor.org/discover/10.2307/4609685, January 5, 2013.

[90] Frances Stonor Saunders, "Modern Art Was CIA 'Weapon,'" *The Independent*, October 22, 1995, www.independent.co.uk/news/world/modern-art-was-cia-weapon-1578808.html, May 1, 2015.

[91] Eva Cockcrover, "Abstract Expressionism: Weapon of the Cold War," *Artforum,* Vol. 15, No. 10, June (1974): 39–41.

[92] For an erudite examination of *Advancing American Art*, a previous and even more controversial modern art exhibition funded for the purposes of cultural warfare, see Michael L. Krenn, *Fall-out Shelters for the Human Spirit: American Art and the Cold War* (Chapel Hill and London: University of North Carolina Press, 2005).

referring to the exhibition, "I saw the show because I saw the show."[93] The influence, however indirect, of the CCF on *The New American Poetry* must be emphasized because it marks an important moment when the efforts of the CCF on behalf of the CIA crossed over from the mainstream to the underground in American arts and letters. The Anglophone poets who were involved with the CCF, purposefully or inadvertently, tended to be those who published in more popular, commercial venues. This was partly because the only publications worth supporting from the CCF's point of view were those with a wide enough distribution to make them effective at disseminating texts, images and ideas to a significant readership. When one considers the thousands of readers, editors, critics and poets who were in touch with projects and publications related to the CCF, it becomes clear how effective a method of cultural warfare this was. American publications funded or supported by the CCF included *Daedalus, The Hudson Review, The Kenyon Review, The Sewanee Review, Poetry, The Paris Review* and *The Partisan Review*.[94] Limiting consideration to prominent American poets who had more or less direct contact with the CCF, even without being aware of it, a short list would include Elizabeth Bishop (who helped host visiting writers sponsored by the CCF in Brazil),[95] Robert Lowell (whose 1962 visit to Brazil was sponsored by the CCF),[96] James Merrill (who attended a CCF meeting in Berlin in 1964 and whose Ingram Merrill Foundation supported the CCF)[97] and John Crowe Ransom (who founded and edited *The Kenyon Review*).[98] All of these poets and publications would have been considered academic and certainly none of them were included in Allen's anthology or were

---

[93] Basil King, Personal Interview, Telephone, April 7, 2018.

[94] Patrick Iber, "Literary Magazines for Socialists Funded by the CIA, Ranked," *The Awl*, August 24, 2015, https://www.theawl.com/2015/08/literary-magazines-for-socialists-funded-by-the-cia-ranked/, January 6, 2018.

[95] Bethany Hicock, *Elizabeth Bishop's Brazil* (Charlottesville: University of Virginia Press, 2016), 6.

[96] Hicock, 6.

[97] Langdon Hammer, *James Merrill: Life and Art* (New York City: Knopf, 2015), 346.

[98] Stonor Saunders, 240. Some commentators have suggested that Ransom was actively working to recruit promising students into the CIA. See: Iber, "Literary Magazines for Socialists Funded by the CIA, Ranked," and Steven P. Meyer and Jeffrey Steinberg, "The Congress for Cultural Freedom: Making the Postwar World Safe for Fascist 'Kulturkampf,'" *The Executive Review*, http://www.larouchepub.com/other/2004/site_packages/3125ccf_kulturkampf.html, January 6, 2018.

publishing in the independent journals he searched for the contents of his anthology.

The figure of Ransom looms large in opposition to Allen and *The New American Poetry* in part because of Ransom's homophobia, as expressed in his rejection of Robert Duncan's previously accepted submission to *The Kenyon Review* following the publication of Duncan's essay "The Homosexual in Society" in 1944,[99] which will be examined at greater length in Chap. 4. The New Critical hegemony represented by Ransom and his connection to *Understanding Poetry* also made him a target toward which Allen aimed his anthology. *The New American Poetry*'s overt opposition to figures such as Ransom and also to the dominant American postwar political ideology makes the influence of that very ideology on the anthology all the more notable.

Allen's use of *The New American Painting* as inspiration was an important breakthrough for the CCF, though it is unclear whether or not the group recognized it as such, or even registered it at all. Nonetheless it can be interpreted as an American development of their European efforts. As Frances Stonor Saunders has written, referring to the CCF, "whether they liked it or not, whether they knew it or not, there were few writers, poets, artists, historians, scientists, or critics in postwar Europe whose names were not in some way linked to this covert enterprise."[100] The efforts of the CCF were by purpose and necessity directed outwardly, toward Europe and elsewhere, especially countries along the Iron Curtain and nations in Asia and South America that were felt to be particularly vulnerable to communist influence. However, when Allen borrowed the title of a CCF-sponsored exhibition, along with the distinctly nationalist focus and the American flag on the cover of his anthology, the international efforts of the CCF were clearly visible at home, and an important document of American culture reflected the image of American culture that had been constructed to be projected to other nations around the world. With the publication of *The New American Poetry*, the influence of the CCF, or at least its picture of post-war American culture, became much more rapidly and thoroughly disseminated in the United States.

As mentioned previously, the pervasive efforts of the CCF were discovered and publicized in the mid-1960s. By the 1970s, the congress had ceased to function in its previous capacity. While several of the

---

[99] Robert Duncan, *Collected Essays and Other Prose*, 15.
[100] Stonor Saunders, 2.

CCF-funded publications listed above continue to publish today, it seems safe to say that their work in the twenty-first century has little connection to current efforts by the CIA.[101] But since this aspect of *The New American Poetry* has yet to be fully investigated, and since the anthology has continued to be extremely influential, there is interesting lineage from the contemporary conception of American poetry to the cultural warfare of the Cold War. As a 2017 exhibition at the Haus der Kulturen der Welt in Berlin, *Parapolitics: Cultural Freedom and the Cold War* showed,[102] the field of research into Cold War cultural warfare and the influence of the CCF is still developing. Allen's anthology and its attendant effects on poets, editors and critics should be taken into this account.

That Allen's anthology was conceived in a climate of pro-American nationalism and Cold War propaganda does not necessarily take away from the uniqueness and importance of his editorial achievement. However, it does suggest that he was not pushing against the status quo—whether political or cultural—nearly as much as commonly believed. It is not that Allen's specific choices for the anthology were dictated by the government but that his style of packaging and presenting these poets, which would have long-term effects both on the way they were received and on the way Anglophone poetry has been interpreted and anthologized, was influenced by the CIA's cultural warfare.[103]

Allen, like the poets he published, was guided by Cold War conflicts that were literary and more generally cultural. But the politics of the poems in the anthology have been downplayed in critical considerations of the anthology and the period as critics focus exclusively on the formal

---

[101] However, as Kent Johnson has pointed out, "Henry S. Bienen, the current President of the Poetry Foundation lists, among others, the following past employment and service connections on his résumé: Consultant for the State Department, the National Security Council, the Agency for International Development, the CIA, the World Bank, and Boeing (the Poetry Foundation intriguingly omits these associations in its own public bio on Bienen)." Kent Johnson, "Dispatch #20 – Unfree poetry for brave Marxists," *Dispatches from the Poetry Wars*, September 14, 2017, https://www.dispatchespoetrywars.com/dispatches/dispatch-20-unfree-poetry-brave-marxists/, October 15, 2017.

[102] *Parapolitics: Cultural Freedom and the Cold War*, Haus der Kulturen der Welt, https://www.hkw.de/en/programm/projekte/2017/parapolitics/parapolitics_start.php, January 6, 2018.

[103] For a penetrating study of the amorphous relationship between planned effects and actual outcomes in cultural warfare, see David Monod, "He's a Cripple an' Needs my Love: Porgy and Bess as Cold War Propaganda," *The Cultural Cold War in Western Europe, 1945–1960*, Giles Scott-Smith and Hans Krabbendam, eds. (London: Frank Cass, 2003), 300.

characteristics of the poems and the supposed tug-of-war between raw and cooked poetries, due in part to Allen's inclusion of the "Notes on Poetics" section, and the way he presented the poets in his introduction to the anthology, which highlights the poets' supposed anti-academic stance while downplaying the content of the poems. Just as the general conception of abstract expressionism circles around the idea of an American sense of spontaneity, obscuring the multicultural backgrounds of the artists who were central to the movement as well as their complex individual journeys from formalism to abstraction, the legacy of *The New American Poetry* tends to be limited to the victory of the liberal, anti-academic individual voice. This is a reduction of a richer complexity.

It's easy now to look back on so many of the supposed lessons and dangers of the Cold War as nothing more than well-meaning or insidious propaganda, depending upon one's point of view. Like the idea that hiding under a desk would protect you from the explosion of an atomic bomb, the perception of communism as hell-bent on overthrowing western society now seems charmingly outdated. Similarly, images and objects from the 1950s tend to inspire a kind of kitsch nostalgia, whether it's the ranch-style home, the hula-hoop, the drive-in or the backyard bomb shelter. But just as pop culture's curiosity for these throwbacks masks the environment of strict social and political conformity, fear and distrust they sprung from, the easy association of *The New American Poetry* with the commonplace narrative of the destruction of the cage of form and the triumph of personal freedom in poetry simplifies and sanitizes the complex way these poems and this book grew out of their era and interacted with it. While no one can go to a drive-in today without the feeling of doing something positively old fashioned, most critics and readers continue to accept Allen's Cold War model of American poetry and its attendant binary split between avant-garde and academic without question.

Reevaluating the anthology and its milieu shows that the common critical narrative of the anthology wars, along with the framework it has given us for talking about American poetry to this day, is a vast simplification of an era when many supposedly antagonistic poets were connected socially, when serious poets of all styles were rethinking their approach to form and when the anti-academicism espoused by many non-academic poets was inspired by a sense of alienation as well as self-promotion. Replacing the depoliticized context in which these poems are most often read with the volatile complexities of the Cold War allows us to come to a fuller understanding of the poems themselves and the way they chaffed against and dovetailed with the designs of their society and their editor. Allen's correspondence with some of the key poets in the anthology also suggests that even he realized there were other, more complex and more political ways to interpret the content and themes of this poetry in contrast to the simplified version he presented in his introduction.

CHAPTER 4

The Community of Love: *The New American Poetry* and Revolutionary Relationships in Cold War America

In a letter to Robert Duncan on November 3, 1959, the day after he turned in the anthology to Grove Press, Donald Allen suggested that the distinguishing trait of the poems included in *The New American Poetry*, as opposed to post-war poetry at large, had nothing to do with form or attitudes toward academia but was rather a "keener analysis of the elements of love and friendship":

> The recurring theme of the anthology (it was only towards the end that I realized this was happening) is love or rather that enormous complex of themes; there are all the themes of lust, desire, hatred, longing, etc., but what profoundly distinguishes much of the New Poetry here from every other group of poets one could assemble from the contemporary scene strikes me as being (what I think of as being the prevailing continuing leavening ethic inherited from Black Mountain): the community of love. Whether we (Olson's the 200 that matter) love each other more today than before, than others have in earlier periods, I can't say; but the work certainly shows a keener analysis of the elements of love and friendship, etc.[1]

[1] Donald Allen to Robert Duncan, November 3, 1959, TL: 1, 1959–1964, Box: 77, Robert Duncan Collection, PCMS-0110, The Poetry Collection of the University Libraries, University at Buffalo, The State University of New York.

© The Author(s), under exclusive license to Springer Nature Switzerland AG 2021
S. Delbos, *The New American Poetry and Cold War Nationalism*, Modern and Contemporary Poetry and Poetics, https://doi.org/10.1007/978-3-030-77352-6_4

88   S. DELBOS

This insightful description of the distinct character and significance of the poetry in *The New American Poetry* differs from Allen's introduction to the anthology, which describes the unifying characteristic of the poets included as "a total rejection of all those qualities typical of academic verse" and suggests that the poets are "closely allied to modern jazz and abstract expressionist painting."[2] Allen's letter to Duncan inspires this chapter's consideration of the anthology's political and social significance, which has often been obscured by debates about poetic form, thanks in part to Allen's introduction. The obscurity of this aspect of the anthology, which necessitates its closer examination, is summed up by Brother Antoninus in a letter to Allen in 1960: "I had thought its emphasis would be vitalist, in the Whitman-Lawrencian sense, but by assimilating it to abstract American art and music, its emphasis becomes experimental, ie., cerebral."[3] The palpable disappointment here speaks to the way that Allen—purposefully or inadvertently—obscured this vitalist, communal aspect of the anthology in favor of a more pronounced division between academic and avant-garde.[4]

"The community of love" is a phrase heavy with connotations. It points backward and forward at once—back to the radical 1930s, when it was used by the Catholic Worker Movement and left-leaning writers and thinkers, and even farther back to nineteenth-century American communes and the work of the German philosopher Georg Wilhelm Friedrich Hegel, who used it to describe the community surrounding Jesus. The phrase also looks forward to the liberal sexual practices of the 1960s. But "the community of love" also had a political meaning in the 1950s, when its underlying features of collectivism and the abolishment of private property would have reminded even the most open-minded American of communism. Allen's use of the phrase to describe the anthology suggests this poetry is more engaged in politics than his introduction and critics such as Kalaidjian suggest.

[2] Allen, xi.

[3] Brother Antoninus to Donald Allen, May 31, 1960, Box 9, Folder 12, Donald Allen Collection, MSS 3, Special Collections & Archives, UC San Diego Library.

[4] It's also important to note the way that critics assumed that Allen's introduction truly spoke for the poets themselves. Katherine Garrison Chapin wrote in her review of *The New American Poetry* that the poets therein "align themselves with abstract painting, experimental music and jazz. They have grown impatient with the New Criticism of the thirties and forties, and they reject whatever they feel is 'academic' in writing – a wide term." Katherine Garrison Chapin, "Fifteen Years of New Writing," *The New Republic*, January 9, 1961, 25.

4 THE COMMUNITY OF LOVE: *THE NEW AMERICAN POETRY...* 89

On November 5, 1959, Duncan responded to Allen with a detailed analysis of the role of love, friendship and community in American poetry:

> I have much the same thot [*sic*] that you have in your letter about the theme of love (the continual creation of the idea of love is the romance tradition... adverse critics use the term "romantic" to obscure the continuity). But I'm not an enthusiast for pan-eros... There are general ideas which my mind would assent to in Ginsberg's democratic vistas but my nerves and heart are not humanitarian. Academic verse (that is verse written by schoolteachers) specifically cannot deal with love at any depth that is disturbing to public respectability. But given that poets who are not public figures can afford to be intense in their sexual lives – i.e. can inherit the responsibilities of the romance tradition or of erotic ceremonies or sacraments.[5]

Duncan's careful consideration of the theme of love, not just in Allen's anthology but also regarding the larger context of contemporary poetry, suggests that the topic was significant for poets of the period. Duncan even claims that attitudes toward love and a willingness to write intensely about sex distinguishes "poets who are not public figures" from those who teach, an important point that reflects back on the debates about so-called academic poets examined above.[6]

Taking Allen's use of the phrase "the community of love" as a framework for this poetry and as a starting point for a consideration of love, relationships and marriage in post-war America reveals important ways the poems in *The New American Poetry* interacted with their Cold War context on levels other than form. This chapter first considers the social and interpersonal context of this exchange between Allen and Duncan before illuminating the history of the phrase "the community of love" and how it would have been interpreted in the late 1950s. Next the chapter examines the changing role of marriage and sexual mores during the Cold War to

---

[5] Robert Duncan to Donald Allen, November 5, 1959, TL: 1, 1959–1964, Box: 77, Robert Duncan Collection, PCMS-0110, The Poetry Collection of the University Libraries, University at Buffalo, The State University of New York.

[6] James Wright had earlier confirmed the idea that poets vying for job security in teaching positions were limited in terms of subject matter. In a letter to Donald Hall in 1958 he wrote, referring to the poetry he had published in *The New Poets of England and America*: "I already felt within myself the secret guilt at my denying the darker and wilder side of myself for the sake of subsisting on mere comfort – both academic and poetic." Anne Wright and Saundra Rose Maley, eds., *A Wild Perfection: The Selected Letters of James Wright* (New York: Farrar, Strauss and Giroux, 2005), 132.

90   S. DELBOS

suggest how poems in the anthology promoted alternative, liberal life-styles during a conservative period. Putting these poems in the larger context of American poetry shows how both Allen's poets and the so-called "academic" poets of the period reflected changes in American society after World War II.

Allen's letter only begins to suggest how the anthology promotes opinions and lifestyles considered subversive during the Cold War. At the same time, it distances the poems from the charges of arid impersonality that conservative critics commonly leveled against left-leaning poets of the period.[7] This sheds light on the complex ways *The New American Poetry* deals with politics and locates it among the stalking horses and public doublespeak of the 1950s. But most immediately, this exchange between two gay men[8] during an especially repressive time and place that has been referred to as "homophobic America,"[9] where "to be out was a dangerous thing, and even gossip could ruin you,"[10] merits a consideration of Allen's use of the phrase "the community of love," and Duncan's response to it, in terms of homosexuality and masculinity in *The New American Poetry*.

4.1   PARTICULARLY VULNERABLE: GAY POETS IN *THE NEW AMERICAN POETRY*

Robert Duncan and Donald Allen were gay (as were Allen Ginsberg and Walt Whitman, the two poets Duncan alludes to in his letter), which suggests that any interpretation of this exchange and the multitude of meanings and connotations of "the community of love" should consider how the phrase reflected on the gay community of the 1950s. Utilizing this framework to examine Allen's letter and Duncan's response, which includes a rejoinder against the "public respectability" of "Academic verse," also reveals the self-censorship many gay men in America felt forced to employ during this period, while adding nuance to the academic and avant-garde divide explored previously.

[7] Filreis, 115.

[8] Thank you to Kevin Killian for confirming Allen's homosexuality.

[9] Ian Thomson, "Cold War Dante: How a Medieval Christian Poet Inspired a Texan, Neo-Dadaist Maverick," *Times Literary Supplement*, September 15, 2017, 5.

[10] Jason Farago, "A Flag Is a Flag Is a Flag," *The New York Review of Books*, March 22, 2018. http://www.nybooks.com/articles/2018/03/22/jasper-johns-flag-is-a-flag/, March 24, 2018.

Duncan's survey of what he refers to as sexual intensity in American poetry and the unwillingness of certain public figures to express or explore it for fear of losing their jobs reveals the pervasive fear that surrounded homosexuality throughout the 1950s, especially in the academy. Many people in positions of power considered homosexuals moral and physical degenerates while equating homosexuality with both alcoholism and communism.[11] Homosexuals in general feared admitting or being forced to admit their sexuality, which would potentially cost them their jobs and public standing. This tense moment forced homosexuals to use extreme caution, even when communicating with one another.

The Lavender Scare began in 1950, when "two statements by U.S. government officials concerning security risks in the State Department captured national attention," one being the supposed infiltration by 205 card-carrying communists and the other the contention that among the individuals considered to be security risks at the State Department 91 were homosexuals.[12] As Johnson writes, "the 1950s generally witnessed a tremendous upsurge in publicity about 'sexual perverts,'"[13] during a period when "three of President Harry Truman's top advisors wrote him a joint memorandum warning that 'the country is more concerned about the charges of homosexuals in the Government than about Communists.'"[14] With the passing of sexual psychopath laws that targeted homosexuals in 21 states and the District of Columbia by the late 1950s, "life for many American gay men and lesbians was now more fearful and secretive than ever before."[15] Over the next decades, more individuals would lose their jobs or be denied jobs because of their supposed homosexuality than for connections to the Communist Party.[16]

This situation affected even individuals who did not hold governmental or academic posts. In an interview with Ekbert Faas conducted in 1980, Duncan asks: "Did you ever talk to Creeley about the letter sent to Olson

---

[11] David K. Johnson, *The Lavender Scare: The Cold War Persecution of Gays and Lesbians in the Federal Government* (Chicago: University of Chicago Press, 2004), 8.

[12] Johnson, 1.

[13] Johnson, 5.

[14] Johnson, 2.

[15] Edward White, *The Tastemaker: Carl Van Vechten and the Birth of Modern America* (New York: Farrar, Straus and Giroux, 2014), 291.

[16] James Kirchick, "The Dark History of Anti-Gay Innuendo," *Politico*, February 13, 2019, https://www.politico.com/magazine/story/2019/02/13/the-dark-history-of-anti-gay-innuendo-224930, February 14, 2019.

where he says something like 'why do you bring this lavender or something into the group?'"[17] Duncan goes on to explain that Creeley was referring to the purple poetry he wrote during this period, yet it is impossible to ignore the homosexual connotations of the phrase. Indeed, Duncan himself, after explaining Creeley's reference, almost immediately links this exchange to the reaction he faced after his essay "The Homosexual in Society" was published in 1944 in Dwight Macdonald's journal *Politics*.

In this essay Duncan outlines, with remarkable clarity and courage, his formulations and reflections about the homosexual's place in society. He also admits that he is homosexual, the first time an American writer had done so publicly in writing. Unsurprisingly, the article caused a stir upon publication. Eventually it led John Crowe Ransom to withdraw his acceptance of Duncan's poem "Toward an African Elegy" in *The Kenyon Review* because Ransom, after reading the essay, considered the poem an advertisement for homosexuality.[18] For Duncan and gay poets like him, the homophobia of American life during the 1950s—especially in the government and the academy—was not an abstraction.

Many of the poets in *The New American Poetry* were gay, including Allen Ginsberg, Robert Duncan, Peter Orlovsky, Jack Spicer, Robin Blaser, Frank O'Hara, John Ashbery, Jonathan Williams, James Broughton, Ebbe Borregaard, James Schuyler, Edward Field and John Wieners.[19] Yet *The New American Poetry* is not exactly an anthology of gay poetry. The lack of explicitly homosexual poetry in the anthology, with a few exceptions, mainly from Allen Ginsberg, would have been caused in part by a harshly repressive American Cold War culture and is possibly attributable to Allen's editorial choices as well.[20] Nevertheless, Allen's sexuality and that

[17] Christopher Wagstaff, *A Poet's Mind: Collected Interviews with Robert Duncan, 1960–1985* (Berkeley: North Atlantic Books, 2012), 358.

[18] Robert Duncan, *Collected Essays and Other Prose*, 15.

[19] Allen's anthology is far less diverse in terms of race and gender, an issue that will be taken up in Chap. 6.

[20] Clearly Allen could have included more explicitly homosexual poems in the anthology. The poem "Rocks and Cocks" by Jack Flynn is indicative of a whole other tradition of controversial poetry being published at this time that Allen would have been aware of from his arduous research in small magazines and independent journals:

> I have a cock
> like a rock –
> meaning – my cock
> shatters

of some of the poets in the anthology were not lost on certain readers, like editor and writer Jory Sherman, who called Allen's anthology "a daisy chain affair with every snotnosed poet running to him with hardon, and ms. clutched in crotch."[21] This type of aggressive anti-homosexual rhetoric and the myriad ways that gay poets responded to it were rooted in the context of the Cold War, when, as Michael Davidson points out, homosexuals often felt compelled to mask and subvert their own homosexuality, even in one another's company.

Davidson cites the "compulsory homosociality"[22] of 1950s avant-garde poets, specifically around Jack Spicer in San Francisco and Charles Olson at Black Mountain College, to whom Allen refers in his letter to Duncan as one source of the community of love. During the Cold War, alongside a greater awareness of homosexuals, there was a constellating of homosexual identities, as different communities interpreted issues of identity and rebellion against a repressive society in different ways.[23] Allen and Duncan locate their ideas about the community of love in distinct contexts. Allen frames it within the rough-and-tumble camaraderie of Black Mountain, a community that, like Allen's anthology, rallied around and in many cases followed the suggestions of Charles Olson. Meanwhile Duncan places contemporary relationships and community in the context of Eros and the romance tradition.

> like a rock when
> I meet
> homosexuals
> who try to
> shatter
> rock cocks
> with
> little
> rocks.

Walter Höllerer Collection, Das Literaturarchiv Sulzbach-Rosenberg, [03] WH / BH [/ 11, 1.]

[21] "Daisy chain" has a specific homosexual connotation relating to oral sex. Jeff Weddle, *Bohemian New Orleans: The Story of the Outsider and Loujon Press* (Jackson: University Press of Mississippi, 2007), 67.

[22] Michael Davidson, *Guys Like Us: Citing Masculinity in Cold War Poetics* (Chicago, University of Chicago Press, 2004), 28.

[23] Davidson, 28.

94 S. DELBOS

In the same letter quoted above, Duncan continues at length with an interesting description of the contemporary poetic landscape regarding sexuality, passion and one's relationship to the physical body:

> Among the new poets, as I hint in the new notes to my *Politics* article, there is a marked search to attack the sensual unity with drugs – aspiring to subject senses to psyche: impotence, constipation, stomach cramps, and paranoiac projection of the "scene" are the result. Self-loathing is almost the mode of Ginsberg, McClure, and Lamantia. Certainly the most rudimentary love suffers in the process... The new poets seem anyway to shift from the genitals to the viscera; the stomach and not the heart is the emotional center; poets of shit (which word they use too for their drugs) and not of blood. The decline in sexuality between *Ulysses* or *Lady Chatterly's Lover* and *The Subterraneans* or *Howl* is major.

Duncan seems to object to depictions of physical relations from his contemporaries because they profane the tradition of romance and locate it in baser instincts. He laments the dissolution of the "lover's quest" in contemporary American poetry, suggesting that promiscuity, which is evident in several of the poems in the anthology, had taken the place of chivalry and courting. This "intensity" that Duncan writes about in regard to relationships and how those without public personas can afford to be intense refers to heterosexual and homosexual relationships alike and cuts across the divide of academic and avant-garde.

The *Politics* article Duncan refers to here is a revised version of "The Homosexual in Society," complete with new notes, which he prepared in 1959.[24] It makes clear the topic of the homosexual in American society was still very much on Duncan's mind in the late 1950s, though he admits his life had changed dramatically in positive ways since the original essay was published. The essay and Duncan's notes reflect interestingly on the exchange between Allen and Duncan regarding the community of love.

There is a revealing portrait of W. H. Auden in Duncan's 1959 notes for the essay,[25] showing the pervasiveness of insecurity among gay poets during this period, even famous poets such as Auden. Auden's comments about his professional life harmonize with Duncan's description of a lack of freedom among academic poets to deal truthfully with their sex lives.

---

[24] Robert Duncan, *Collected Essays and Other Prose*, James Maynard, ed. (Berkeley: University of California Press, 2014), 444.

[25] Duncan, *Collected Essays and Other Prose*, 446.

According to Duncan's 1959 notes, he wrote to "an eminent poet in 1945 asking if I could attempt an essay on his work in the light of my concept that his language had been diverted to conceal the nature of his sexual life and that because he could never write directly he had failed to come to grips with immediacies of feeling."[26] Auden declined to give permission, in large part because of his work in academia:

> As you may know, I earn a good part of my livelihood by teaching, and in that profession one is particularly vulnerable. Further, both as a writer and as a human being, the occasion may always arise, particularly in these times, when it becomes one's duty to take a stand on the unpopular side of some issue. Should that ever occur, your essay would be a very convenient red-herring for one's opponents. (Think of what happened to Bertrand Russell in New York.)[27]

In 1940, Bertrand Russell was given a post as professor at The City College of New York, a position that was rescinded after a court ruled that the philosopher was "morally unfit" to teach, due to his beliefs about marriage and relationships.[28] Clearly this exchange was on Duncan's mind when he was writing to Allen, having just revisited it for his notes to the new version of his essay. In 1975, when Duncan was filmed for a documentary, he suggested that the impossibility of an academic career for a non-closeted homosexual like himself had been a turning point of his life:

> When I was 17 and 18 and in love with a college professor and living with a college professor, what I saw there was the double life that homosexuals lived in the academic world. And I knew another thing about myself that was after all a strength… one thing I was never going to have, and maybe I was not capable of it, but certainly I also had a moral conviction against it… I was not going to have a double life.[29]

The awareness among homosexual poets that there was simply no place for them in the academy if they did not repress their sexuality, that in fact

[26] Duncan, *Collected Essays and Other Prose*, 15.

[27] Duncan, *Collected Essays and Other Prose*, 15.

[28] Daniel Schugurensky, "1940: Bertrand Russell Unwelcome to Teach in New York," *History of Education: Selected Moments of the 20th Century*, http://schugurensky.faculty.asu.edu/moments/1940russell.html, October 28, 2017.

[29] Cody Carvel, "Robert Duncan…A Life in Poetry," *YouTube*, May 28, 2018, www.youtube.com/watch?v=WC1EwgBqEUU, March 15, 2019.

96   S. DELBOS

they could not be an openly gay poet and also an academic poet, sheds new light on the academic and avant-garde debate and also suggests that arguments such as Golding's that the academy was not "an external and easily located 'enemy'"[30] have not taken into account the real ways that academic employment was incompatible with homosexuality during the Cold War.

At the beginning of his commentary on the new publication of "The Homosexual in Society" in 1959, Duncan emphasized that although his life had improved since he wrote the essay, "all this sense of danger remains" because homosexuality was still considered a "crime."[31] He goes on to describe sexual love as a "singular adventure," and suggests that he didn't consider homosexual and heterosexual love as mutually exclusive. As Duncan wrote:

> The sense of this essay rests then upon the concept that sexual love between those of the same sex is one with sexual love between men and women; and that this love is one of the conditions of the fulfillment of the heart's desire and the restoration of man's free nature. Creative work for the common good is one of the conditions of that nature. And our hope lies still in the creative imagination wherever it unifies what had been thought divided, wherever it transforms the personal experience into a communal good.[32]

This contradicts Barrett Watten, who argues, citing Sherman Paul's description of "homoeros" in Duncan's work, that "the object of love in Duncan's poetry is male."[33] While Duncan doesn't explicitly mention the community of love in "The Homosexual in Society," the title makes clear that the essay is concerned with the gay individual in the overtly heterosexual society, thus suggesting that homosexuals formed a kind of subcommunity. Over the course of the essay Duncan draws connections between personal experience and the communal good and also remarks on what he calls a "community of thoughtful men."[34] The final paragraph of Duncan's essay can also be read as calling for a community of love. Though he does not identify it by name, he writes that his social ideal is "that

---

[30] Golding, 204.

[31] Duncan, *Collected Essays and Other Prose*, 12.

[32] Duncan, *Collected Essays and Other Prose*, 13.

[33] Barrett Watten, "The Lost America of Love: A Genealogy," *Genre* XXXIII Fall-Winter, (2000): 307.

[34] Duncan, *Collected Essays and Other Prose*, 6.

4 THE COMMUNITY OF LOVE: *THE NEW AMERICAN POETRY...* 97

fulfillment of desire as a human state of mutual volition and aid, a shared life,"[35] which is very close indeed to the community of love.

In his letter to Allen, Duncan also writes about several of his contemporaries, judging them according to the descriptions of love and relationships in their work and, perhaps intrusively, whether he believes they have "been in love":

> Lamantia's efforts to achieve the bizarre does not disguise his anti-sensual bias, his hatred of his body and attempt to achieve a separate psychic entity. It is a striking fact that he does not seem to have been in love; the women he addresses are objects of the search for the unusual or prestigious, not objects of passionate love... Whalen writes conceptual about love, and does not have any anti-sensual program: but it is a sad fact there too that he does not belong to the romance tradition either. He has never "been in love." Snyder has, but then his work shows few affinities with the group he is often put with.
>
> It's Ginsberg's work and life then that comes into the romantic, romance tradition. He has been in love, and is ardent and constant in that service... Let the above be as it is, impulsive and not definitive. I was roused by your "Whether we (Olson's the 200 that matter) love each other more today than before, than others have in earlier periods..." and the sense of how poor our literature is, as erotic sensibility, compared with *The Tale of the Genj* [*sic*].[36]

It is significant that Duncan refers to *The Tale of Genji*, a work of classic Japanese fiction that includes several homoerotic scenes.[37] Distinguishing the poets in *The New American Poetry* by whether or not their depictions of sexuality and relationships fit into the romance tradition, Duncan suggests how many of the poems in the anthology describe non-traditional approaches to love. Homosexuality is just one of the alternative styles of relationships that these poets advocate.

[35] Duncan, *Collected Essays and Other Prose*, 13.

[36] Robert Duncan to Donald Allen, November 5, 1959, TL: 1, 1959–1964, Box: 77, Robert Duncan Collection, PCMS-0110, The Poetry Collection of the University Libraries, University at Buffalo, The State University of New York.

[37] Andrew Calimach, "The Beautiful Way of the Samurai: Native Tradition and Hellenic Echo," *The World History of Male Love*, 2008, http://www.gay-art-history.org/gay-history/gay-customs/japan-samurai-male-love/japan-samurai-homosexual-shudo.html, October 28, 2017.

98   S. DELBOS

"The community of love" is a phrase with complex connotations that developed over time and took on specifically political meanings during the Cold War. Allen's use of the phrase points to a myriad of possible interpretations, including those concerning homosexuality and the place of the homosexual in society. Considering how homosexuality was conflated with radical politics and social aberration during the Cold War crisis known as the Lavender Scare, any consideration of *The New American Poetry* should take into account the era's rampant homophobia, which highlights the fact that the anthology was unusually inclusive of homosexual poets during an era of extreme repression. This also adds a new dimension to the post-war divide between the academy and the avant-garde, revealing that one key element of the rebellion of gay poets against the academy was the fact that it was not possible to be both openly homosexual and a teacher or professor. Approaching *The New American Poetry* this way fits the anthology squarely within a discussion of Cold War politics and culture, democracy, capitalism, Catholicism, sexuality and freedom.

4.2   Freedom from the Pursuit of Insane Objectives: The Cold War Community of Love

Donald Allen didn't invent the community of love. The concept, if not the exact phrase, was on the minds of several poets during this period. Ginsberg's "A Supermarket in California," included in *The New American Poetry*, asks of Walt Whitman: "Will we stroll dreaming of the lost America of love past blue automobiles in driveways, home to our silent cottage?"[38] Robert Creeley, writing his poem "For Love" in September 1960,[39] just after the publication of Allen's anthology, concluded: "Into the company of love / it all returns." Libbie Rifkin shows how this echoes Hart Crane's "The Broken Tower," which declares the poet's task "to trace the visionary company of love," an allusion that gives a sense of completion to Creeley's volume, which opens with an elegy for Crane. Rifkin also proposes a reading of these lines as "bespeaking the certainty of professional affirmation, a return on a decade's careful investment, as much as the

[38] Allen, 182.
[39] Libbie Rifkin, *Career Moves: Olson, Creeley, Zukofsky, Berrigan, and the American Avant-garde* (Madison: University of Wisconsin Press, 2000), 69.

optimism of a new marriage."[40] This focus on love in American poetry would become even more pronounced as the 1960s progressed.

Allen may have been thinking of Ginsberg in his description of the anthology to Duncan. Other important uses of "the community of love" as a phrase or concept came from Kenneth Rexroth, the Catholic Worker Movement, American communes of the nineteenth century and Hegel, all of whom used the concept of the community of love as an ideal for human existence based on mutual affection rather than commerce or competition. However, what began as an essentially religious idea had become politically charged by the 1950s, due largely to outspoken individuals like Rexroth. In an interview from 1959, Rexroth gives his own colorful definition of the community of love as "the organic community of man":

> This doesn't mean that it's all a great gang fuck. In fact, it doesn't have anything to do with that at all. It means that what holds a natural society together is an all-pervading Eros which is an extension and reflection, a multiple reflection, of the satisfactions which are eventually traced to the actual lover and beloved. Out of the union of the lover and the lover as the basic unit of society flares this whole community of love. Curiously enough, this is Hegelianism, particularly the neo-Hegelians who are the only people who ever envisaged a multiple absolute which was a community of love... But, irrespective of the metaphysical meanings, this is what makes a primitive society work... This sounds very romantic but it is actually quite anthropological.[41]

The intersection of physical love, public love and politics resonates with much of the poetry in *The New American Poetry*. Rexroth posits the community of love as an anthropological fact found not just in Hegel's study of the early Christian community but also in Native American tribal culture. Elsewhere in this interview, Rexroth suggests the community of love is the natural condition of mankind but has been eradicated by the ruling powers of American capitalist democracy who feel threatened because a community that is bound together this way cannot be controlled or

---

[40] Rifkin, 69. This is a line also cited by Barrett Watten in a consideration of language poetry, by which time its meaning had contracted to "literary community." Anne Dewey, Libbie Rifkin eds., *Among Friends: Engendering the Social Site of Poetry* (Iowa City: University of Iowa Press, 2013), 110.

[41] Kenneth Rexroth, "The Social Lie," *Liberation*, June 1959, 13–14.

100 S. DELBOS

commodified. In promoting the community of love Rexroth was in fact promoting an alternative system of governance.

During the Cold War, any suggestion of alternatives to American democracy would have been interpreted as communist sympathizing at best; in many cases this would have been accurate. Rexroth later mentioned the community of love in his obituary for Muriel Rukeyser, who died in 1980. The phrase's communist connotations, and its connections to Whitman, here come to the fore:

> After all, poetry in the tradition of the American Dream must be tragic, because the Community of Love of Whitman (and of all the communalist communities that flourished in his youth) has not been realized.
>
> Muriel Rukeyser believed in the Community of Love, not because she was convinced that it was going to win but because it is true, it is the right way for human beings to live. She has been accused of optimism, and this in a country where the Left thinks the revolution is around the corner and the rest of the population continuously invent euphemisms for graveyards. I think gravediggers (undertakers) now call themselves bereavement counselors.
>
> Like Walt Whitman, as the horizons darkened and the Community of Love seemed to grow more distant, Muriel sought ever deeper into her self for its meaning.[42]

Using the phrase to refer to Rukeyser, a poet well known for her leftist sympathies, Rexroth suggests a connection between the community of love and radical politics and reveals the way that words like "love," "community" and "communalism" were used to sanitize leftist politics in public discourse during the Cold War. Rukeyser is a fulcrum in this discussion because of the way she, like many left-leaning poets in the post-war period, was maligned by critics such as Louise Bogan for writing poetry that "outlawed personal emotion," was "deficient in the sense of human life" and was devoid of "rough joy and silly pleasure."[43] Such sentiments—which, as Filreis shows, were used broadly by conservative critics to attack in quasi-aesthetic terms a poet whose politics they disagreed with—reveal the deeper political implications of Allen's use of the phrase "the community

---

[42] Kenneth Rexroth, "Rukeyser: A Partisan of Love," *Los Angeles Times*, March 2, 1989, 3.
[43] Filreis, 114–115.

of love" in 1959. Utilizing the terms of Cold War cultural debate, Allen suggests that the poets in the anthology had indeed begun to write the personal, emotional poetry that conservatives had long called for. This allowed them to sneak the countercultural message of their poems under the radar.

Despite the seemingly innocent nature of the phrase "the community of love," in the climate of the Cold War it suggested an alternative worldview that would have put those who used it in opposition to the country's prevailing values. The relationship between those with power in America and those without it was an issue that Rexroth commented upon at length. And clearly, if the community of love were an established fact, it would not have been necessary for a poet like Rukeyser to be a "partisan" for love. As Nixon's kitchen debate with Khrushchev suggested, the increased commercialization of American culture during this period, as lower unemployment and lower costs of commodities saw the standard of living rising rapidly,[44] was the trump card for the American capitalist system against communism. Materialism was politicized, and Rexroth unsurprisingly locates the enemy of love not only in government but also in commercialism. The state and state-sponsored capitalism employ what Rexroth called the social lie in order to maintain the status quo and to keep the population in check. As a result, they deny the possibility of the community of love:

> The masters, whether they be priests or kings or capitalists, when they want to exploit you, the first thing they have to do is demoralize you, and they demoralize you very simply by kicking you in the nuts. This is how it's done. Nobody is going to read any advertising copy if he is what the Reichians call orgastically potent. This is a principle of the advertising copy writer, that he must stir up discontent in the family. Modern American advertising is aimed at the woman, who is, if not always the buyer at least the pesterer, and it is designed to create sexual discontent... with the adult, the young married couple, which is the object of almost all advertising, the copy is pitched to stir up insatiable sexual discontent. It provides pictures of women who never existed. A guy gets in bed with his wife and she isn't like that and so he is discontented all the time and is therefore fit material for exploitation.[45]

---

[44] Cecil Bohanon, "Economic Recovery: Lessons from the Post-World War II Period, *Mercatus Center*, September 10, 2012, http://mercatus.org/publication/economic-recovery-lessons-post-world-war-ii-period, March 27, 2016.

[45] Lawrence Lipton, *The Holy Barbarians* (New York: Julian Messner, 1959), 295–296.

102   S. DELBOS

Concern about the increasing materialization of American society in the post-war years was not limited to Rexroth. It is one of the themes of Charles Olson's *The Maximus Poems*, which he began in the mid-1940s. In one of these poems in *The New American Poetry*, "I, Maximus of Gloucester, To You," Olson writes:

> But that which matters, that which insists, that which will last
> where shall you find it, my people, how, where shall you listen
> when all is become billboards[46]

Allen was obviously familiar with Olson's poem and also with Rexroth's writing (Allen lived in San Francisco and edited the San Francisco issue of *The Evergreen Review*, to which Rexroth contributed a long essay). Even a passing knowledge of Rexroth's work would have made Allen aware of the older poet's use of the phrase "the community of love" in his poetry, essays and interviews. He was also likely aware of "The Dragon and the Unicorn," Rexroth's long poem of post-war personal and philosophical recovery, which was published in 1952 and greeted enthusiastically by critics and poets including Olson and Duncan.[47] In this work Rexroth insists upon the community of love's opposition to the government.

"The Dragon and the Unicorn" investigates the relationship between the individual and society, time and the universe, and post-war American culture in contrast to the older cultures of Europe, suggesting naturalism in place of nationalism.[48] Rexroth mentions the community of love several times in the poem, as well as phrases including "community of lovers,"[49] "community of persons"[50] and "love relationship,"[51] along with the suggestion that "love is reciprocal."[52] Much of Rexroth's poetry is sensuous and he often found poetic and personal transcendence in the communion of lovers. Yet the recurrence of these phrases—especially in the context of

---

[46] Allen, 8.

[47] Rachel Katz Lerner, "Rexroth's 'The Dragon and the Unicorn,'" *Jacket 2*, December 24, 2012, http://jacket2.org/article/rexroths-dragon-and-unicorn, September 20, 2015.

[48] For an insightful interpretation of the poem, see Sam Hamill, "The Poetry of Kenneth Rexroth," *Jacket Magazine*, August 2003, http://jacketmagazine.com/23/rex-hamill.html, May 1, 2015.

[49] Sam Hamill and Bradford Morrow, eds., *The Collected Poems of Kenneth Rexroth* (Port Townsend: Copper Canyon Press, 2003), 407.

[50] Hamill and Morrow, 520.

[51] Hamill and Morrow, 515.

[52] Hamill and Morrow, 460.

4 THE COMMUNITY OF LOVE: *THE NEW AMERICAN POETRY...* 103

this poetic quest for meaning in the aftermath of what Rexroth viewed as the inevitable failure of capitalism to remain peaceful—proves that the community of love for Rexroth had both political and personal resonance. His adherence to this ideal, with its alienating consequences in a capitalist society, is summed up in the following lines from "The Dragon and the Unicorn":

> This is what free love is, freedom
> From the destructive power
> Of a society coerced
> Into the pursuit of insane
> Objectives. Until men learn
> To administer things, and are
> No longer themselves organized
> And exploited as things, there can
> Be no love except by intense
> Effort directed against
> The whole pressure of the world.
> In other words, love becomes,
> As it was with the Gnostics,
> The practice of a kind of cult.[53]

For Rexroth, the community of love was the one answer to the devastation of World War II. Only by joining together in a community of mutual empathy could humanity hope to overcome the promotion of murder and evil in the name of profit. At times, Rexroth's actual definition of the community of love is more metaphysical:

> A community of mutual
> Indwelling, in which each member
> Realizes his total
> Liability for the whole.[54]

But at other times Rexroth places the community of love in patent opposition to contemporary American society, which he writes is characterized by "frigid fucking for frigidaires,"[55] a phrase that briskly summarizes the

---

[53] Hamill and Morrow, 426.
[54] Hamill and Morrow, 481
[55] Hamill and Morrow, 500.

104   S. DELBOS

intensified materialism and conformity in American domestic life after World War II.

Rexroth's leap from love to politics may seem vast in Cold War America, as love has little to do with politics in a country preoccupied by war. But therein lies one element of love as a political stance: when the government in power takes conflict as its primary directive—as several political scientists including William Appleman Williams suggest the United States did during this period[56]—then an insistence on love is in fact political, since it promotes alternative practices and values. This commingling of love and politics had been explored three decades earlier by the Catholic Worker Movement, a leftist social group founded in 1933 by Dorothy Day and Peter Maurin.[57]

According to the thoughts on love and community expressed in Maurin's poetry, the community of love is united with Catholicism and the active fellowship enacted by public service, which was crucial to the lasting political and social significance of the Catholic Worker Movement. Maurin connects the concept not only to religion but to art as well, most clearly in his poem "Prostitution of Art":

> When the artists
> were artisans
> they had the community spirit.
> They had the community spirit
> because they believed
> in the doctrine
> of the Common Good.
> Now that the artists
> do no longer believe
> in the doctrine
> of the Common Good
> they sell their work
> to art speculators.
> As Eric Gill says,
> "they have become
> the lap-dogs
> of the bourgeoisie."[58]

[56] See William Appleman Williams, *The Tragedy of American Diplomacy* (New York: W.W. Norton, 1959).

[57] See Kenneth Rexroth, *An Autobiographical Novel* (New York: New Directions, 1991).

[58] Peter Maurin, *Easy Essays*, http://www.easyessays.org, May 15, 2015.

4 THE COMMUNITY OF LOVE: *THE NEW AMERICAN POETRY*... 105

Citing Eric Gill, a British socialist artist, Maurin quickly moves from art to community to politics, suggesting like Rexroth that capitalism is the enemy of community. In the poem "Up to Catholics," He places community and Catholicism in even starker contrast to capitalism. Suggesting that Catholics should start a movement "back-to-the-land," Maurin writes that Catholics "realize"

> more clearly than any others
> the shortcomings
> of the old capitalist
> industrial system.
> They, better than others,
> see the threat
> that impends.
> They alone understand
> that while the family
> is the primary social unit,
> the community comes next.
> And there is
> no sound
> and righteous
> and enduring community
> where all its members
> are not substantially
> of one mind
> in matters of the spirit–
> that is to say,
> of religion.[59]

Passages like this make Maurin's radical Catholicism clear. Religion has often, though not always, been important to the practice of a community of love. In the late nineteenth century, most Americans would have associated the phrase with communities like Brook Farm, which was officially secular, and the Oneida Community, whose founder believed Jesus had returned in 70 AD.[60] Readers such as Rexroth, who were familiar with the writing of Hegel, however, would also have connected the phrase to Jesus.

Hegel deals explicitly with the community of love in his early writings on Christianity, specifically "Christianity and its Fate" and a fragment

---

[59] Maurin, *Easy Essays.*
[60] Gay Talese, *Thy Neighbor's Wife* (Garden City: Doubleday, 1980), 306.

106   S. DELBOS

called "Love." In these essays, Hegel meditates on the formation of the Christian community around Jesus, detailing the social aspects of the movement, as well as its ultimate failure to realize the Kingdom of God on earth. For Hegel, the Kingdom of God was synonymous with the community of love:

> A loving circle, a circle of hearts that have surrendered their rights against one another over anything their own, that are united solely by a common faith and hope, and whose pleasure and joy is simply the pure single-heartedness of love, is a Kingdom of God on a small scale. But its love is not religion.[61]

Hegel's description of the community of love here both clarifies its meaning and indicates why he thought the community failed. The dual oppositions of powerful government and human nature virtually ensure the impossibility of realizing the community of love while relegating it to a minority of society or, as Rexroth writes, a kind of cult or, as Allen writes, the avant-garde.

For Hegel, love is a unity between self and other. The community of love is the Kingdom of God, a community without private property. Hegel's writings on love make this connection to property blatant, claiming that property "makes up such an important part of men's life"[62] that the community of love is unlikely to be realized. His definition of lovers is "a multiplex opposition in the course of their multiplex acquisition and possession of property and rights."[63] This is the main challenge the community of love faces in the modern world. It is also what connects it to communism.

The community of love for Hegel can only flourish when the individual cedes his importance to the group, when everything is shared and nothing is held back. It is thus in clear opposition to the democratic capitalism the United States promoted during the Cold War. The following quotes sum up the connection of love and property according to Hegel's definition of the community of love:

---

[61] Georg Wilhelm Friedrich Hegel, *On Christianity: Early Theological Writings*, Trans., T. M. Knox, (New York: Harper & Brothers, 1961), 289.

[62] Georg Wilhelm Friedrich Hegel, *On Christianity: Early Theological Writings*, Trans., T. M. Knox, (New York: Harper & Brothers, 1961), 307.

[63] Georg Wilhelm Friedrich Hegel, *On Christianity: Early Theological Writings*, Trans., T. M. Knox, (New York: Harper & Brothers, 1961), 307.

4 THE COMMUNITY OF LOVE: *THE NEW AMERICAN POETRY...* 107

Abolition of property, introduction of community of goods, common meals... The essence of their group was (a) separation from men and (b) love for one another; (a) and (b) are necessarily bound together... By love's extension over a whole community its character changes; it ceases to be a living union of individualities and instead its enjoyment is restricted to the consciousness of their mutual love... Love is indignant if part of the individual is severed and held back as a private property.[64]

Clearly there are connections between Hegel's community of love and communism as a community of individuals who cede their individualism and property to the collective.

Allen may have been aware of the historic implications of the phrase when he used it in his letter to Duncan, and he was certainly familiar with Rexroth's work and thought. This is not to suggest that *The New American Poetry* is a communist anthology or that Allen was a communist. Based on his lifestyle, interests and homosexuality, one might assume that he was liberal. Allen's archive doesn't contain many clues about his politics in this regard, though writing a reader's report on communist poet Tom McGrath's *Letter to an Imaginary Friend* in late 1957, Allen took pains to distance himself from the book's politics, stating:

McGrath echoes many of Rexroth's opinions about modern poetry. He keeps harping on his left-wing experiences and summoning up an older tradition. I would guess he is not now a Communist, but was once close to the party; but is aware too of the IWW tradition and the anarcho-socialist tradition. I wish I could recommend this poem because it stands for many things that need encouraging today: I mean the use of free verse, the attempt to deal with reality (not the left wing stuff), the positive point of view, etc.[65]

Despite Allen's misgivings here, by their very existence, by their language and focus and by the way of life they profess, many of the poems in *The New American Poetry* anthology were radical, both socially and politically. As such, they represent a vitalization of American literature and express an insistence on the potency of love, friendship and community that had appeared only irregularly, even though Allen downplayed this important

---

[64] Georg Wilhelm Friedrich Hegel, *On Christianity: Early Theological Writings*, Trans., T. M. Knox, (New York: Harper & Brothers, 1961), 286.
[65] Donald Allen, November 24, 1957, Box 8, Folder 6, Donald Allen Collection, MSS 3, Special Collections & Archives, UC San Diego Library.

108   S. DELBOS

element in his introduction. In this sense Allen's anthology was the culmination of a long-standing desire—stretching back a century—for a more human, communal, physical literature to break from the country's Puritanical roots.

There is evidence that some American writers desired a community of love well before the Cold War or the 1930s. Rexroth cites Walt Whitman as one precursor to this movement, and in the poet's boisterous passion and insistence on the purity of the body one can see clear connections to the exuberant physicality of the Beats. Underlying this was a feeling expressed by numerous American writers in the early twentieth century, namely that American literature and society have always taken a conservative approach to matters of love and passion. H. L. Mencken and George Santayana, for example, worked against what they called the genteel sensibility of American art and culture.[66] Even earlier, Henry Adams gave keen insight into the presentation of the female body in American literature and popular culture at the end of the nineteenth century, showing the society's dominant conservatism:

> Adams began to ponder, asking himself whether he knew of any American artist who had ever insisted on the power of sex, as every classic had always done; but he could think only of Walt Whitman; Bret Harte, as far as the magazines would let him venture; and one or two painters, for the flesh-tones. All the rest had used sex for sentiment, never for force; to them, Eve was a tender flower, and Herodias an unfeminine horror. American art, like the American language and American education, was as far as possible sexless.[67]

The absence of sexuality Adams describes is reminiscent of Duncan's description of dispassionate public poets at mid-century and Ginsberg's complaints about "prissy lifeless"[68] academic poetry. With this in mind, the shift in sexual mores that was taking place in America after World War II and especially in the 1960s, as evidenced and foreshadowed by *The New American Poetry*, seems even more revolutionary.

[66] See Charles C. Alexander, *Here the Country Lies* (Bloomington: Indiana University Press, 1980).

[67] Henry Adams, *The Education of Henry Adams* (Boston and New York: Houghton Mifflin Company, 1918), 384.

[68] Allen Ginsberg to Donald Allen, May, 1958, Box 10, Folder 15, Donald Allen Collection, MSS 3, Special Collections & Archives, UC San Diego Library.

Inasmuch as the community of love depended on the abolition of private property in order to flourish, it never had much of a chance in the United States. But that does not mean it was insignificant. Tracing the origins of the phrase shows just how radical it was in the 1950s to insist on a community of individuals united by mutual sympathy rather than commerce and capitalism. This suggests that the critical discourse on post-war American poetry, which has privileged a formal narrative over a consideration of content, has blunted the socially significant writing in Allen's anthology, thanks in part to Allen's own introduction. The connections between the Beat Generation and the Free Love Generation are clear, and many of the values the Beats championed in the 1950s found their way into the culture by the 1960s. Clearly the social implications of this poetry remained potent and provided an alternative viewpoint and alternative possibilities, both social and literary, for generations of writers and readers. How did these cultural shifts manifest themselves in *The New American Poetry*?

4.3 I Love My Love: *The New American Poetry*'s Reconsideration of Traditional Relationships

The critical tendency to read *The New American Poetry* as a collection of largely apolitical poems is as limiting as it is widespread. Many of the poems in the anthology that deal with love—and the most obvious societal institution of love, marriage—do so cynically or in ways that empower women by allowing them to speak for themselves. What emerges is that many of these poets were questioning the roles of men and women in relationships and in marriage and were also experimenting with alternatives to the accepted style of family life, at least in part because many of them were gay. These poets were also approaching the relationship between poet and reader in fresh ways, suggesting a sense of community with the audience and one another. There is an evident reconsideration of social roles and a range of reactions to them in these poems, from irony about marriage to earnest suggestions of alternatives. This section examines the concepts of community, relationships and marriage as presented by the poems in *The New American Poetry*. Rather than delving directly into the content of the poems, however, it is revealing to begin with their dedications.

110   S. DELBOS

The concept of the community of love pervades Allen's anthology, from its organization to the content of the poems, both of which display a sense of poetic community that seems at least in part a result of what Golding has called the anthology's "communal construction."[69] Perhaps the clearest indication that these poets and their work form a community is the number of poems dedicated to peers. Two of David Meltzer's poems are dedicated to John Wieners;[70] one of LeRoi Jones's poems is dedicated to Gary Snyder;[71] one of Richard Duerden's poems is dedicated to "R.D. & J.C.," who are likely Robert Duncan and his partner Jess Collins;[72] one of Jack Spicer's poems is dedicated to Robin Blaser;[73] Helen Adam's "I Love My Love" begins with a quote by Robert Duncan;[74] one of Robert Creeley's poems is dedicated to Robert Duncan;[75] and a section of Duncan's "Poem Beginning with a Line by Pindar" is dedicated to Charles Olson.[76] These are only the dedications to individuals also included in the anthology. In contrast, *The New Poets of England and America* has only a few poems with dedications, none of which are to poets also included in the anthology. More often than not these poems are dedicated to historical and literary figures such as William Cowper or Katharine of Aragon.[77] This sense of community wasn't merely an aspect of Allen's anthology; it was also evident in the life and work of several of its key poets.

Much has been written about Frank O'Hara's poetics of coterie, which can also be seen as an extension or interpretation of the community of

---

[69] Golding, "*The New American Poetry* Revisited, Again," *Contemporary Literature* 39.2 (1998): 181. This is an insightful discovery, thanks to Golding's admirable archival work. But Allen was always careful to assert his editorial independence, writing to James Broughton in 1959: "During these past two years I've discussed the changing plans for the anthology with many of the poets, listening attentively to what each has offered by way of advice. Charles Olson has given me the greatest encouragement and the most useful but my final decisions are of course my own and do not completely [align] with the views (often political) of the poets consulted." Donald Allen to James Broughton, August 10, 1959, Box 10, Folder 3, Donald Allen Collection, MSS 3, Special Collections & Archives, UC San Diego Library.

[70] Allen, 382–383.

[71] Allen, 358.

[72] Allen, 152.

[73] Allen, 142.

[74] Allen, 114.

[75] Allen, 83.

[76] Allen, 52.

[77] Hall, Pack and Simpson, 52.

4 THE COMMUNITY OF LOVE: *THE NEW AMERICAN POETRY...* 111

love.[78] The concept also connects directly to O'Hara's theory of "Personism," set forth in a 1959 essay in which he describes a realization he had while writing a love poem:

> While I was writing it I was realizing that if I wanted to I could use the telephone instead of writing the poem, and so Personism was born… It puts the poem squarely between the poet and the person, Lucky Pierre style, and the poem is correspondingly gratified. The poem is at last between two persons instead of two pages.[79]

This renews the function of the poem as communication and not merely verbal icon. Or rather, if a poem has always been communication, what is privileged here is the communication between poet and audience, rather than poet and poet, or poet and tradition, as is suggested by placing the poem between "two pages." The mention of Lucky Pierre, a slang term for someone in a threesome both giving and receiving, suggests the nonchalance with which O'Hara could question traditional sexual roles and relationships. O'Hara's conflation of sexuality and poetics is similar to the way that Jack Spicer placed dedications on all the poems of *After Lorca* (1957) and *Admonitions* (1957) in order to establish a community among his audience. Spicer's insistence on the physicality of the relationship between poet and reader and on the primacy of the communication between a poem and its reader, rather than the tradition out of which it developed, is evident in one of the letters from *After Lorca* that sounds remarkably like O'Hara:

> Some poems are easily laid. They will give themselves to anybody and anybody physically capable can receive them… I swear that if one of them were hidden beneath my carpet, it would shout out and seduce somebody.[80]

Here Spicer suggests that the poem is more interested in its readership than in tradition; thus the poem forms a kind of community, if a sexual one, with its readers. Spicer grants the poem an agency that is not present in O'Hara's description of his work. But both poets share the idea that the

---

[78] See Lytle Shaw, *Frank O'Hara, The Poetics of Coterie* (Iowa City: University of Iowa Press, 2013).

[79] Frank O'Hara, "Personism: A Manifesto," *Yugen* 7, 1961, 27–29.

[80] Peter Gizzi and Kevin Killian, *My Vocabulary Did This to Me: The Collected Poetry of Jack Spicer* (Middletown, CT: Wesleyan University Press, 2008), 138.

112   S. DELBOS

poem should be judged by how readily it communicates with those for whom it is intended.

Spicer and O'Hara provocatively update "the Whitmanian notion that there should be marriage between poet and people, poet and public, or poet and 'reader.'"[81] For poets in Allen's anthology, the community of love included but was certainly not limited to their readership. John Simon was one critic who recognized this in his largely negative review of *The New American Poetry*:

> What connects these poems most strongly is the vociferous variations on the theme of love. No less than fourteen poems of the anthology, for instance, even though they have little to do with loving, have the word "love" appear, climactically, in their last lines. This may be either a clamorous demand for love, or the display of one's unparalleled grip on it, or the mere trumpeting of its magic name. These last lines run the gamut from such elaborateness as O'Hara's "and dying in black and white we fight for what we love, not are," or Ginsberg's "who loves himself loves me who love myself," or Lamantia's "There is this look of love Throne Silent look of love," through such purer and simpler forms as Creeley's "and love her as hard as you can," or Ray Bremser's more pregnant "and love!" or Philip Whalen's ecstatically capitalized and italicized "LOVE <u>YOU</u>" – all the way down to Michael McClure's basic and irreducible "love." But you cannot capture love by sprinkling salt on its tail, or even by liberally sprinkling the tails of your poems with its name. Indeed, all this dragging in of love as a <u>deus ex vagina</u> is only a sorry testimonial to the essential lovelessness of these poets: the great climax proves merely a grand climacteric.[82]

The disappointment and disgust are palpable here, as is the limiting of love to vaginal-focused heterosexuality. Simon rightfully points out the prominence of the theme of love in the anthology, but he is clearly prejudiced against the book. I would argue that these declarations of love are not evidence of lovelessness but instead display new approaches to love and relationships that would have been unrecognizable or even abhorrent to conservative readers in post-war America.

As Simon suggests, many of the poems in the anthology deal directly with love and relationships, and many take a modern approach to love or

---

[81] Nathanial Tarn, "Is There, Currently, an American Poetry?, Republished in *Dispatches from the Poetry Wars*, March 14, 2019, https://www.dispatchespoetrywars.com/wp-content/uploads/2019/03/Tarn-Is-there-an-American-Poetry-1986-red.pdf, April 22, 2019.

[82] John Simon, "Sleight of Foot," *Audit*, 1.6, October 26, (1960): 6–7

4 THE COMMUNITY OF LOVE: *THE NEW AMERICAN POETRY...* 113

freshly conceptualize the subject, from Bruce Boyd, who writes "For love is the kind of a tree whose fruit / Grows not on the branches but at the root,"[83] to the free love and communal feelings espoused by much of the poetry of Allen Ginsberg, such as "The Shrouded Stranger," "Sunflower Sutra" and "Sather Gate Illumination."[84] Poems about family life are less common, though they are present. The most domestic poems in the book are Joel Oppenheimer's. Two of his poems, "The Bath" and "The Feeding," are focused on life at home, with acute observations of domesticity heightened by the recognition of each family member as a complete and autonomous being interacting with other members of the family community and, where the adults are concerned at least, actively deciding to stick together. The understated amorousness of "The Bath" is complemented by a rather pervasive feeling of reverence. The narrator admits that "he will insist on / reading things into her simplest act" and then proceeds to do just that, describing the "ritual" of his wife's bath, which she is undertaking "to ready herself." The poem ends:

> and himself more often than not decides
> she wants him unbathed manlike.
> what he is most pleased about is
> her continuing bathing.
> in his tub. in his water. wife.[85]

The pre-coital implications here are clear, but there is a quiet sense of communion throughout the poem, even though it ends with a tone and suggestion of ownership that reflects the masculine dominance of the 1950s. There is a sense of unabashed voyeurism too, on the part of the narrator and by extension the reader, which indicates a disavowal of the private boundaries of family life that would grow more frequent in the late 1950s and early 1960s in the work of the confessional poets.

Oppenheimer's "The Feeding" has a similar tone, though it is more sensitive and humorous. Describing "the child" feeding from a "she" who is presumably his mother, the narrator observes how the child "fought back" and the narrator asks "what does / he know of fruitfulness." Finally, after the child "spilled his milk" in the poem's final lines he

---

[83] Allen, 158.
[84] Allen, 178–179.
[85] Allen, 110.

looked up. smiling at her,
pleasantly, and, damn it, without
malice, even.[86]

The poem expresses a stubborn joy in the pleasures and frustrations of parenthood. Again the narrator observes the members of his family, all of them individual yet interconnected. It is a plain-speaking, practical and clear-eyed approach to parenthood that contrasts the rhetoric of many other domestic poems of the period.

Robert Creeley, "probably the best love poet of his generation,"[87] is another poet in Allen's anthology who often wrote about love and relationships, though his love poems employ a cynicism that borders at times on violence, as in the eight-line poem "The Warning":

For love – I would
split open your head and put
a candle in
behind the eyes.

Love is dead in us
if we forget
the virtues of an amulet
and quick surprise.[88]

Creeley here, as in many of his poems about relationships, is playfully violent. As Foster has written, "Love in Creeley's poetry is marked by peculiarly modern situations and anxiety and tension."[89] A dangerous insistence lies at the edge of these lines. Love is a threat, or even "an agony of gendered subjectivity split in terms of its objects."[90] While they do clearly draw on traditional tropes and forms, these are certainly not traditional love poems.

Creeley's "A Marriage" and "Ballad of the Despairing Husband" are no less ominously humorous. In these poems Creeley repurposes the

[86] Allen, 111.
[87] Foster, 104.
[88] Allen, 78.
[89] Foster, 105.
[90] Barrett Watten, "The Lost America of Love: A Genealogy," *Genre* XXXIII Fall-Winter, (2000): 287.

4 THE COMMUNITY OF LOVE: *THE NEW AMERICAN POETRY...* 115

forms and tropes of chivalric poetry, bringing classical rhetoric into a modern mode. This is evident especially in the latter poem. After the narrator's wife has left him, he lives by himself, passing his days "with little cheer." The third stanza follows:

> Oh come home soon, I write to her.
> Go fuck yourself, is her answer.
> Now what is that, for Christian word,
> I hope she feeds on dried goose turd.[91]

The wife's reply modernizes the language and sensibility of the romantic poem. Here Creeley turns the tables on a more traditional mode of address and is more equal and seemingly more inclusive:

> Oh wife, oh wife – I tell you true,
> I never loved no one but you.
> I never will, it cannot be
> another woman is for me.
>
> That may be right, she will say then,
> but as for me, there's other men.
> And I will tell you I propose
> to catch them firmly by the nose.
>
> And I will wear what dresses I choose!
> And I will dance, and what's to lose!
> I'm free of you, you little prick,
> and I'm the one can make it stick.[92]

The colloquialism of the final lines is refreshing and seems particularly contemporary for the period. By allowing the wife to speak, the poem casts an unflinching (if good-humored) gaze at the dark side of love in post-war America, illustrating the difficulties of keeping relationships together. Significantly, the poem also enlivens a traditional form with a modern sensibility, rather than rejecting the form entirely. Creeley was not the only poet in the anthology to do so.

---

[91] Allen, 80.
[92] Allen, 80–81.

116   S. DELBOS

Helen Adam's "I Love My Love" takes a mythical approach to love and marriage, allowing a female protagonist to speak for herself while also putting an old form to contemporary use. The title refrains throughout the poem, becoming more ominous as the love between maid and man becomes more repressive and violent. When the man strangles his wife to escape her, her golden hair comes back from the dead for revenge. The penultimate stanza reads:

> The hair rushed in. He struggled and tore, but whenever he tore
> a tress,
> "I love my love with a capital Z," sang the hair of the sorceress.
> It swarmed upon him, it swaddled him fast, it muffled his every
> groan.
> Like a golden monster it seized his flesh, and then it sought the
> bone,
> Ha! Ha!
> And then it sought the bone.[93]

Using a ballad form like Creeley, Adam not only reverses the typical power structure of marriage, suggesting that the woman has more power than the man, but also suggests that the woman, rather than being a passive member of the relationship, is endowed with mystical power and may at any moment take revenge on a trying husband. Again, it is the content of the poem, rather than its form, that distinguishes it.

While humor and imagination are evident in Adam and Creeley, ambivalence is often the primary tone in poems dealing with relationships in Allen's anthology. Barbara Guest's "Parachutes, My Love, Could Carry Us Higher" suggests a wariness about being bound to others through romance, fidelity and commitment. The poem begins:

> I just said I didn't know
> And now you are holding me
> In your arms,
> How kind.
> Parachutes, my love, could carry us higher.[94]

---

[93] Allen, 117.
[94] Allen, 216.

4 THE COMMUNITY OF LOVE: *THE NEW AMERICAN POETRY...* 117

Throughout the poem, Guest questions the female's traditionally silent or passive role and presents an alternative, giving voice to a female counterpart who is skeptical, ironic and bitingly eloquent. Sure of her own autonomous self, the narrator here questions the benefit of being linked to another person and suggests that a relationship may actually distract and weigh down an otherwise independent woman. The poem ends:

> I am closer to you
> Than land and I am in a stranger ocean
> Than I wished.[95]

This is the image of a woman cut off from her own desires and is at odds with the prescribed role of women in post-war America. The fact that Allen's anthology gives voice to these women, who were themselves giving voice to liberal ideas about women's roles in relationships, is one of its significant contributions, despite the fact that the number of women in the anthology is small.

The troubling sense of domestic difficulty evident in the above poems is found throughout the anthology. Jonathan Williams's "The Switch Blade (or, John's Other Wife)" is indicative of the generally casual exploration of marital issues in the book. It begins:

> men share perceptions (and
> their best friends' wives, in lieu of
>
> a perverse tangling of arseholes.[96]

Here the topic of an open marriage, or at least knowing infidelity, is broached in an off-hand and ironically humorous style, suggesting along with, perhaps, a desire to shock, a liberal approach to love, marriage and relationships and one that could be interpreted as foreshadowing the love revolutions that coincided with the invention of the birth control pill, the gradual acceptance of pornography and the emergence of sex clubs and swingers in the 1960s and 1970s.[97] Critics such as David McReynolds pointed out in 1959 that "there is a lot of bisexual behavior and a greater freedom in having sexual relations" among "hipsters" and "beats... not because the hipster is trying to turn life into one long orgy, but because he

[95] Allen, 216.
[96] Allen, 107.
[97] See: Gay Talese, *Thy Neighbor's Wife* (Garden City: Doubleday, 1980).

118   S. DELBOS

believes in carrying relationships with people as far and as deep as possible."[98] Surveying Allen's anthology and poems from poets like Jonathan Williams, who was more southern aristocrat than hipster, suggests that these liberating tendencies were not limited to those who identified as Beats or hipsters, though certainly there are many of these poets in the anthology as well.

The most famous relationship poem in Allen's anthology is also one of the most famous marriage poems of the era. Gregory Corso's "Marriage" is a five-and-a-half-page meditation on the first line's two questions: "Should I get married? Should I be good?"[99] The poem wittily excoriates the institution of marriage and the courting rituals of the post-war middle class.

> When she introduces me to her parents
> back straightened, hair finally combed, strangled by a tie,
> should I sit knees together on their 3rd-degree sofa
> and not ask Where's the bathroom?
> [...]
> But I should get married I should be good
> How nice it'd be to come home to her
> and sit by the fireplace and she in the kitchen
> aproned young and lovely wanting my baby
> and so happy about me she burns the roast beef
> and comes crying to me and I get up from my big pap chair
> saying Christmas teeth! Radiant brains! Apple deaf!
> God what a husband I'd make! Yes, I should get married![100]

The poem presents a conception of love that privileges human relationships over institutions. At the same time, it questions the mores of love in a commodity culture, promotes the autonomy of the individual and suggests alternative ways of pursuing love and happiness from those prescribed by preceding generations. Corso here seeks to deflate the institution of marriage, holding up its most sacred rituals—such as the suitor's first meeting with his beloved's parents—and ridiculing them with such

[98] David McReynolds, "After the Beat Generation: Hipsters Unleashed," *Liberation*, June, 1959, 8.
[99] Allen, 209.
[100] Allen, 209–212.

enthusiasm that his language at times veers into babble, suggesting that convention itself is nonsense agreed upon by society.

The poems in Allen's anthology concerning love and relationships do not always take a cynical approach, however. A number of them, including Gary Snyder's "For a Far-Out Friend" and Paul Blackburn's "The Once-Over," present women as objects of lust, the female form eliciting praise and sexual feelings from the male narrator. "Feasts of Death, Feasts of Love" by Stuart Z. Perkoff is concerned with a more literal interpretation of the word "community." An ambitious seven-page poem that achieves a kind of chiaroscuro through its juxtaposition of memories of attending a Jewish camp with images of the Holocaust, the poem charts the narrator's attempts to come to grips with tragedy, while presenting the summer camp as an idyllic experience that has fostered a lifetime of memories and practices. Citing the Hebrew blessing said over food on Shabbat, Perkoff writes:

> at the edge of the water
> the glass house eye of God
> embraced us, pure
> in white
>
>   clean after communal showers
> & communal food
> [...]
>
> sitting on the benches, bodies warm & throats filled with joy &
>   love
> we offered worship
> sitting warm to warm, our eyes & skins touching, love flowing
> we offered worship
> [...]
>
> o living communities
> men & women who love & are loved
> o living bodies
> men & women who love & are loved
> o loving cities
> men & women who live & are lived[101]

---

[101] Allen, 302–303.

120   S. DELBOS

It is telling that the young Jewish group must go on retreat to achieve this rapturous sense of community. This connects with Hegel's sense of the community around Jesus as cut off from the larger community and Rexroth's suggestion that such a community in post-war America must remain a kind of cult. The bardic tone used to invoke and so lovingly describe these "living communities" of "men & women who love & are loved" contrasts with the next section of the poem, which describes a far bleaker vision:

> I see clothes piled in great heaps
> against grey sky
> with the smoke & sun in the air
> of human flesh
> [...]
>
> there are bodies
> naked
> not talking of love
> in their last waters
> naked
> not talking of love[102]

Here the individuals of the previous stanzas, the active agents of life and love, are reduced by the powers of evil to indiscriminate bodies. The community of love becomes a lost principle, an experience that inspires longing yet only serves to add to the confusion and despair of the narrator as he confronts the Holocaust. Love, in this forced gathering of individuals not given the agency to form a community, has been lost even to language. Yet Perkoff's juxtaposition of the community of love with concentration camps grants love an equal power, one that must be reckoned with and recalled even in the face of evil.

It is difficult to imagine a clearer description of Hegel's concept of the community of love. For Perkoff, love is a force commensurate to death. And while the community of love, which is represented in his poem by the Jewish community, may not be able to escape evil, it is the opposite of death. In this poem, as in the other poems of love and community in Allen's anthology, love involves a looking beyond oneself; elsewhere it is bounded by marriage and here by modern social life.

[102] Allen, 304.

4 THE COMMUNITY OF LOVE: *THE NEW AMERICAN POETRY...* 121

In Philip Whalen's "Two Variations: All about Love" the narrator's ecstatic expression of love has overtones of a mature, Rilkean sensibility in American vernacular:

> All I would tell is you
> And love; I must tell
> Me, that I am a world
> Containing more than love
>
> Holding you and all your other
> Lovers wherein you
> And I are free from each other
> A world that anyone can walk alone
> [...]
> Refuse to see me!
> Don't answer the door or the telephone
> Fly off in a dragon-chariot
> Forget you ever knew me
>
> But where you are
> Is a corner of me[103]

This is not the attitude displayed in a typical post-war love poem, nor is it an expression of sadistic or lowbrow attitudes about wife swapping. Rather, the poem suggests that love connects individuals even if they are separated by distance. It is not an avant-garde idea, as readers of John Donne would know. But in the post-war context, this poem presents an alternative to the sacrament and social tradition of marriage. The colloquial language Whalen uses, especially in the second, more ecstatic section of the poem, updates the conceit with an inventive, irrepressibly optimistic energy:

>   F
> Train
> Absolutely stoned
> Rocking bug-eyed billboards waff:
> No more bridge than adam's
>   off ox
>   Pouring over it 16 2/3 MPH sodium –
>   vapor light yellow light
>
>   LOVE YOU

---

[103] Allen, 281–282.

122 S. DELBOS

Got you on
	like a coat of paint
Steamy girder tile

LOVE *YOU*[104]

Even more than the reinvention of old tropes in the previous section of the poem, this second section, entitled "(BIG HIGH SONG FOR SOMEBODY)," is indicative of Whalen's postmodern sensibility, which was influenced by Beat poetics and drugs as well as his study of Zen Buddhism.[105] The tone and diction are colloquial and bound by no familiar form, an effect emphasized by the layout of the poem. These characteristics infuse Whalen's declarations of love with an unabashed joy. Both in its suggestions of love without attachments and in its unrestrained outbursts of feeling, Whalen's "Two Variations" seems worlds apart from the domestic poetry of the post-war years, which more accurately expressed the expectations of American society and its attendant feelings toward marriage and commitment.

While most of the poets in Allen's anthology stop short of promoting free love and promiscuous sex, nearly all of the poems concerning love, marriage and relationships in the anthology take a liberal approach. Whether the poems offer down-to-earth considerations of the mundane aspects of marriage like bathing and breastfeeding, refreshing revisions of the balance of power between man and woman, a casual comment on marital infidelity, or an imaginative, if violent, tale of love and loss, they offer revolutionary reconsiderations of love and relationships. The number of poets in the anthology who dedicate poems to friends who are also included in the anthology shows that they themselves composed a unique community in post-war Anglophone poetry. At the same time, the diversity of approaches to physical, relational and sexual liberation in Allen's anthology suggests that this shift wasn't limited to Beats and hipsters but was something on the minds of many individuals.

---

[104] Allen, 281–282.
[105] See David Schneider, *Crowded by Beauty: The Life and Zen of Poet Philip Whalen* (Oakland: University of California Press, 2015).

The avant-garde's poetic meditations on love, marriage and relationships provide numerous counter-narratives to popular behavior in America during the Cold War. Edward Brunner has described the dynamics of family life at a time when the atomic bomb cast a shadow over a society enjoying a higher rate of marriage and childbearing as well as more economic independence and employment than previous generations.[106] Despite the latent dread of nuclear war, these conditions allowed many poets, especially those with steady jobs, to "help raise their children and take pleasure in watching them grow."[107] Elaine Tyler May in her study of the Cold War family points out that 96.4 percent of the women and 94.1 percent of the men who came of age during and after World War II got married.[108] Another significant text in this regard is F. W. Dupee's review of *The New Poets of England and America*:

> Marriage is obviously an attractive as well as advisable state for the young poets, and it provides them with a stock of poetic objects. Home, wife, children, parents, pets, gardens, summer resorts, travel en famille make up the unromantic romance of their poetry.[109]

This is clearly evident in poems like Donald Hall's "My Son, My Executioner," included in *The New Poets of England and America*. It is a poem in which the combination of love and rue the father feels for his newborn son is beautifully expressed, while traditional meter and rhyme remove the poem from the communicative language of the everyday home. The poem begins:

> My son, my executioner,
>   I take you in my arms,
> Quiet and small and just astir,
>   And whom my body warms.
>
> Sweet death, small son, our instrument
>   Of immortality,
> Your cries and hungers document
>   Our bodily decay.[110]

---

[106] Brunner, 230.

[107] Brunner, 230.

[108] Elaine Tyler May, *Homeward Bound: American Families in the Cold War Era* (New York: Basic Books, 1988).

[109] Brunner, 230.

[110] Hall, Pack, Simpson, 94.

124   S. DELBOS

The poem continues in this fashion, weighing conflicting feelings of fatherhood and attempting to come to terms with the balance of life and death the son represents. In Hall's words, this dilemma is "the mortal paradox."[111] This poem inhabits a similar field of experience as Oppenheimer's "The Feeding," but one feels that for Hall, the quality of the poem lies in its artfulness, whereas for Oppenheimer, quality resides in clear observation and sharp documentation of both scene and the poet's individual voice. But perhaps more importantly, in Oppenheimer's poem the son is presented as an equal member of the family, whereas in Hall's poem the son is portrayed as an intruder—if a welcome one—and more forebodingly, and frankly more "poetically," as a harbinger of death. While Hall's poem evinces a hierarchical approach to childbearing, Oppenheimer's colloquial language brings his poem into the everyday discourse of the family unit.

Louise Bogan was inaccurate when she wrote, in her review of *The New American Poetry*, that the poets included "abjure lyricism and all tender emotions."[112] On the contrary, the poems cited above from Allen's anthology provide alternatives to the domestic poetry of the period, expressing a more personal sense of lyricism and emotion. Whereas domestic life in much of 1950s poetry was presented as a secure, blissful state (with occasional difficulties), in Allen's anthology, marriage is a social institution that an intelligent individual should hesitate to join. Whether these poems explore homosexual themes, describe open marriages or narrate relationships from the woman's point of view, they suggest different possibilities from the overtly conservative approach to romance and relationships prescribed by American society in the 1950s, when more people were getting married younger and having more children than previously. These poems make the book truly revolutionary. And while Allen's description of the community of love as central to *The New American Poetry* may at first seem idiosyncratic, it stands up to closer investigation. Allen's use of the phrase also points to the crucial ways that the poets in the anthology achieved a sense of community that is missing from later American avant-gardes including language poetry, which "cannot come up with a coherent notion of community or politics."[113] *The New American Poetry* did both. Reading the poems this way provides a more complete social and political

---

[111] Hall, Pack, Simpson, 94.
[112] Louise Bogan, "Verse," *The New Yorker*, October 8, 1960, 200.
[113] Kaufmann, 132.

4 THE COMMUNITY OF LOVE: *THE NEW AMERICAN POETRY...* 125

framework for this anthology than has been widely realized. The political ramifications of the community of love—and this section's examination of poems—make clear that these poets' re-evaluations of social mores brought them close to radical politics and distinguished their work from mainstream poetry in ways that are more significant than form.

4.4   A SOCIAL FEELING: BEYOND FORMAL DIVISIONS IN POST-WAR AMERICAN POETRY

Allen's use of the phrase "the community of love" places his anthology within the Cold War context in ways he does not account for in his introduction. Had he included this description in the anthology, he might have helped push discussions of post-war American poetry beyond Lowell's binary as well as the stereotypes of the formal breakthrough narrative.[114] Arguments based on the idea of a formal revolution in post-war poetry cannot explain the ballads of Robert Creeley or Helen Adam or the rhymes of poets like Brother Antoninus and Bruce Boyd in *The New American Poetry*. It is more revealing to examine the content of these poems, as this helps us distinguish the work in new and perhaps more accurate ways. Exploring how the poems in Allen's anthology reconsidered relationships shows how they interacted with the rapid changes taking place in the United States after World War II, as did more formally conservative poets such as Donald Hall. Rather than two opposing camps, post-war American poetry might be best thought of as a continuum on which individual poets registered societal changes in their own distinct ways.

American citizens were expected to align their beliefs and behavior with conservative social values in the years following World War II. One result was more marriages and more couples devoted to materialism than any preceding generation.[115] Domestic life and relationships were matters of national politics during this period, and alternative practices, be they homosexual or communal, were generally perceived as an affront to the heteronormative drift and puritanical foundation of American society. Change would come, however, and *The New American Poetry* was an early

---

[114] James Longenbach, *Modern Poetry After Modernism* (Oxford: Oxford University Press, 1997), vii.

[115] "Women and Work after World War II," *PBS*, http://www.pbs.org/wgbh/americanexperience/features/general-article/tupperware-work/, May 1, 2015.

126   S. DELBOS

sign of that change, even if Allen blunted the book's most socially revolutionary aspects with his formalist, anti-academic stance.

Alan Filreis cites John Crowe Ransom speaking during this period to a literary gathering about "'Urbanization' [which] had caused poets to replace 'the love of nature' with 'a social feeling.'"[116] The quote is important because it both registers the development and voices complaint against it, showing the conservatism that would hold back such changes as long as possible, in poetry and in society. Filreis also suggests that Ransom was using a kind of doublespeak common to the Cold War, which allowed critics and editors to broach political topics in non-political language. There is a clear line from Ransom's "social feeling" to the community of love, as well as the heightened domesticity of the post-war period. Urban and suburban poets, in contrast to Ransom's agrarian ideals, necessarily developed new subjects. Rather than writing about nature, they wrote about their surroundings: friends in the city or families in the living room. As Frank O'Hara exclaimed, "I can't even enjoy a blade of grass unless I know there's a subway handy, or a record store or some other sign that people do not totally regret life... The clouds get enough attention as it is."[117] Elsewhere during the same period, Gregory Corso wrote: "Fields, streams, mountains, groves, sky, flower, bird, frightful euphemisms...to the 1958 poetic eye. Sad. Sad, and funny, too, because the field the stream can't understand what they did to lose their publicity-agents. The field still bloom; the strem [sic] still flows. Wasn't them that changed."[118] The poets had changed, of course. More marriages and relationships were reflected in American poetry after World War II, enlarging the possibilities of the genre. Meanwhile the poets in Allen's anthology were imagining new kinds of community, not agrarian associations of citizens (with the exception of Black Mountain College) but congregations of poets and readers, the transient, temporary urban coteries and transnational epistolary networks around which Allen organized his anthology. This reflected a larger shift in American life.

As poets during this period reflected changes in American life in what and how they wrote, editors and critics supported or refuted these changes

---

[116] Filreis, 181.

[117] Frank O'Hara, *The Selected Poems of Frank O'Hara*, Donald Allen, ed. (New York City: Vintage Books, 1974), 87.

[118] Walter Höllerer Collection, Das Literaturarchiv Sulzbach-Rosenberg, 03 WH / BH / 6, 5.

4 THE COMMUNITY OF LOVE: *THE NEW AMERICAN POETRY...* 127

through their interpretations of poetry. Wallace Fowlie's introduction to Daisy Aldan's *A New Folder* anthology registers this shift: "The inspiration of nature would be today the bizarre, love would be possibly Eros, God might be the subconscious."[119] And, as Robert Pack explained in his introduction to the second selection of *The New Poets of England and America*:

> Love, in these pages, is experienced more in the contexts of sexual desire, need, marriage and divorce, than in the contexts of romance or spiritual striving. The traditional theme of unfaithfulness has become more specifically adultery; parting has become divorce; union (transcendence) has become harmony, compatibility.[120]

This poetry is new too, despite the fact that it was largely written in received forms. While some poets in the late 1950s were moving to cities and writing about alternative lifestyles, others were buying homes, starting families and finding inspiration in these experiences. A specifically domestic style of poetry emerged following World War II alongside the poetry that Allen claimed was new. Any poet worth reading reflected these societal changes in their own way.

The New American Poetry must be read as a reaction to social conventions as much as literary ones. Throughout the 1950s, influential individuals, from sociologists like C. Wright Mills to comedians like Lenny Bruce, voiced doubts about the conservative social values that the United States had so enthusiastically embraced. Beginning in the mid-1950s, as court rulings in cases such as those involving Grove Press and City Lights Books pushed back obscenity laws, the lifestyles that poets in Allen's anthology, and Allen himself, could only hint at became more widely expressed.[121] Even the least politically engaged of these poets, by writing about more liberal styles of relationships, was voicing dissatisfaction with the prescribed social values of the period. But Allen's introduction to the anthology overlooks the politics of the poetry in favor of a formal debate, following terms that had been set by conservative critics who used

[119] Daisy Aldan, *A New Folder, Americans: Poems and Drawings* (New York: Folder Editions, 1959).

[120] Donald Hall and Robert Pack, eds. *New Poets of England and America: A Second Selection* (New York: Meridian, 1962), 179.

[121] In fiction, these changes were registered in books like Hubert Selby, Jr.'s *Last Exit to Brooklyn* (1964), which deals explicitly with drugs, homosexuality and prostitution. Like *The New American Poetry*, it was published by Grove Press with cover art by Roy Kuhlman.

complaints about form to object to leftist politics in poetry. In contrast, Allen's letter to Duncan hints at the radical nature of the book and the way that it could be interpreted as a rejoinder to critics such as Bogan who accused left-leaning poets like Rukeyser of being devoid of personal feeling.[122]

Allen's two explanations about the unifying characteristic of *The New American Poetry*, in his introduction and his letter to Duncan, show the complexity of the book's interactions with Cold War politics and society. The debate about form in American poetry that accelerated after World War II is perhaps a timeless one. But by drawing attention to the significant ways these poems deal with love and relationships, Allen (if only in private correspondence) reveals how the poets in his anthology shut down one central thrust of conservative arguments against politically and socially subversive American poetry since the 1930s. Critics who focus solely, or even mostly, on the formal character of these poems obscure this larger significance. The importance of love and community to the post-war avant-garde has not completely escaped critical attention, however. Writing in 1986, Nathanial Tarn described how the promise of new ways of conceiving love and relationships that flourished in the 1950s, at least in poetry, had been obscured:

> At a critical junction in the self-recognition of American poetry, we had, in Williams, a move away from the over-writerly and over-hermeticist (read here also, in many cases, fascist) components of modernism. The stress on the oral and the speakerly enabled the question to be raised of marriage with a reader through a shared national idiom. Whatever the difficulties with this praxis (in the matter of the definition of "nation"), it did for a time allow of the thought of an "America of Love," as consistently marital critics like Sherman Paul and Paul Christensen have pointed out. The scramble to return to the writerly, consistent with the political hues of the passage in time from the 1960s to the 1970s and 1980s, has once again obscured this praxis.[123]

A case in point of this obscuring of the rich possibilities and complex meaning of "the community of love" is Barrett Watten's definition of Bob

---

[122] Filreis, 115.

[123] Nathanial Tarn, "Is There, Currently, an American Poetry?, Republished in *Dispatches from the Poetry Wars*, March 14, 2019, https://www.dispatchespoetrywars.com/wp-content/uploads/2019/03/Tarn-Is-there-an-American-Poetry-1986-red.pdf, April 22, 2019.

Perelman's citation of Creeley's phrase "the company of love" in the 1970s as, simply, "literary community."[124] Considering Allen's anthology from this perspective in the twenty-first century is therefore both revelatory and elegiac.

Ultimately, *The New American Poetry* is both liberal and conservative at once, breaking away from Cold War conventions yet mired in them. While Allen's anthology is dominated by males, many of them were homosexual, and much of the love poetry in the book expresses a view of relationships that privileges the narratives and freedom of women and suggests alternative lifestyles that would be more fully explored in the coming years. The newness of the poems in the anthology is most distinctly located in the attitudes they express, which links them to larger developments in American society as a social avant-garde began to embrace a more open-minded approach to life and love in reaction to the country's prevailing conservatism. Allen's anthology was part of these liberal tendencies, even if his editorial decisions muted some of the most significant aspects of the poetry. But Allen's decisions also helped *The New American Poetry* to conservatively shift the debate about innovation in Anglophone poetry, obscuring the internationalism of the modernists and misleadingly limiting a transnational development in post-war poetry with a national framework that fit perfectly into Cold War nationalism and cultural warfare.

---

[124] Anne Dewey, Libbie Rifkin eds., *Among Friends: Engendering the Social Site of Poetry* (Iowa City: University of Iowa Press, 2013), 110

CHAPTER 5

This Thing Is Most National: Nationalism and Assimilation in *The New American Poetry*

Considering the title of his anthology, Donald Allen's decision to exclude foreign poets from *The New American Poetry* may seem like a foregone conclusion. But given the fact that most previous anthologies had insisted on the shared tradition of American and British poetry, *The New American Poetry*'s American nationalism was a conscious decision that has helped shape the accepted narrative of the anthology as a breakthrough for American poetry. The exclusion of poets who were writing innovative poetry in English in countries other than the United States after World War II means that *The New American Poetry*'s presentation of the post-war poetic avant-garde as a movement based specifically in the United States is a simplification. The milieu was far more diverse and international than Allen's anthology suggests, and even the poets included in *The New American Poetry* often lived, wrote and published beyond the borders of the United States. Allen's American framework harmonized with the conservative, nationalistic Cold War climate and perpetuated a limited picture of a transnational literary development in ways that would have satisfied the Cold War cultural warriors in the American State Department and the CIA, who sought to promote capitalist-democratic values through American culture in contrast to the seemingly rigid, officially prescribed communist culture. Allen located the center of avant-garde poetics in the United States, which is an incomplete understanding of innovation in Anglophone post-war poetry and one that continues to influence the way

© The Author(s), under exclusive license to Springer Nature 131
Switzerland AG 2021
S. Delbos, *The New American Poetry and Cold War Nationalism*,
Modern and Contemporary Poetry and Poetics,
https://doi.org/10.1007/978-3-030-77352-6_5

132   S. DELBOS

that we interpret American poetry as inherently innovative and British poetry as inherently traditional. Allen's new Americans were more international than is now generally perceived, and his anthology is more conservative than most critics have been in a position to understand.

This chapter begins by examining Allen's correspondence with poets in *The New American Poetry* to reveal how his nationalist conception developed as he worked on the anthology and how it only became central to the anthology at a late stage in preparation after specific suggestions from Charles Olson. The chapter then turns to the way Allen missed or misidentified significant transnational elements of this poetry and included Scottish and British poets residing in the United States, Helen Adam and Denise Levertov, while excluding others like Scottish poet Gael Turnbull because he wasn't an American citizen, thus presenting the post-war avant-garde as a united movement generated by American culture. Reading *The New American Poetry* through a transnational lens not only affords a new point of view on the anthology and its effects on subsequent editors, poets and critics, it also suggests fruitful new ways of interpreting the post-war avant-garde and the tradition of innovation in Anglophone poetry. Examining the anthology's use of the American flag as a cover image and considering how that symbol was germane to the nationalism of the Cold War, the chapter further suggests how the anthology's presentation of these poets as an American phenomenon fits into the Cold War climate. This is coupled with an examination of Allen's use of similar titles and cover images in subsequent publications, which helped him create a consensus about the Anglophone avant-garde as specifically American. Finally, the chapter considers the misleading effect Allen's anthology continues to have on the Anglophone canon and our perception of both British and American poetry in the twenty-first century, suggesting that Allen's model is both outdated and inaccurate.

5.1   Poems and Passports: *The New American Poetry*'s Nationalist Conception of Post-war Anglophone Poetry

Allen's landmark anthology began as his personal perception of dozens of individual poets writing in numerous styles and locations in the post-war years. The editor's correspondence and his own commentary on the gestation of the book reveal how he conceived of the anthology and its

5 THIS THING IS MOST NATIONAL: NATIONALISM AND ASSIMILATION... 133

organization. Writing in 2003, Allen reminisced about his stay at the writer's colony Yaddo in 1957, when he "began to ponder what I saw happening in American poetry, beginning to think that this new writing connected... a possible movement, and I began to think about the possibility of doing an anthology."[1] Allen's correspondence concerning the anthology with poets including Robert Creeley and Charles Olson from the late 1950s is a curious mix of specificity and vagueness and shows the flexibility of the editor's conception of his project. Writing to Olson on September 24, 1958, Allen lays out the details for the first time:

> As you know, I am compiling an anthology of modern American poetry (1948 to 1958-9)... My aims in compiling this anthology are: (1) to show the continuation of the modern movement in American poetry during the past decade, (2) to show what new trends have developed, and what new conceptions of the poem have emerged during the period. (3) to demonstrate, too, the continuation and modification of several of the older, basic traditions in American verse, (4) to present a number of the younger poets who have appeared in the last few years. My bases for selecting poems are derived in part from William Carlos Williams' essays (especially Measure) and Charles Olson's Projective Verse; they are, very briefly: (1) voice, and breathing (2) heat of the poem, energy, feeling, (3) use of the American language, (4) stance of the poet in the poem (5) strategy: use of techniques – traditional or newly recovered from ancient or primitive literature, as well as newer devices (dream effects, cutting, montage, dissolve, etc., etc.,)... The academic poets of the decade are well enough represented in the Meridian Books anthology edited by Donald Hall, and others, and I do not plan to include their work in the anthology I am compiling... The anthology will be published by Grove Press in 1959.[2]

Here Allen lays the groundwork for *The New American Poetry*, although much of what he describes in this letter would remain in flux over the next two years. Allen goes on to elucidate the layout of the anthology, which would include 10 to 15 pages of poetry by an older generation of American poets including Ezra Pound and William Carlos Williams. This particular idea was abandoned because the community of the new would soon become the central focus. Even what is seemingly Allen's simplest

[1] Maud, 7.
[2] Maud, 46.

134 S. DELBOS

condition—that he would include poetry by Americans only—would not be fixed until later.

In a letter to Robert Creeley written on April 17, 1958, Allen had written: "Thank you for notes on the anthol[ogy]. Since this will be limited to American poets I'll not be including [Canadian poet Irving] Layton and [Scottish poet Gael] Turnbull."[3] Whether owing to diplomacy or the fact that the exact designs of the anthology remained fluid, Allen's correspondence with others, including Turnbull himself, reveals a less determined editorial attitude.[4] Writing to Charles Olson in early September, 1959, a year after his letter to Creeley and after he'd decided on the title of the anthology, Allen mentions that he is "also think[ing] of throwing in a couple of poems by Layton and Gael Turnbull to round it out, taking American in the wider sense."[5]

But Olson's unequivocal response to Allen's suggestion of including Turnbull, on September 12, 1959, would set Allen's tone for deciding who would and would not be included in the anthology.

> Anyway, the important thing to my mind is to leave the group alone: don't drag in those other gooks of the past – & present solely because they hang around (don't die !... yr anthology ought to be the decisive defining factor, that American writing went into a new gear, which is what it is now running on, and going over to Canada, England Scotland and out (and by god none of those older ghosts like – even the papas were international, this thing is most national[6]

[3] Donald Allen to Robert Creeley, April 17, 1958, Box 10, Folder 15, Donald Allen Collection, MSS 3, Special Collections & Archives, UC San Diego Library.

[4] The precise designs of the anthology remained fluid from beginning to end. That timespan begins in early 1958, when Allen wrote: "Barney [Rosset] has okayed my plans to put together an anthology of postwar American poetry..." Donald Allen to Charles Olson, February 27, 1958, Series II: Correspondence, undated, 1910–1970, the Charles Olson Research Collection, Archives & Special Collections at the Thomas J. Dodd Research Center, University of Connecticut Libraries. It wasn't until late 1959 that Allen had decided on the title, writing to James Broughton, "I propose to call the anthology "The New American Poetry." Donald Allen to James Broughton, September 4, 1959, Box 9, Folder 3, Donald Allen Collection, MSS 3, Special Collections & Archives, UC San Diego Library.

[5] Donald Allen to Charles Olson, September 9, 1959, Box 93, Folder 5, Donald Allen Collection, MSS 3, Special Collections & Archives, UC San Diego Library.

[6] Maud, 61.

5 THIS THING IS MOST NATIONAL: NATIONALISM AND ASSIMILATION... 135

Olson's presumptuous nationalism and his disturbingly casual use of the word "gooks" just six years after the conclusion of the Korean War betray his desperation. He needed Allen to follow his directives so that the anthology would best showcase his work and that of his chosen contemporaries. John Woznicki has noted how this letter displays Olson's "sense of himself as an American poet with no ties to the European cosmopolitanism functioning in the poetics of Pound and T. S. Eliot"[7] without pointing out the dramatic nationalism in Olson's stance.[8] There seems to be some confusion about this element of Olson's worldview and by extension that of *The New American Poetry*, as recent critics have written of Olson as an "internationalist"[9] and of his and the anthology's "commitment to a poetics of internationalism."[10] Nothing could be further from the truth.

Francis Fukuyama defines nationalism as "a doctrine that political borders ought to correspond to cultural communities, with culture defined largely by shared language."[11] Substituting the word "political" with "poetic" suggests how Olson's letter confirmed the nationalist focus of Allen's anthology. This would extend to every aspect of the book, from its title to the cover image of a stylized version of the American flag, to its organization according to geographic areas of the North American continent. In his introduction, Allen seems to paraphrase Olson when he writes "the new American poetry [is] now becoming the dominant movement in the second phase of our twentieth-century literature and already exerting strong influence abroad."[12] This national focus created the image of a united poetic community that differentiated itself both from tradition and from the poetry of other English-speaking countries. The fragility of this framework is revealed by considering poets who fell outside Allen's somewhat permeable editorial borders.

---

[7] Woznicki, 30.

[8] Nationalism and politics were inherent in Olson's conception of poetry. This is the poet who, at the 1965 Berkeley Poetry Conference, "only half playfully proposed appointments to his poetry cabinet..." and declared "if you don't know... that poetics is politics, [that] poets are political leaders today, and the only ones... you shouldn't have come." Clark, 324–325.

[9] Woznicki, 98.

[10] Woznicki, 160.

[11] Francis Fukuyama, *Identity: Contemporary Identity Politics and the Struggle for Recognition* (London: Profile Books, 2018), 62.

[12] Allen, xii.

136   S. DELBOS

Born in Scotland in 1928, Gael Turnbull would seem to have been immediately ineligible for Allen's consideration. Yet the poet's situation was somewhat more nuanced. Although he had been raised and educated in the United Kingdom (by a Scottish father and American mother),[13] Turnbull lived in Ventura, California, between 1958 and 1964[14] and was well known as a contributor to avant-garde Anglophone poetry journals. He published a collection of poems with Toronto's Contact Press (which is listed in the "Short Bibliography" of *The New American Poetry*) in 1954, published a collection with Cid Corman's Origin Press in 1956, interviewed William Carlos Williams for *The Massachusetts Review* in 1958,[15] and between 1957 and 1966 ran the influential Migrant Books, an important small magazine and publisher dedicated to promoting avant-garde Anglophone writing from both sides of the Atlantic.[16] Turnbull's poetry would have fit nicely in the anthology. His poem "Now That April's Here," for example, has the wit of Kenneth Koch's "Fresh Air" and the same attitude toward the poetry establishment. It is written in rhyming quatrains reminiscent of some of Robert Creeley's poetry in the anthology. Turnbull's poem concludes:

> Put the Great back in Great Britain.
> Write a letter to *The Times*.
> Lots of fun with Billy Butlin.
> It's a poem if it rhymes.[17]

Poets including Robert Creeley, Robert Duncan and Allen Ginsberg suggested to Allen in correspondence that Turnbull's work should be included in *The New American Poetry*. Allen's letters with others regarding Turnbull,

---

[13] "Gael Turnbull 1928–2004," *The Poetry Foundation*, https://www.poetryfoundation.org/poets/gael-turnbull, January 24, 2018.

[14] Clay and Phillips, 149.

[15] Gael Turnbull, "A Visit to WCW: September, 1958," *The Massachusetts Review*, 3.3 (Winter 1962): 297–300.

[16] The origin story of Migrant Books, which was headquartered in Ventura, California, and Worcester, United Kingdom, attests to its transnational roots and reach. Turnbull began the press "by purchasing stock from several presses, including Origin, Jargon, and Divers Press..." According to Turnbull, "In the summer of 1957, I published *The Whip*, a small volume of selected poems by Robert Creeley, who arranged and managed the printing for me on Mallorca... The bulk of the edition went out through Jargon (Jonathan Williams) in the United States." Cited in Clay and Phillips, 149.

[17] Gael Turnbull, *While Breath Persist* (Erin, Ontario: The Porcupine's Quill, 1992), 22.

5 THIS THING IS MOST NATIONAL: NATIONALISM AND ASSIMILATION... 137

and with the poet himself, show both the initial fluidity of the editor's idea of "American in the wider sense" and the narrow definition of "American" he ultimately utilized for the anthology.

> Dear Gael Turnbull... are you now becoming an American citizen? The limits I've set for this anthology of modern American poetry I'm preparing excludes poets who aren't actually Americans, unfortunately. If you are becoming, I'd very much like to include some of your poems.[18]

The fact that Turnbull's inclusion hinges not on the quality or style of his work, nor on the poetic milieu in which he had established himself, nor on the impact he'd had on the work of his American contemporaries, but on the fact that he didn't possess American citizenship shows the non-literary nature of this limit of eligibility and its centrality for Allen. There is an important shift in Allen's thinking here, from citizenship based on language to one based on passports. Turnbull responded facetiously to Allen's request:

> I'm rather tickled that you should think of me for your anthology. Gregory Corso already gave me a temporary honorary alternative citizenship for some group of US and Canadian poems he chose for some German anthology. However, otherwise, I expect to travel on my British Passport for some time to come. Which may sound a bit like flag-waving. I don't mean it quite like that. Actually, when I'm in England, I am often dubbed a Canadian or a "yank". Never mind. Lawrence lived abroad a good bit too, if I recall.[19]

The Scottish poet subtly, if definitively, deflates Allen's concept of nationalism while illustrating the elasticity of national identity, a fact accentuated

---

[18] Donald Allen to Gael Turnbull, September 8, 1959, Box 70, Folder 17, Donald Allen Collection, MSS 3, Special Collections & Archives, UC San Diego Library.

[19] Gael Turnbull to Donald Allen, September 12, 1959, Box 70, Folder 17, Donald Allen Collection, MSS 3, Special Collections & Archives, UC San Diego Library. The poetry anthology that Turnbull refers to here is the bilingual anthology *Junge Amerikanische Lyrik*, edited by Gregory Corso and Walter Höllerer and published in Munich in 1961. The first anthology to introduce many of Allen's poets to a German audience, *Junge Amerikanische Lyrik* is another example of the transnational reach of these post-war poets. Ironically, considering the way that Turnbull's Scottish origins led him to be excluded from Allen's anthology, Turnbull is described in the biographical notes as being born in Canada and living in England. Gregory Corso and Walter Höllerer, *Junge Amerikanische Lyrik* (Munich: Hanser, 1961), 269.

by the example of D. H. Lawrence, which raises an interesting question: if a British writer composes a poem or novel in the United States, is it a work of American literature? This question would help inspire the recent development of transnational literary criticism[20] and would continue to vex Allen and his co-editors in future "new American" publishing projects. In a letter concerning *The Postmoderns: The New American Poetry Revised* in 1977, co-editor George Butterick queried Allen about the possible inclusion of Cid Corman but quibbled with the definition of "American poet," writing: "though as far as I'm concerned anyone who was out of the country for half of the period the anthology covers, from before the Kennedy assasination [*sic*] and through the resignation of Nixon, missed the point of being an American poet even if he once was 'new.' Thump, thump, thump!"[21]

For Allen in the late 1950s, the nationality of a poem depended on that of its writer. Turnbull contrasts this by mentioning how poets like him might fall through the cracks: in the United Kingdom he was "often dubbed a Canadian or a 'yank,'" while in the United States also he was an outsider. Curiously, though Allen declined to include Turnbull's poetry in *The New American Poetry*, he did cite his international Migrant Press in the anthology's "Short Bibliography" of significant presses and publications.

Ben Hickman, among others, has written about the importance of Turnbull's Migrant Press in promoting the newest American post-war poets to British audiences. The fact that a Scottish poet living and publishing a journal in the United States could directly influence poets in the United Kingdom suggests just how transnational the poetry of the

---

[20] This question has also provided fruitful areas of research including *The Multilingual Anthology of American Literature*, Werner Sollors's collection of American literature written in other languages.

[21] George Butterick to Donald Allen, February 24, 1977, Box 14, Folder 6, Donald Allen Collection, MSS 3, Special Collections & Archives, UC San Diego Library. The problem of nationalism in poetry has continued to vex editors even into the twenty-first century. As William Logan wrote about Rita Dove's *The Penguin Anthology of Twentieth-Century American Poetry* (2011): "Dove's rule is that poets had to live in America and write in English. She doesn't set a term for residence, but presumably it had to be longer than a two-week vacation. Auden is in, meagerly, but not Joseph Brodsky; Paul Muldoon, but not Anne Carson." William Logan, "Guys and Dove," *The New Criterion*, June 2012, https://www.newcriterion.com/issues/2012/6/guys-dove, April 18, 2018.

5 THIS THING IS MOST NATIONAL: NATIONALISM AND ASSIMILATION... 139

moment truly was.[22] Yet Hickman's description of Turnbull as one of the "British followers of *The New American Poetry*"[23] rather than one of its innovators shows the effects on reception that Allen's exclusions have had. These effects were not limited to the United States, as "the single most influential book on British avant-garde poetry"[24] helped form the poetic consciousness of poets and critics on both sides of the Atlantic and also "polarized British poetry in a way that was damaging to it, and to both sides' attempts to find an audience."[25] This puts in a new light Golding's comment that "[Allen's] commitment to his project overrode his reservations about individual contributors' work."[26] This is true only insofar as Allen's project was national and, considering his exclusion of Steven Jonas for aesthetic reasons,[27] racially homogenous.

Turnbull provides a specific example of nationalism at work in the creation of Allen's anthology, but the issue is not as simple as a strong editorial policy against one poet. The question is made even more complex by the inclusion of Helen Adam and Denise Levertov, born in Scotland and Britain, respectively. Adam was a San Francisco-based poet and a member of the poetic community surrounding Robert Duncan and Jack Spicer.

---

[22] Another case in point for the era's transnationalism is the April 1957 issue of *COMBUSTION*, published by Turnbull's Contact Press in Canada and containing part three of Ginsberg's "Howl," as well as poetry from Sergei Esenin, F. R. Scott, Jonathan Williams, Henry Moscovitch and Michael McClure, an essay by Turnbull on Olson's *Maximus* and reviews of Denise Levertov and Cid Corman. A copy of this journal was sent from Contact Press in Toronto to Ginsberg, care of the US Embassy in Tangiers, Morocco, then redirected to his residence in Paris, and finally ended up in the possession of German poet and editor Walter Höllerer. Walter Höllerer Collection, Das Literaturarchiv Sulzbach-Rosenberg, 03 WH / BH / 10, 1.

[23] Woznicki, 82. Obituaries for Turnbull highlight his outsider status. John Lucas notes how Turnbull "promoted the cause on both sides of the Atlantic." John Lucas, "Gael Turnbull: Poet and doctor who promoted the cause on both sides of the Atlantic," *The Guardian*, July 12, 2004, https://www.theguardian.com/news/2004/jul/12/guardianobituaries.booksobituaries, March 12, 2017. Nicholas Johnson writes that "Critics were unsure whether Gael Turnbull was Canadian, American or Scottish." Nicholas Johnson, "Gael Turnbull: Internationalist poet whose Migrant Press pointed the way to the British poetry renaissance," *The Independent*, July 7, 2004, https://www.independent.co.uk/news/obituaries/gael-turnbull-550057.html, March 12, 2017.

[24] Woznicki, 82.

[25] Woznicki, 100.

[26] Golding, 202.

[27] Donald Allen to Marjorie Perloff, June 19, 1999, Box 57, Folder 12, Donald Allen Collection, MSS 3, Special Collections & Archives, UC San Diego Library.

140   S. DELBOS

Born in Glasgow, Adam did not move to the United States until the age of 30, in 1939.[28] As one of only four female poets included in the anthology, and as one whose work was regularly praised in reviews, Adam's inclusion makes *The New American Poetry* a decidedly richer collection. Further, given her importance as a proto-Beat poet and playwright living in San Francisco, as well as her close association with Robert Duncan, who played an important role in the creation of the anthology, Adam's inclusion in some ways appears assured, even as Allen's insistence on nationalism would seem to render her ineligible.[29] For it is certain that Allen knew she was Scottish.[30] This is just one example of the problematic complexities of Allen's nationalist policy of inclusion.

The case of Denise Levertov is similar. Born in England in 1923, she published her first book in London in 1946 and lived in Europe until settling in New York at the end of 1948. Before her move, Kenneth Rexroth had included her work in his anthology *The New British Poets* (1947).[31] Allen seems not to have questioned her inclusion. Again, this may have been due to Duncan's influence—his intense epistolary relationship with Levertov began in 1952 and as early as 1956 he had written to Allen, including Levertov, Helen Adam and Madeline Gleason in a list of

[28] Adam's Wikipedia page describes her as "a Scottish poet." Helen Adam, *Wikipedia*, http://en.wikipedia.org/wiki/Helen_Adam, May 1, 2014.

[29] According to Ron Silliman, Duncan claimed to have played an extremely active role in choosing who was to be included in the anthology. He writes: "Listening to Duncan personally in San Francisco, on several occasions. He made it sound as if Allen had been his amanuensis or grad student assistant." Ron Silliman, Personal Interview, December 27, 2014. However, Allen's correspondence indicates that he considered Duncan more of a nuisance than an aide. Writing to Robert Creeley in August, 1959, Allen commented: "Duncan has been a considerable problem." Donald Allen to Robert Creeley, August 10, 1959, Box 9, Folder 12, Donald Allen Collection, MSS 3, Special Collections & Archives, UC San Diego Library.

[30] See James Broughton's letter to Allen on October 7, 1959: "I have one major questions about your SF lineage: That is Helen Adam, who is very much out of the mainstream, an 'original,' and also Scottish rather than American." James Broughton to Donald Allen, October 7, 1959, Box 9, Folder 3, Donald Allen Collection, MSS 3, Special Collections & Archives, UC San Diego Library.

[31] The existence of this anthology, a collection of British poetry edited by an American and published by New Directions, an American publisher, suggests the degree to which American and British poetry were considered part of a shared tradition in the post-war years, a point that will be taken up below.

5 THIS THING IS MOST NATIONAL: NATIONALISM AND ASSIMILATION... 141

important post-war American poets.[32] The inclusion of Helen Adam and Denise Levertov, and the exclusion of Gael Turnbull, suggest the fluidity of nationalism in poetry and the problematics of a poetry anthology based on national identity.[33] For one thing, lines of influence that exceed the United States are overlooked, a fact that critic Katherine Garrison Chapin touches on in her review of Allen's anthology for *The New Republic*:

> Nearly all of these poets have travelled; lived, worked and gathered impressions (and clichés) in different corners of the globe from the far East to the West; they have read and listened to foreign rhythms, languages, and music. But this experience only seems to have added a dimension to the depth of their spiritual bankruptcy.[34]

Other reviewers also noted the international influences of the poets in the anthology. Vincent McHugh claimed that the style of the poetry in the anthology, "the prosodic attack (this is what confuses people brought up in the tradition of English poetry) comes out of world poetry, mainly French, or French via... '20s Americans."[35] Douglas Woolf suggested that Canadian poet Irving Layton and French poet Jacques Prevert should have been included because they had conspicuously contributed to the style and form of the poets in *The New American Poetry*.[36]

Even James Schuyler wrote to Allen in late 1959 about the international influences of the New York School:

---

[32] Robert Duncan to Donald Allen, December 16, 1956, Box 63, Folder 5, Donald Allen Collection, MSS 3, Special Collections & Archives, UC San Diego Library.

[33] A letter from Levertov to William Carlos Williams on September 21, 1960, suggests the complexity of any questions of nationalism, poetic voice and influence: "You must take into consideration that I grew up not in an American, and not in an English, but a European atmosphere; my father was naturalized in Eng. only around the time I was born – his background was Jewish, Russian, Central European – and my mother, herself proudly Welsh; had lived in Poland, Germany, & Denmark etc. all the years between 1910 & 1923. And then, when I came to the U.S., I was already 24 years old..." Denise Levertov and William Carlos Williams, *The Letters of Denise Levertov and William Carlos Williams*, Christopher MacGowan, ed. (New York: New Directions, 1998), 100.

[34] Katherine Garrison Chapin, "Fifteen Years of New Writing," *The New Republic*, January 9, 1961, 25.

[35] Vincent McHugh, "What IS That New, Unlabeled Streak Across the Sky Saying?" *San Francisco Sunday Chronicle*, June 12, 1960, 25.

[36] Douglas Woolf, "Radioactive Generation," *Inland*, Autumn (1960): 33–34.

142 S. DELBOS

> If there is a New York 'school' now, it certainly began elsewhere, even abroad… Continental European literature is, really the big influence: the Greats, plus Auden, seemed to fill the scene too completely – so one had to react with or against them, casting off obvious influences as best one can. In the context of American writing, poets like Jacob and Breton spelled freedom rather than surreal introversion. What people translate for their own pleasure is a clue: Frank, Holderlin and Reverdy; John A. (before he'd been to France), Jacob's prose poems; Kenneth and I have both had a go at Dante's untranslatable sonnet to Cavalcanti; I've translated Dante, Leopardi and, fruitlessly, Apollinaire and Supervielle… But Pasternak has meant more to us than any American poet. Even in monstrous translation his lyrics make the hair on the back of one's neck curl.[37]

The idea that Pasternak, a Russian poet, "meant more" to the New York School "than any American poet" is crucially insightful. Schuyler's description and these readings of the anthology effectively argue against Olson's suggestion that these poets were less international than their predecessors. Turnbull, Adam and Levertov further prove the permeability, not to say randomness, of Allen's national exclusionism. Allen seems to have cherrypicked his poets, ignoring their international roots where convenient (Adam, Levertov) and foregrounding them in the case of other poets (Turnbull). This selective use of nationalism would continue as "the New American" project continued. As Warren Tallman explains in his preface to *The Poetics of the New American Poetry* (1973):

> We scarcely need more than mention that the 'new' we have in view has to do with poetry written in the English language, specifically by Americans, and we hope no one will mind too much our adopting García Lorca and D. H. Lawrence into this company. They, after all, didn't hesitate to adopt both America and Whitman into their own searches for the new.[38]

The adoption of "America and Whitman" would certainly apply to Turnbull and many others who were excluded from *The New American Poetry*. So why would Allen, following Olson, insist on nationalist criteria?

There is a sense that Olson's insistence on a specifically national project fits into his worldview. In an essay from 2010, Martha King described

---

[37] James Schuyler to Donald Allen, September 20, 1959, Box 1, Folder 11, Donald Allen Collection, MSS 3, Special Collections & Archives, UC San Diego Library.

[38] Warren Tallman, "Preface," *The Poetics of the New American Poetry* (New York: Grove, 1973), ix.

5 THIS THING IS MOST NATIONAL: NATIONALISM AND ASSIMILATION... 143

Olson as a "jingoist."[39] Asked to elaborate on her comment in the context of this study, King reiterated:

> I stick by the word jingoist. There was a romantic concept about America being an exceptional place on earth. That was something [Olson] held very much in [his] mindset and I'm sure that Olson's interest in politics came out of wanting to influence that, especially during the FDR era. It is nationalistic, but in a very romantic way, that there's a new world and a new way to be a human being and America's got an edge on it. There was a whole body of intellectuals and artists whose feelings about America were influenced by that.[40]

As Basil King elaborated, "that was one of the things that absolutely annoyed Charles, that his parents were immigrants."[41]

It may be easier to recognize the clear nationalism that animates *The New American Poetry* in the twenty-first century, when American exceptionalism has proved itself a farce, than it was in the heady pro-American post-war days of the late 1950s. And for American allies like Britain, still flush from the glow of victory in World War II, American nationalism wasn't necessarily seen as limiting. Just the opposite in fact, as Hickman notes: "in essence, *The New American Poetry* had initiated a choice for British poets that was national as much as aesthetic between a nationalistic Little Englandism on the one hand and a perceived American internationalism on the other."[42] The word "perceived" is crucial here.

Clearly though, this is a multifaceted issue and one that has much to do with point of view. The complexity of this subject can be unpacked by considering three further concepts. First, transnationalism as opposed to the nation-as-community, which has been suggested by theorists including Benedict Anderson and applies to the poets included in *The New American Poetry*, who were a heterogeneous group living and working in many parts of the world, although the anthology presents them as a united group of Americans. Second, the anthology's utilization of an American identity and the American flag, a symbol that gained new emphasis during

---

[39] Martha King, "Three Months in 1955: A Memoir of Black Mountain College," *Jacket 2*, 2010, http://jacketmagazine.com/40/king-martha-black-mountain.shtml, March 23, 2018.

[40] Martha King, Personal Interview, Telephone, April 7, 2018.

[41] Basil King, Personal Interview, Telephone, April 7, 2018.

[42] Woznicki, 89.

144   S. DELBOS

the 1950s. And third, the national effort to promote a specific version of American culture during the Cold War, so that the differences between communism and democracy could be accentuated to America's advantage. The remainder of this chapter will deal with these issues separately and will then conclude by considering the portrait of American poetry that emerges from the anthology.

5.2   AMERICAN IN THE WIDER SENSE: READING *THE NEW AMERICAN POETRY* TRANSNATIONALLY

In his seminal study of nationalism, *Imagined Communities*, Benedict Anderson writes: "Since World War II every successful revolution has defined itself in *national* terms."[43] Inasmuch as the American post-war poetry avant-garde as presented by *The New American Poetry* can be said to comprise a revolution in literature, Anderson's observation holds true, as does his definition of a nation as an imagined community, united by a shared narrative and an imaginary conception of unity. Allen established precisely this sense of community with his description of the poets included in the anthology as "a strong third generation... our avant-garde, the true continuers of the modern movement in American poetry."[44] Clearly, Allen's use of "our" foregrounds the nationalism of the anthology, as it presupposes an American readership and context. In that light, this section examines the other key term here, "American poetry," to argue that what Allen presented as a specifically American literary movement was not actually confined by the borders of the United States.

Bearing in mind Anderson's arguments about the necessity of a shared narrative for communal cohesion, the importance of Allen's national and chronological strictures is evident. Within the confines of an anthology entitled *The New American Poetry*, which has an American flag on the cover and in which the majority of the biographical notes begin "Born [year] in [American city]," the national heritage of the poets is asserted before the qualities of the poetry. But Allen's national focus does not only limit the way the poetry in the anthology is read. Claiming that innovative post-war poetry belonged to the United States alone discounts the significant experimental poetry being written around the world by poets such as Turnbull, Basil Bunting and Roy Fisher from Britain, Samuel Beckett,

---

[43] Benedict Anderson, *Imagined Communities* (London: Verso, 1996), 5.
[44] Allen, xi.

5 THIS THING IS MOST NATIONAL: NATIONALISM AND ASSIMILATION... 145

Brian Coffey and Thomas MacGreevy from Ireland, Irving Layton from Canada and the Nigerian poet Christopher Okigbo, among many others. These far-flung individuals were also using a new, more speech-based approach to writing poetry in English, which Allen limited to the "American language"[45] when compiling the anthology. Allen does not explicitly claim that no innovative poetry was being written in other countries during this period, but the fact that he insisted on a separate American strand of innovation that was exerting "strong influence abroad"[46] without admitting to any international influence certainly gives one that impression.[47]

As Alan Riach has written about poet Ed Dorn (who appears in *The New American Poetry*), "the key qualities" of the "new forms of address in the American poetry of the 1950s and what was to come in the 60s" are

> hard observation, moral commitment, fierce independence, self-determination, irrepressible humour, ironic flair, a flourishing sense of engagement, and literary and poetic structures to match and convey all these things. They were as essential to Edward Dorn as they were to Hugh MacDiarmid.[48]

That a Scottish poet could have been as innovative with English-language form and content as American poets during this period does not seem to have occurred to Allen or poets such as Olson. The stylistic tendencies the editor identified as the defining characteristics of new poetry in the United States, and the actual places of production for this poetry, were more international than Allen's anthology suggests.

Allen's ideas about the new poetry of his nation were gleaned from contemporary publications. Fortunately, the 1950s were a boom time for small presses. In the "Short Bibliography" of *The New American Poetry*, there are 15 addresses of independent poetry publishers and 37 magazines and journals listed under "Chief Periodicals" and those that are "Also of

---

[45] Maud, 46.

[46] Allen, xii.

[47] This is similar to the treatment of abstract art during this period, when the dominant American critical narrative Americanized tendencies taking place in art communities around the world.

[48] Alan Riach, "What Can We Learn from Ed Dorn?," *The National*, April 1, 2016, http://www.thenational.scot/culture/alan-riach-what-can-we-learn-from-edward-dorn.15780, April 1, 2016.

146   S. DELBOS

Value." Many of these were located outside the United States. The journal *Contact* was located in Toronto; *Fragmente* was located in Freiburg im Bresigau; *Jabberwock 1959* was from Edinburgh; *Artisan* was from Liverpool; *Prospect* was located in Cambridge, England; and *Botteghe Oscure* was from Rome, and incidentally published in Italian, French, Spanish and German as well as English, a fact that allowed it to promote "a new international spirit and the opening to a larger literary world for a generation of writers who would find each other through its pages."[49] One of the presses mentioned, Gael Turnbull's Migrant, had addresses both in California and in England.[50] So even on the level of publication, there was less that was specifically American about innovative Anglophone poetry in the decade after World War II than the anthology makes apparent. The very existence of foreign presses that are considered American opens interesting cracks in the façade of a supposedly united national avant-garde. It also shows that the conception of American poetry as something taking place within the borders of the American continent is inaccurate.

The internationalism of Allen's poets is exemplified most clearly by Robert Creeley, who was, along with Charles Olson, one of the most significant movers of post-war American poetry and someone who kept up a voluminous correspondence with Allen during the conception of the anthology and afterwards. Creeley spent most of these years outside of the United States, and even his editorship of *The Black Mountain Review* and Divers Press, which published seminal books including volumes by Paul Blackburn, Larry Eigner, Robert Duncan and Creeley himself, took place in Mallorca.[51] Martha King reveals how Creeley's international

---

[49] Helen Barolini, "The Shadowy Lady of the Street of Dark Shops," *Virginia Quarterly Review*, Spring 1998, http://www.vqronline.org/essay/shadowy-lady-street-dark-shops, May 15, 2015.

[50] Allen, 451–452

[51] Duberman, 412. Olson alludes to this in "Letter 9" of *The Maximus Poems*:

> as the news that the almond
> was in bloom Mallorca
> accompanied the news
> that that book was in print
> which I wish might stop
> the workings of my city

Charles Olson, *The Maximus Poems*, ed. George F. Butterick (Berkeley: University of California Press, 1983), 45.

5 THIS THING IS MOST NATIONAL: NATIONALISM AND ASSIMILATION... 147

lifestyle—as much as his innovative style of writing—was intriguing for young American readers of these publications:

> Was this before or after I bought a copy of the *Black Mountain Review* at the Bullshead Bookshop in the basement of the university library?... What was this magazine typeset and published in Palma de Mallorca? I looked it up to find out where it was. Balearic Islands. Spain. I still didn't know where it was. Spain meant Franco to me. A curtain had closed over the whole country after the loss of the Spanish Civil War. But Black Mountain College was not in Spain. It was right here: Black Mountain, North Carolina.[52]

Born in Arlington, Massachusetts, in 1926, Creeley served in the American Field Service in India and Burma during World War II, then attended Harvard, but left without a degree. He moved with his wife and children to Provence in 1951, then to Mallorca the following year. After a stint at Black Mountain College, he relocated to Guatemala, then to New Mexico, then to British Columbia, before finally resettling in the United States during the last decades of his life. For a poet so closely identified with "New American" poetry, Creeley didn't spend much time in the United States during the post-war years, nor did he seem particularly interested in nationalism. As he wrote in 1952: "my place is so much on the paper, and not where it might, even ought, to be. I'm real portable these days, like the fucking typewriter. I argue against 'place,' and that false sense of what it counts as, which is usually generator for an altogether dead memory, etc."[53] It is a striking statement from a poet who was so influential to post-war American poetry and yet seemed to believe that living in Cold War America would have a detrimental effect on his work.[54]

The limitations of nationalism as a critical category have become even more apparent with the passing of time, especially given the recent transnational turn of American literary studies. Allen's Amero-centric approach

---

[52] Martha King, "Three Months in 1955: A Memoir of Black Mountain College," *Jacket 2*, 2010, http://jacketmagazine.com/40/king-martha-black-mountain.shtml, March 23, 2018.

[53] Smith, Baker and Harris, 92.

[54] Creeley wrote to Olson in 1950: "I.e., one thing else, i.e., thinking of yr comment, to be where there is nothing American, i.e., against that, wd put this: that the thing is, somehow, not so much that as to be, in a place so much its own way, any, that it cd make you, push you, somehow to a difference, not that change, i.e., to the 'new' personality, but to that shade, variation, cd plot you, new, the line to yr self, etc., to the in." Smith, Baker and Harris, 54.

148 S. DELBOS

now contrasts with a critical discourse that insists on the permeability of national borders in literature. Numerous literary critics of the past two decades, including Jahan Ramazani, Wai Chee Dimock, James Clifford and Donald E. Pease, have insisted on reading American literature in a global context, privileging what James Clifford has called routes of influence rather than roots.[55] This transnational framework is specifically relevant to any discussion of the Cold War, when American studies was first instituted as an academic discipline, which is only one example of the era's assertion of American culture and widespread nationalism. Ramazani's *A Transnational Poetics* is particularly relevant in this regard, as it "proposes various ways of vivifying circuits of poetic connection and dialogue across political and geographic borders and even hemispheres, of examining cross-cultural and cross-national exchanges, influences, and confluences in poetry" by taking into account "globalization, migration, travel, genre, influence, modernity, decolonization, and diaspora."[56] Contrary to what *The New American Poetry* presents, poetic influence and innovation are never hermetically sealed by national borders.

Taking issue with the continued prevalence of poetic nationalism, Ramazani identifies this framework across various media:

> In studies of modern and contemporary poetry in English, single-nation genealogies remain surprisingly entrenched: an army of anthologies, job descriptions, library catalogs, books, articles, and annotations reterritorializes the cross-national mobility and migrancy of modern and contemporary poetry under the banner of the single-nation norm.[57]

Ramazani locates the source of these single-nation genealogies in a "pre-Romantic concept of literature as an expression of national identity [that] rigidifies in the Cold War American academy."[58] It is true that American Studies was founded in the nationalistic period of the Cold War. But what the nationalism of *The New American Poetry* shows us is that a single-nation concept of poetry was promoted both inside and outside the

---

[55] James Clifford, *Routes: Travel and Translation in the Late Twentieth Century* (Cambridge: Harvard University Press, 1997), 3.

[56] Jahan Ramazani, *A Transnational Poetics* (Chicago: University of Chicago Press, 2009), x–xi.

[57] Jahan Ramazani, *A Transnational Poetics* (Chicago: University of Chicago Press, 2009), 23.

[58] Ramazani, 23.

academy. Allen's anthology, which was conceived of as a "total rejection of all those qualities typical of academic verse,"[59] also participates in the Cold War calcification of an old notion of what Ramazani refers to as the citizenship of a poem.[60] While many of the poets in Allen's anthology were existing and writing transnationally—traveling and living in foreign countries, interacting and communicating with foreign cultures, languages and literatures—they were presented and read as being American above all.

Bearing in mind these relatively new ways of tracing poetic influence across borders, Olson's claim that the innovative Anglophone poetry that Allen collected in his anthology was specifically the product of American culture seems less an accurate, objective reading of that poetry and the post-war landscape and more a statement that blends self-promotion with Cold War American nationalism. Even leaving aside examples such as Gael Turnbull, the idea that American poets between 1945 and 1960 had shaken off the influence of the internationally minded modernists in order to create a poetry that was completely indigenous to the United States is disingenuous to say the least. Thus the seeming contradiction among critics who call Olson an internationalist, citing his interest in Mayan culture and others, despite the fact that he had a key role in creating the nationalizing apparatus of Allen's anthology. None of the poets in *The New American Poetry* were completely free of international influences and in fact many of them openly embraced these influences, whether through reading and admiration, translation, communication with non-American poets or by actually living in foreign countries. Poetic influence is not something that can be turned on and off. Nor is it something that segregates itself along national borders, especially among Anglophone countries, contrary to what Tallman suggests in his preface to *The Poetics of the New American Poetry*: "Yeats is a magnificent poet but is perhaps nearer to some endpoint of a great British line than to the emergence of a new American poetry."[61] As Clifford, Ramazani and other transnational scholars have pointed out, literary influence is not compartmentalized in such a convenient way. This is not something that would be apparent to readers of *The New American Poetry*, which Allen confined to a single continent and organized according to American geography.

---

[59] Allen, xi.
[60] Ramazini, 31.
[61] Allen and Tallman, x.

150   S. DELBOS

Allen's geographical organization of the anthology and his division of poets into communities based mostly on where they lived and worked further emphasized his national framework. The difficulties Allen had in organizing the book this way, and the opposition he faced with poets such as Robert Duncan, who vocally disputed some poets' claims to be San Francisco poets, point to the heterogeneity of the post-war avant-garde and also to the fact that such regional communities were, in Anderson's terms, "imagined." Allen all but admits this in his introduction:

> I have adopted the unusual device of dividing the poets into five large groups, though these divisions are somewhat arbitrary and cannot be taken as rigid categories... The first group includes those poets who were originally closely identified with the two important magazines of the period, *Origin* and *Black Mountain Review*... the second group, the San Francisco Renaissance... The Beat Generation, the third group, was originally associated with New York, but they first attracted national attention in San Francisco... John Ashbery, Kenneth Koch, and Frank O'Hara, of the fourth group, the New York School Poets, first met at Harvard... The fifth group has no geographical definition... Occasionally arbitrary and for the most part more historical than actual, these groups can be justified finally only as a means to give the reader some sense of milieu and to make the anthology more a readable book and less still another collection of "anthology pieces."[62]

The editor's caginess here is apparent, and with good reason. As late as December 1959 Allen had written, in another context, that the "New York poets... can scarcely be said to exist as a group, though there are correspondences between them."[63] Nonetheless, Allen's insistence on organizing his anthology this way would alter the popular perception of American poetry, defining it along geographical lines that drew focus away from New England (and old England) as traditional centers of literary production.[64] It would also present the avant-garde as a nationwide phenomenon that was stylistically varied, taking inspiration from different parts of the country. This is exactly what Louise Bogan picked up on in her

---

[62] Allen, xii–xiii.

[63] Donald Allen, December 11, 1959, Box 8, Folder 7, Donald Allen Collection, MSS 3, Special Collections & Archives, UC San Diego Library.

[64] On a related note, Duberman mentions how the category of Black Mountain Poets, which Allen says in his introduction is centered around *Origin* and *The Black Mountain Review* rather than the college, has been conflated with poets who attended the college. Duberman, 411.

5 THIS THING IS MOST NATIONAL: NATIONALISM AND ASSIMILATION... 151

review of the anthology: "This group (or series of groups), [is] more numerous than one might suppose, and more widely spread over the land – from Massachusetts to Oregon and California, plus a detour into the South by way of North Carolina."[65]

From the earliest stages of planning the anthology, Allen seems to have considered a geographical style of organization, so apparently his sense of American poetry as divided along geographical lines was inherent in his conception of the milieu, and anything that complicated this style of organization, such as foreign poets or those not living in major cities,[66] would likely be ignored. Writing to James Broughton in early September 1959, Allen described his concept of an arrangement that would be "somewhat historical as well as being geographical."[67] But it wasn't until the previous generation of poets was excluded from the book that place became Allen's primary means of organization. But it is important to note that poets including Creeley attempted to dissuade Allen from using these categories. As Creeley wrote: "[Labels] have bred enough confusion as it is. Again they generalize the people to whom they are attached, and... seem to misplace finally people to whom they may first draw attention."[68] Nonetheless, Allen pushed on. As he phrased it in a letter to Creeley the following month, it was simply a "problem" of deciding "where does the muscle begin."[69]

By 1960 Allen had decided. That year he wrote in a letter to Larry Eigner that his purpose in arranging the anthology geographically was "to give a somewhat historical presentation of a whole new movement & generation and to arrange it so that it would be interesting to read and easily informative as well." In the same letter he explains how his designs took precedence over the wishes of some of the poets:

[65] Louise Bogan, "Verse," *The New Yorker*, October 8, 1960, 199.

[66] David Clippinger applies this argument to William Bronk, apparently the last poet to be cut from consideration in Allen's anthology. See: David Clippinger, "Neither Us nor Them: Poetry Anthologies, Canon Building, and the Silencing of William Bronk," *The Argotist Online*, http://www.argotistonline.co.uk/Clippinger%20essay.htm, December 19, 2016.

[67] Donald Allen to James Broughton, September 4, 1959, Box 10, Folder 3, Donald Allen Collection, MSS 3, Special Collections & Archives, UC San Diego Library.

[68] Robert Creeley to Donald Allen, August 17, 1959, Box 9, Folder 12, Donald Allen Collection, MSS 3, Special Collections & Archives, UC San Diego Library.

[69] Donald Allen to Robert Creeley, September 8, 1959, Box 9, Folder 12, Donald Allen Collection, MSS 3, Special Collections & Archives, UC San Diego Library.

152   S. DELBOS

> Outside of Duncan, I didn't really worry about what... a poet would feel about his location in the book. And by setting up the fifth section I proceeded to deny the validity of the geographical as of now. However, in a new edition I have been thinking I'd rearrange the whole thing, presenting poets chronologically by year of birth, drop a couple of names and add several new ones.[70]

This style of organization would be influential for future anthologists and critics. Yet it was one of the most controversial features of Allen's anthology and one which brings the local aspects of American nationalism into focus while suggesting the degree to which Allen's geographically dispersed communities were imagined rather than actual. The fact that several of the poets chafed against his editorial restraints suggests the idiosyncrasy and the inappropriateness of these categories.

Allen's regional conception of post-war American poetry seems to have emerged in 1956 when he was considering a San Francisco-focused issue of *The Evergreen Review*. Through his correspondence, Duncan established himself as something of a gatekeeper for the San Francisco scene. The poet would become a thorn in Allen's side, withdrawing his poems from the issue at first and generally being difficult to work with. Ultimately he would call Allen's idea of a "regional anthology... Strange."[71] Duncan took particular umbrage at Allen's suggestion of including Gregory Corso in *The Evergreen Review*, writing:

> I will not tolerate the inclusion of Corso... Corso was imported to San Francisco for a period of one month so that Ginsberg could present his gang as San Francisco poetry. Corso's claims to inclusion in that category are entirely fraudulent.[72]

In a later letter, Duncan writes to Allen:

---

[70] Donald Allen to Larry Eigner, June 10, 1960, Box 63, Folder 25, Donald Allen Collection, MSS 3, Special Collections & Archives, UC San Diego Library.

[71] Robert Duncan to Donald Allen, March 13, 1957, Box 63, Folder 5, Donald Allen Collection, MSS 3, Special Collections & Archives, UC San Diego Library.

[72] Robert Duncan to Donald Allen, December 15, 1956, Box 63, Folder 5, Donald Allen Collection, MSS 3, Special Collections & Archives, UC San Diego Library.

5 THIS THING IS MOST NATIONAL: NATIONALISM AND ASSIMILATION... 153

> As I wrote to you before should Corso be included in an anthology of San Francisco work I will not permit the appearance of any of my work... This is entirely based on the fact that he is not a San Francisco poet.[73]

Finally, Corso's work was not included in the issue, and in Allen's anthology he would be placed in the Beat Generation section. Duncan's dispute with Allen suggests that the editor's avant-garde was not as united nor as geographically organized as the anthology made it seem.

Lawrence Ferlinghetti was also skeptical about Allen's geographic system of organization, writing to the editor:

> Your anthology is big historical-type event even if your groupings are kind of artificial, though cool. It's real cool editing job, but the geographical classification is really irrelevant these days, what with everyone commuting between metropolises. Then too, 6 or 7 out of the 11 poets you list in Section 5 have been more closely associated with San Francisco than anywhere else, and they have also been here most of the time. I think the geographical shd [*sic*] have been ignored completely, but, as it is, I certainly feel somewhat out of place in the "SF Group" which seems to be mostly leftovers from the "Berkeley Renaissance" or the "SF Renaissance" of a dozen years ago, plus a few young arrivals. As to the new poets in SF section, I don't see how you could choose the ones you did instead of Kaufman, Brautigan. (How come you ignored Kaufman, anyway?)[74]

A good question.[75] It is telling that Ferlinghetti, a San Francisco poet if there ever was one, felt uncomfortable being presented as such. His and Duncan's comments indicate that Allen's arrangement of his material was less than organic. While many of the poets argued against geographical strictures, Allen insisted on them. And it wasn't only poets who objected to the organization of the anthology. The geographical boundaries inevitably riled regional feelings in readers and critics as well.

---

[73] Robert Duncan to Donald Allen, February 11, 1957, Box 63, Folder 5, Donald Allen Collection, MSS 3, Special Collections & Archives, UC San Diego Library.

[74] Lawrence Ferlinghetti to Donald Allen, June 6, 1960, Box 63, Folder 5, Donald Allen Collection, MSS 3, Special Collections & Archives, UC San Diego Library.

[75] Robert Duncan suggested that Kaufman simply hadn't played a large enough role in the poetry of the day to be included. Duncan wrote: "No amount of arrangement... can make Kaufman seem to have done the work, have been the creative spirit that Corso was and is, in the creation of the 'Beat' vision." Golding, 191.

154   S. DELBOS

Reviewing the anthology for the *San Francisco Sunday Chronicle*, Vincent McHugh complained that the effect of Allen's organization was "a false displacement toward New York" when San Francisco deserved more credit for supporting modern poetry, "even if we don't have the money to publish big anthologies."[76] Eight years after the publication of the anthology, Charles Olson was even more outspoken about what he called Allen's "terrible mistake" of organizing the anthology the way he did:

> No, I think that whole "Black Mountain poet" thing is a lot of bullshit. I mean, actually, it was created by the editor, the famous editor of that anthology for Grove Press, Mr. Allen, where he divided – he did a very – but it was a terrible mistake made. He created those sections – Black Mountain, San Francisco, Beat, New York, New, Young, huh? Oh, I mean, imagine, just for the hear of it, "Young." Hear the insult, if you're young. You're suddenly classified into a thing – by one of the great editors, the founder of *Evergreen Review*. And the first issues of *Evergreen*, the first four issues of *Evergreen* were, really, first rate. But he made a big mistake; he made a topological error. I mean he had the wrong topology. And he created something which is very unhappy. For example, poets who just can't get us straight because they think we form a sort of club or a claque or a gang or something.[77]

In later years, Allen himself was less than enthusiastic about his geographic organization, which ironically has been one of the anthology's most lasting legacies. Writing to George Butterick in 1976, Allen commented: "One lesson I did finally learn, though I resisted it for years, is that the divisions should not be so evident as were mine. Best to set it up chronologically by date of birth and then follow that through the book."[78]

The wide readership of *The New American Poetry* and the way that it has been used as a teaching tool while creating a model for future anthologists and critics suggest that the anthology played a not-insignificant role in the continued national conception of Anglophone poetry. Allen both perpetuated and was influenced by the Cold War emphasis on American nationalism. His editorial decisions limited and normalized the rich development of post-war Anglophone poetry that had its roots in countries around the world. *The New American Poetry*'s insistence on a specifically

---

[76] McHugh, 25.

[77] Quoted in Smith, Baker and Harris, 426.

[78] Donald Allen to George Butterick, December 13, 1976, Box 14, Folder 6, Donald Allen Collection, MSS 3, Special Collections & Archives, UC San Diego Library.

5 THIS THING IS MOST NATIONAL: NATIONALISM AND ASSIMILATION... 155

American collective, which is now taken for granted, was not appreciated by all of his early correspondents. Even some of his supporters were skeptical at first about the necessity of publishing a specifically American poetry anthology. As Cid Corman wrote to Allen in early 1958:

> I don't know how you can make such an anthology pertinent without taking a particular stand. I have pushed for such an anthology for several years, and then when it was in hand, I realized that in all honesty there wasn't enough material to fill 75 pages. There are too many anthologies, too many predigested "books." All the more reason to take what may seem a biased position... I can't give you any names that are unknown to you. (I might, if American weren't the gimmick – which I think is provincial in itself)[79]

Corman here suggests that the concept of an American anthology is unique enough to be a "gimmick." Calling on Allen to take a "particular stand," Corman chastises the editor for utilizing a focus he deems cheap. What Corman did not realize, however, is that Allen's decision to include only American poets was in fact a stand and one that involved more imagination than may be apparent. For the American avant-garde poetry scene of the 1940s and 1950s was much less *American* than Allen's anthology suggests.

Much can happen between conceiving of a poetry anthology and publishing it. There is no doubt that between 1957, when Allen "began to ponder what I saw happening in American poetry, beginning to think that this new writing connected... a possible movement,"[80] and November 3, 1959, when he would write in his diary "Turned in the New American Poetry antho[logy] yesterday (Monday). Great fatigue, lassitude last night...,"[81] countless difficult decisions, revisions, excisions and changes of mind had taken place. In the end, Allen remained committed to a national idea of post-war poetry. As a professional editor he must have been aware that much of his anthology's commercial success would depend on its national cohesion. A disparate collection of unrelated poets is much easier to ignore than a cohesive group embodying "our

---

[79] Cid Corman to Donald Allen, April 16, 1958, Box 11, Folder 1, Donald Allen Collection, MSS 3, Special Collections & Archives, UC San Diego Library.

[80] Maud, 7.

[81] Donald Allen, Diary, November 3, 1959, Box 64, Folder 2, Donald Allen Collection, MSS 3, Special Collections & Archives, UC San Diego Library.

avant-garde."[82] But the success that nationalism brought for the anthology has come at the price of a limited conception of post-war Anglophone poetry.

By the late 1950s, any American poet who had taken any interest in their craft and its history would have internalized the work of the modernists, along with their international influences. As William Carlos Williams famously wrote about Eliot's "The Waste Land," the model of the international modernist poem if there ever was one: "It wiped out our world as if an atom bomb had been dropped upon it and our brave sallies into the unknown were turned to dust."[83] *The New American Poetry* was its own kind of bomb, one that seemed to eradicate the international influence of the modernists at a moment when it had been truly assimilated by American poets. What was left when the smoke cleared was a national model that continues to be influential to this day.

Examining more closely the poets included and excluded from *The New American Poetry*, as well as the group dynamics among the poets and their opinions about Allen's editorial choices, makes clear that what Allen presented as a flourishing of specifically American poetry after World War II was more transnational and heterogeneous than it appears. Not only are Allen's decisions regarding inclusion somewhat arbitrary[84] but the American poets he presents as a homogeneous avant-garde are both less united and more international than he suggests. Bearing in mind the actual locations of production for American post-war avant-garde poetry, as well as the examples of Turnbull, Adam, Levertov and the peripatetic Robert Creeley, it is clear that the "thing" Olson described was not exactly "most national." Yet Allen's national presentation of this poetry was foregrounded even in the graphic design of the anthology.

---

[82] Allen, xi.

[83] William Carlos Williams, *The Autobiography of William Carlos Williams* (New York: Random House, 1951), 174.

[84] Nationalism is always arbitrary to a certain degree: "Surely, if people were to understand how arbitrary nationalism is, the concept would appear ludicrous." Robert Sapolsky "This Is Your Brain on Nationalism: The Biology of Us and Them," *Foreign Affairs*, March/April, 2019, 47.

5 THIS THING IS MOST NATIONAL: NATIONALISM AND ASSIMILATION... 157

5.3   RED, WHITE AND RECOGNIZABLE: THE DESIGN AND TITLE OF *THE NEW AMERICAN POETRY*

The most immediately apparent features of *The New American Poetry* are its title and cover, a stylized version of the American flag. These made the anthology instantly recognizable as American during a time when demonstrations of one's nationality took on a heightened significance. Representing the dominant political and cultural ideologies of the era, during which "the postwar order that is generally seen as the non plus ultra of American hegemony was built on the hardened divisions of the Cold War,"[85] these features would be retained in several of Allen's subsequent publications. This helped to form the consensus that avant-garde Anglophone poetry after World War II was an American innovation.

The cover of *The New American Poetry* was designed by the artist Roy Kuhlman, the house designer for Grove Press during the 1950s and 1960s.[86] An abstracted version of the American flag in keeping with Kuhlman's signature style, which often featured graphics influenced by abstract expressionism and utilized the brushstroke technique most recognizable in the work of Franz Kline, the cover of the first edition hardcover features five crooked or broken horizontal red brushstrokes, mimicking an American flag waving in the wind. On the top left corner, the text reads: "The New American Poetry" in black, "1945–1960" in red and "Edited by Donald M. Allen" in gray, and this against a white background. As mentioned previously, the dates in the anthology's title are somewhat misleading, as very few poems therein date from before 1950. The back cover lists the title in black and red, with the names of the poets included. If one opens the cover all the way, it appears as if the names of the poets on the back cover are the stars of the flag suggested by the front cover.[87] The simplicity of the graphic layout bespeaks a quiet confidence in the claim that this is the new poetry from the United States, while the abstracted

---

[85] Adam Tooze, "Is this the end of the American century?: America Pivots" *The London Review of Books*, April 4, 2019 https://www.lrb.co.uk/v41/n07/adam-tooze/is-this-the-end-of-the-american-century, April 5, 2019.

[86] For insightful commentary on Kuhlman's work for Grove Press, excepting *The New American Poetry*, see Loren Glass, *Counter-Culture Colophon: Grove Press, The Evergreen Review and the Incorporation of the Avant-Garde* (Stanford: Stanford University Press, 2013).

[87] With 44 poets, the cover is only 4 short of the 48 stars that would have appeared on the American flag until 1959, when Alaska and Hawaii were granted statehood.

158   S. DELBOS

version of the American flag suggests a new vision of what it means to be American.

The national focus and intent of the cover of *The New American Poetry* is in clear contrast to the cover of *The New Poets of England and America*, which features a black-and-white photograph of what appears to be a sparkler shooting sparks from a white-hot center. This suggests the explosive energy and excitement of the poetry contained therein. Nation-state nationalism is downplayed not only by the title of the anthology but by the cover itself, which brings our attention to the qualities of the poetry rather than its national identity. Interestingly, the title of the anthology is not capitalized on the cover, although "An Anthology" and the names of the editors are in all-capital letters. Here the text draws our attention to the particular role of the trio of editors with the phrase "edited and selected by," further activating and emphasizing the role of the editors and their critical taste.

The title of the Hall, Pack and Simpson anthology also needs special attention because it has often been confused. The original title of the first edition of the anthology is *The New Poets of England and America*. In the "Second Selection" of the anthology published in 1962, the title was shortened to *New Poets of England and America*, which downplayed the original anthology's claims to definitiveness because, as Donald Hall has said, "The definite article was criticized!"[88] After the publication of Allen's anthology it was much more difficult to claim such definitiveness, as the two anthologies shared no single poet but both claimed to be new.

Roy Kuhlman was not the only American artist reconsidering the flag as a symbol of American life and patriotism in the years following World War II. Readers familiar with modern American art in the 1950s—the very milieu that Allen sought to connect with poetry in his introduction to *The New American Poetry*—would have been reminded, upon seeing the anthology's cover, of Jasper Johns's painting *Flag*, completed in 1955 and first exhibited in New York City at The Leo Castelli Gallery, one of abstract expressionism's home bases, in 1958. Due to Allen's and Kuhlman's connections to New York City's art world, it is not unlikely that they would have been aware of Johns's painting, but by examining Kuhlman's use of the America flag motif on the anthology's cover I do not mean to suggest that he was copying Johns. The potency of the American flag as a symbol ripe for reconsideration was central to the cultural climate of the Cold

---

[88] Donald Hall, Personal Interview, Email, February 11, 2014.

War, from the establishment of Flag Day as an Act of Congress in 1949 to the addition of "under God" in the Pledge of Allegiance in 1954. As Michael Davidson writes, the anthology's cover "reminds us that the NAP was engaged in a project of national redefinition as much as a poetic one."

> The flag on the cover was partly patriotic but mostly satiric because it marked a set of alternative political and social positions to American consensus that would not be found in the reigning college anthology of the period, Brooks's and Warren's *Understanding Poetry*. As Golding and others have indicated, it was an era of "anthology wars" where poetic turf was being defended for the hearts and minds of English teachers in the expanded educational system of the 1960s.[89]

While I disagree that the flag is "mostly satiric," Davidson is right to point out that the cover suggests a reconsideration of symbols of Americanness, which was in itself a political act during this period.

The cover of *The New American Poetry* has parallels with Johns's famous painting in at least one other important way. Just as Johns would regularly revisit and recreate *Flag* in a fashion that was significant for him, the painting and American culture, Allen would reuse and reconfigure his title and cover in subsequent publications. Later editions of *The New American Poetry* used a design similar to Kuhlman's original, although the jagged paint strokes would be replaced by somewhat smoother lines. Allen also made use of the original anthology's design concept in publications that revisited *The New American Poetry*'s legacy and helped to ensure its continued relevance, including *New American Story* (1965), *The New Writing in the USA* (1967), *The Poetics of The New American Poetry* (1973) and *The Postmoderns: The New American Poetry Revised* (1982), all of which contain a reference to *The New American Poetry*, in their title, on their cover or in their introductions. *New American Story* has a very similar cover design as the original anthology, with seven waving red lines interspersed by white, an abstract flag waving in heavier wind, perhaps, than *The New American Poetry*. *The Poetics of the New American Poetry* features an American flag with seven red stripes bent in a similar style to the original waving pattern from 1960. This time the stars are also present. In direct homage to Jasper Johns, *The Postmoderns: The New American*

---

[89] Michael Davidson, *Guys Like Us: Citing Masculinity in Cold War Poetics* (Chicago: University of Chicago, 2004), 200.

160 S. DELBOS

Poetry Revised uses his painting *Three Flags* (1958) on the cover, confirming both the importance of this national symbol for Allen's project and the importance of Johns's reconfiguration of that symbol.

By continually revisiting his original project in this way, Allen consolidated its canonical position. This is not something that was unfamiliar to Johns, as art critic Fred Orton has pointed out:

> [*Flag*] achieves this status not only by becoming established as the work that begins "Jasper Johns" but by being repeated by Johns himself. He continually returns to it and retrieves it, makes another *Flag* or paints another *Stars and Stripes*, to mark the progress of the changing surface appearance of his art and thus reassure those, including himself, who need the ideological and financial security it provides, that all his work is indexed to it and to the "Jasper Johns" who produced it and whom it produces. That is to say, the dynamic of repeating *Flag* keeps "Jasper Johns-ness" present even as a new beginning is made and a new kind of "Jasper Johns" is created.[90]

In the same way, by revisiting the success of *The New American Poetry* in various publications over two decades, Allen not only reassured himself and critics that his own work as an editor was indexed to his original breakthrough anthology but also suggested to critics, poets and readers that all of avant-garde or postmodern American poetry was indexed to *The New American Poetry*, thus ensuring the continued relevance of the original project while providing a roadmap for the critical discourse. Ultimately, *The New American Poetry* does not actually refer to a single publication but rather a host of publications that together form a consensus about post-war American poetry, continually referring to one another and to the poetry itself. While other poetry anthologies of the past 60 years would reference the rivalry between academic and avant-garde, or insiders versus outsiders, or play up the rebellious nature of non-academic poets, no anthologist has so completely laid claim to such a specifically national project as Allen or has so dramatically reorganized what might have been a transnational literary discourse. In so doing, Allen and his anthologies have helped create the American poetry we know today.

---

[90] Fred Orton, *Figuring Jasper Johns* (London: Reaktion Books, 1994), 97.

5.4 The Decisive Defining Factor: Donald Allen's Construction of American Poetry

In one sense, as explored above, *The New American Poetry* was the end point in a debate that stretched back to colonial days about the possibility of a specifically American poetry. There is an alternative narrative of American poetry, however, one that takes into account the internationalism of the first generation of modernists, about whom Olson admitted, "even the papas were international."[91] By the early twentieth century, American poetry had more convincingly than ever established its independence from Britain, according to critics including Harriet Monroe.[92] But Modernist American verse was transnational, as is evident in the French-infused poetry of Eliot, and Pound's Provençal, Chinese and Greek translations, and more generally in the wealth of international quotations and literary allusions in their work as well as their lives in Europe. So by the 1920s, Rexroth could write of a "Fundamental Disagreement with Two Contemporaries," referring to André Breton and Tristan Tzara.[93] Another index was the Armory Show of 1913 which profoundly influenced not only the development of American art but also its literature, as Wallace Stevens, Williams and Rexroth (who attended the show as a young boy with his parents) would attest.[94] Polyglot poets like Édouard Roditi, who was born in Paris to American parents and who wrote in and translated poetry from several languages, are indicative of this transnational milieu.[95]

The argument for a world literature or an international modern idiom during this period was compelling, and it would grow even more so by the late 1930s with the arrival of the surrealists in New York City, allowing American and European art to confront one another again.[96] But by that time, New Critical ideology had begun to standardize the American cur-

---

[91] Maud, 61.

[92] Harriet Monroe, "Colonialism Again," *Poetry*, X (May 1917): 94, http://www.poetryfoundation.org/poetrymagazine/browse/10/2#!/20571230/2, May 1, 2015.

[93] Kenneth Rexroth, *The Complete Poems of Kenneth Rexroth*, Sam Hamill and Bradford Morrow, eds. (Port Townsend: Copper Canyon Press, 2003), 83.

[94] Tom McCormack, "The 1913 Armory Show: America's First Art War," *Art 21*, http://www.art21.org/texts/the-culture-wars-redux/essay-the-1913-armory-show-americas-first-art-war, May 1, 2015.

[95] "Édouard Roditi, 1910–1992," *The Poetry Foundation*, https://www.poetryfoundation.org/poets/edouard-roditi, April 2, 2018.

[96] See Serge Guilbaut, *How New York Stole the Idea of Modern Art* (Chicago: University of Chicago Press, 1985).

riculum by focusing on received forms and the Anglophone poets who utilized them. In the 1920s and 1930s poets such as Rexroth, Kenneth Patchen and Kenneth Fearing, among many others, were writing poetry that fit alongside the work of figures from other countries like Octavio Paz, Pablo Neruda and Nazim Hikmet, a poetry embracing a left-leaning modern idiom and sensibility and an international sense of citizenship regardless of language. But as Alan Filreis has shown, by the early 1940s, strong forces were at work in American poetry to brand such writers—and their style of poetry—as anti-American, a gesture that increased in intensity during the Cold War.[97]

Subscribing to the narrative that American poetry embraced an international modernism in the early twentieth century before being stifled and provincialized in the 1930s and 1940s, and bearing in mind the transnationalism of the poets in *The New American Poetry* as well as the international locations of the journals and presses that published them, necessitates an important revision in how we think about the impacts of Allen's anthology. Generally, *The New American Poetry* is seen as an anthology that opened up new possibilities in American poetry. But from another point of view, just as a new, younger generation of poets emerging after World War II began to explore and expand the internationalism of the modernists and connect with poets internationally, Allen's anthology nationalized them. This deepened the supposed split between cooked and raw American poetry while also strengthening the conflation of so-called academic poetry with dusty British formalism, which fit perfectly into Cold War cultural positions. This interpretation and its persistent influence continue to provincialize American poetry while also diverting attention from the political ramifications of the avant-garde in favor of divisions between free and formal verse.

There is a sense, in terms of literary history, that Allen's provincialization of American poetry was inevitable, the result of decades of lobbying by conservative critics to erase the political poetry of the 1930s from the modernist legacy. Marcus Klein is worth quoting at length on this crucial point, arguing how "The institution of literary studies cooperated and

---

[97] Rexroth persisted in his international outlook, publishing important transnational essays such as "The Influence of French Poetry on American" during the height of Cold War literary nationalism, while also translating hundreds of poems from Japanese, French and German. Today most know Rexroth solely as a precursor to the Beat Generation, but his insistence on pushing the sensibilities of young American poets toward other cultures is perhaps even more important.

5 THIS THING IS MOST NATIONAL: NATIONALISM AND ASSIMILATION... 163

eliminated the names of political poets from the ongoing conversation of the discipline."[98]

> It is remarkable how rapidly we lost the rich literary and social heritage of modern poetry. By the 1950s a limited canon of primary authors and texts was already in place. The names in the canon continued to change, but a substantial majority of interesting poems from 1910–1945 had already been forgotten. Academic critics had come to concentrate on close readings of a limited number of texts by "major" authors. University course requirements were increasingly influential in shaping the market for new anthologies. And the professorate, largely white and male and rarely challenged from within its own ranks, found it easy to reinforce the culture's existing racism and sexism by ignoring poetry by minorities and women... As a result of these and other factors, modernism came to be seen in part as an oppressive burden – the unassailable, unrepeatable achievements of a few masters... Poets also believed they couldn't compete with the major modernists, that modernism left them no resources to exploit on their own... For Paul Carroll it seemed "all of the major poetic discoveries and innovations had been accomplished."[99]

The key element here, and where Allen's anthology fits in, is that this conservative reshaping of the legacy of modernism to do away with its social heritage and sweeping inclusion, as well as its fruitful internationalism, is generally considered the work of conservatives in the interwar and post-war academy. *The New American Poetry*, interpreted as a liberal rejoinder to the conservatism of the Cold War, participated in this refashioning of American modernism in ways that remain influential long after the efforts of the era's conservative critics have been called out. Klein's quotation of Paul Carroll, who was included in *The New American Poetry*, is also crucial because it suggests how a simplified, not to say falsified, reading of modernism was predicated on conservative efforts and indelibly shaped the postmodern project that Carroll and his generation, including Donald Allen, were part of. Just as modernism wasn't the singular, homogenous edifice it was presented as during the post-war period, the post-war avant-garde wasn't as simple and homogenous as *The New American Poetry* presents it. Allen's anthology not only ignores the heritage of left-leaning

---

[98] Marcus Klein, *Foreigners: The Making of American Literature 1900–1940* (Chicago: University of Chicago Press, 1981), 10.

[99] Klein, 35.

164   S. DELBOS

poets of the 1930s, it also completely fails to register vital poets like Langston Hughes, Gwendolyn Brooks and those active in the Harlem Renaissance and the Civil Rights Movement. As Klein argues, "The canon is not only a model of a particular culture's notions of literary quality; it is a guide to how literature should engage such matters as sexuality, politics, race, religion and individuation,"[100] a list to which we should add nationality.

The image of American poetry presented by *The New American Poetry* is skewed in ways few were in a position to understand in 1960. Indeed, at that time even a boldly national suggestion about art like John Cage's comment that "Beauty is now underfoot wherever we take the trouble to look. (This is a deeply American discovery.)"[101] would pass unnoticed, as if the discovery of quotidian beauty was somehow both new and also specifically American. Only later revelations would show the forces at work in crafting the post-war image of America, at home and abroad. Allen's anthology renovated a manufactured image of American newness as it sought to redefine the landscape in which discussions of literature and culture took place. Ultimately, Allen's anthology entrenched a sense of American exceptionalism that remains dominant. The Anglophone canon is impoverished as a result.

Poetry anthologies always raise questions of canons, and canons help create nations. Yet, as David Wheatley writes, "Few forms of literary production are simultaneously more revealing and more concealing of the nature of contemporary poetry than the anthology."[102] Furthermore, Allen's choice to create an anthology of "Americans" resulted in a redefining of the broader Anglophone canon, making experimental poetry seem like the property of the United States alone and formal poetry ultimately British. Many literary critics and readers continue to associate traditional poetic form with Britain and voice-based free verse with American poets descended from William Carlos Williams's insistence on the American idiom,[103] as well as Noah Webster's insistence, in 1789, that "language, as

---

[100] Klein, 38.

[101] John Cage, "On Robert Rauschenberg, Artist, and His Work," *Silence* (Middletown: Wesleyan University Press, 1961), 98.

[102] Wheatley, 9.

[103] Paul Mariani, *William Carlos Williams: A New World Naked* (New York: Norton, 1981), 758–759.

5 THIS THING IS MOST NATIONAL: NATIONALISM AND ASSIMILATION... 165

well as government should be national."[104] There can be no question that Allen was engaged in the recreation of the identity of American poetry and that in achieving this goal his anthology was as limiting as it was liberating. The significance of any successful anthology amounts to far more than increased visibility for individual poets. As Robert Von Hallberg has written:

> Canonists worry about what will enable a community of readers to distinguish first- from second-rate thought and expression. A national canon stands as proof that such distinctions can be made so as to command assent; that the nation asks from its writers support for its policies, at the very least its educational policies; that one national objective is to preserve, by education, a hold on the past and a claim on the future.[105]

What Allen achieved with *The New American Poetry* was a redefinition of the Anglophone canon. But his new American canon was influenced by the efforts of conservatives who had worked hard during the 1940s and 1950s to purge American poetry of any so-called radical influence. As these influences were erased, and as a politically and formally conservative orthodoxy solidified its dominance through academic posts and popular publications, an alternative poetic community was thriving in discrete locations throughout the country and abroad, and writers around the world were innovating the English language. But by drawing on an impoverished perception of modernism and presenting post-war poetry in national terms, Allen's anthology confirmed the efforts of conservative critics while seemingly rebelling against them.

The exclusion of writers such as Gael Turnbull juxtaposed with the inclusion of Helen Adam and Denise Levertov may seem unfortunate, at least for Turnbull. But this nationalism had a focusing effect for the anthology even as it signified an inward—and conceptually conservative—turn for American poetry. While Allen's original goals for the collection were simply to "get [Grove Press] other books by poets but also build name [*sic*] of press,"[106] his accomplishment was far more significant: a nationalist

---

[104] Noah Webster, *Dissertations on the English Language: with Notes, Historical and Critical* (Boston: Isaiah and Company, 1789), 179.

[105] Robert Von Hallberg, *American Poetry and Culture 1945–1980* (Cambridge: Harvard University Press, 1988), 27.

[106] Donald Allen to Barney Rosset, April 6, 1958, Box 75, Folder 2, Donald Allen Collection, MSS 3, Special Collections & Archives, UC San Diego Library.

reorientation of Anglophone poetry and the establishment of American poetry as a separate entity from Britain, a geographical decentralization of mainstream American poetry and a reconsideration of the role of the anthology in canon formation. This critical reexamination of Allen's anthology shows that to do so it concealed as much as it revealed.

The New American Poetry's nationalism isn't a self-contained issue; it bleeds into and influences other problematic elements of the anthology because "nationalism has no affinity for democracy... It shows scant tolerance for self-conscious minorities in its midst,"[107] an argument that does not bode well for the single poet of color included in the anthology, LeRoi Jones, nor for the few women included. What many consider to be an anthology that blew open the doors of American poetry to allow more inclusivity was actually exclusionary to a remarkable degree, not only in terms of style and nationality but also regarding race and gender.

---

[107] Robert H. Wiebe, *Who We Are: A History of Popular Nationalism* (Princeton: Princeton University Press, 2002), 10.

CHAPTER 6

Post-war to Post-truth: Reassessing the American Avant-Garde Canon

The American poetry scene of the twenty-first century is very different from that of 1960. The proliferation of cheap printing which developed in the 1970s into what has been termed "the mimeograph revolution"[1] changed the publishing landscape, ushering in a revolutionary democratization of print and publicity that was only a precursor to the effects of digital printing and internet publishing. Coupled with the increased ubiquity of MFA programs, there are now more poets publishing—and more places to publish—than ever before. The binary model of American poetry seems less fitting in light of the contemporary plurality of poets and publishing venues. Poets today have a variety of formal and conceptual stances to choose from, and the traditional division of academic and avant-garde no longer fits at a time when the academy is a stronghold for both sides of a debate that caused so much intellectual hand-wringing after World War II. Yet the presence of *The New American Poetry* remains palpable.

In recent years, identity has become one of the most contentious topics in American poetry, manifesting in controversies such as Kenneth

---

[1] See: Steven Clay and Rodney Phillips, *A Secret Location on the Lower East Side: Adventures in Writing, 1960–1980* (New York: Granary Books, 1998).

© The Author(s), under exclusive license to Springer Nature Switzerland AG 2021
S. Delbos, *The New American Poetry and Cold War Nationalism*, Modern and Contemporary Poetry and Poetics, https://doi.org/10.1007/978-3-030-77352-6_6

167

Goldsmith's use of Michael Brown's autopsy report in performance[2] and Vanessa Place's tweeting of racist content from *Gone with the Wind*.[3] Interrogating such episodes, critics including Cathy Park Hong, John Keene and CAConrad[4] have suggested that the American avant-garde is racially insensitive at best and that this insensitivity originates, at least in part, with *The New American Poetry*.[5] The links between Allen's anthology and today's debates over identity and inclusion suggest not only how Allen's anthology helped create the contemporary conditions of these debates but also how the center of American poetry has shifted over the past half-century. As printing and publication have been decentralized,[6] the critical discourse on Anglophone poetry, once focused on a split between academic and avant-garde, has shifted considerably. The so-called outsider poets of Allen's anthology have entered the canon and the academy while generations of women and writers of color have created their own movements, gaining wider recognition alongside debates about race and gender in American society. At the same time, both prominent conservative and liberal critics have seemingly aligned against further inclusivity in the canon. As Silliman writes, "the history of poetry since the Allen

---

[2] Alec Wilkinson, "Something Borrowed," *The New Yorker*, October 5, 2015, http://www.newyorker.com/magazine/2015/10/05/something-borrowed-wilkinson, November 13, 2015.

[3] Edward Helmore, "Gone with the Wind Tweeter Says she Is Being Shunned by US Arts Institutions," *The Guardian*, June 25, 2015, http://www.theguardian.com/books/2015/jun/25/gone-with-the-wind-tweeter-shunned-arts-institutions-vanessa-place, June 26, 2015. The "Yellowface" controversy of Michael Derrick Hudson's use of a Chinese pen name could also be discussed in this regard, but is less germane to the focus of this study. See: David Orr, "Michael Derrick Hudson Posed as a 'Yi-Fen Chou': Did the Name Sell His Poem?" *The New York Times*, September 9, 2015, http://www.nytimes.com/2015/09/10/books/michael-derrick-hudson-posed-as-a-yi-fen-chou-did-the-name-sell-his-poem.html?_r=0, September 11, 2015.

[4] CAConrad, "Kenneth Goldsmith Says He Is an Outlaw," *Poetry Foundation*, June 1, 2015, https://www.poetryfoundation.org/harriet/2015/06/kenneth-goldsmith-says-he-is-an-outlaw, January 4, 2018.

[5] For a deeply considered overview of these recent events and the intersection of poetry and race in American poetry of the twenty-first century, see the 2019 issue of *New Literary History* "Poetry and Race," edited by Jahan Ramazani. Jahan Ramazani "Poetry and Race: An Introduction." *New Literary History* 50, no. 4 (2019): vii–xxxvii. doi:https://doi.org/10.1353/nlh.2019.0050

[6] Ron Silliman argues that this decentralization is "grounded in economic circumstance," but curiously says that "so much of the discussion of the politics of literature has been fixated on the lone aspect of content." Ron Silliman, *The New Sentence* (San Francisco: Roof, 2003), 27.

6 POST-WAR TO POST-TRUTH: REASSESSING THE AMERICAN AVANT-GARDE... 169

anthology has been one of decentralization, of the destruction of this founding false binary premise."[7] This is true, but that destruction is still happening and in slow motion. If postmodern poetry has lived up to its promise to destabilize "the modernist polarities of old versus new, canonical versus avant-garde"[8]—which is certainly debatable—it has been despite *The New American Poetry*, not because of it. The shortcomings of Allen's anthology set the stage for debates that continue to this day.

This chapter will examine the ways that Allen's anthology foreshadowed today's debates about racial and sexual imbalances in the American avant-garde—and also the role that critics have played in perpetuating this state of affairs since 1960. It also considers recent controversies concerning race and identity in American poetry anthologies to consider how the foundations of the critical establishment have shifted dramatically since 1960 as issues of identity and subjectivity have taken prominence among poets, critics and readers, even while the formalist framework that Allen's anthology helped establish remains entrenched in most mainstream criticism. *The New American Poetry* cannot and should not be blamed for all the problems of American poetry in the twenty-first century, but clarifying the ways that today's avant-garde and the discourse surrounding it can be traced back to Allen's model—and the ways that it has diverged—is useful for coming to a more complete understanding of recent controversies and clearing a path beyond them.

6.1 Hallucinations of Homogeneity: *The New American Poetry*'s White, Male Legacy

Chapter 2 mentioned Walter Lowenfels's ironic description of the mainstream poets of the 1950s as "Bards of the White Citizens Councils,"[9] a remark that also fits Allen's anthology, which contains only one poet of color. Where that chapter established *The New American Poetry*'s lack of racial and sexual inclusivity, this chapter examines how the conception of the American avant-garde as primarily composed of Caucasian males remains influential. Without blurring the distinction between race and gender, these two issues can be fruitfully juxtaposed to argue that, due to

---

[7] Silliman, *The New Sentence*, 135.

[8] Mutlu Konuk Blasing, *Politics and Form in Postmodern Poetry* (Cambridge: Cambridge University Press, 1995), 12.

[9] Walter Lowenfels, "Poetry and Politics," *Liberation*, June, 1959, 12.

170 S. DELBOS

the significance of *The New American Poetry*, we must trace our contemporary concept of the poetic avant-garde back to Allen's anthology, with all its unfortunate shortcomings in regard to race and gender. But at the same time, while rightfully citing the racial and gender exclusionism of the anthology—which is not a new gesture—we should not obscure the ongoing role that critics and poets themselves play in policing the borders of the avant-garde.

Recently, critics such as Cathy Park Hong have called for a revision of our understanding of the importance of people of color in regard to formally experimental poetry in English. As Hong writes in her essay "Delusions of Whiteness in the Avant-garde":

> Poets of color have always been expected to sit quietly in the backbenches of both mainstream and avant-garde poetry. We've been trotted out in the most mindless forms of tokenism for anthologies and conferences, because to have all white faces would be downright embarrassing. For instance, Donald Allen's classic 1959 [*sic*] and even updated 1982 anthology *New American Poetry* [*sic*], which Marjorie Perloff has proclaimed "the anthology of avant-garde poetry," includes a grand tally of one minority poet: Leroi Jones, aka Amiri Baraka. Tokenism at its most elegant.[10]

Has *The New American Poetry* become a scapegoat for the homogeneity of the contemporary avant-garde? This is not the first time that Allen has been called out in the name of poets who were excluded from the anthology. Writing to Marjorie Perloff in the late 1990s regarding complaints from Michael Palmer and others about the exclusion of African American poets Steven Jonas and Norman Pritchard, Allen lamented: "If a white poet wrote so badly you know they'd criticize it – it's all exoticism or rather careerism but it gets so tiresome!"[11] Perloff was similarly dismissive of concerns about a racial imbalance in *The New American Poetry*, commiserating with Allen about a conference on the anthology in 1999 at which "Alan Golding made a lot of silly remarks about the absence of

---

[10] Cathy Park Hong, "Delusions of Whiteness in the Avant-garde," *Lana Turner*, http://www.lanaturnerjournal.com/7/delusions-of-whiteness-in-the-avant-garde, October 28, 2017.

[11] Donald Allen to Marjorie Perloff, June 19, 1999, Box 57, Folder 12, Donald Allen Collection, MSS 3, Special Collections & Archives, UC San Diego Library.

women and/or blacks."[12] Allen's anthology is certainly a large target for contemporary critics looking for the cause of ongoing injustices. But it is important to think deeply about those injustices, as well as Allen's editorial practices, the period that conditioned them and the anthology's changing reception when accounting for the shortcomings of today's avant-garde.

Hong's essay was occasioned by conceptual poet Kenneth Goldsmith's appropriation of the autopsy report of Michael Brown, an 18-year-old African American killed by a police officer in Ferguson, Missouri, in 2014. Several months after this incident, Goldsmith read a piece titled "The Body of Michael Brown" as part of a conference at Brown University. The backlash was immediate and sweeping. Dozens of critics and poets took to social media and online publications, castigating Goldsmith for his inappropriate performance and framing it in terms of white supremacy.[13] Hong mentions the Goldsmith controversy in another essay, tying the backlash against the poet to a burgeoning movement in American poetry that harmonizes with the racial and sexual politics of the moment:

> The more interesting, relevant, and current story is that the poetry world has been riven by a crisis where the old guard – epitomized by Goldsmith – has collapsed. I thought it was essential to contextualize Goldsmith's scandal within a new movement in American poetry, a movement galvanized by the activism of Black Lives Matter, spearheaded by writers of color who are at home in social media activism and print magazines; some poets are redefining the avant-garde while others are fueling a raw politics into the personal lyric. Their aesthetic may be divergent, but they share a common belief that as poets, they must engage in social practice.[14]

Leaving aside the questionable assertion that Goldsmith represents "the old guard" of "the poetry world," Hong here clarifies just how much is at stake in these debates about the canon, although, as David Kaufmann argues, she "never actually shows how this [racism and tokenism] works

---

[12] Marjorie Perloff to Donald Allen, June 4, 1999, Box 57, Folder 12, Donald Allen Collection, MSS 3, Special Collections & Archives, UC San Diego Library.

[13] Alec Wilkinson, "Something Borrowed," *The New Yorker*, October 5, 2015, https://www.newyorker.com/magazine/2015/10/05/something-borrowed-wilkinson, December 29, 2017.

[14] Cathy Park Hong, "There's a New Movement in American Poetry and It's Not Kenneth Goldsmith," *The New Republic*, October 1, 2015, https://newrepublic.com/article/122985/new-movement-american-poetry-not-kenneth-goldsmith, October 28, 2017.

172   S. DELBOS

with poetry," despite her allusion to *The New American Poetry*.[15] But if Hong is correct, Anglophone poetry is currently undergoing a radical reorientation that should render previous models obsolete.

Goldsmith's performance at Brown, in addition to a similarly racially charged publication project by Vanessa Place,[16] has been considered irrefutable evidence of the racial insensitivity of the conceptual avant-garde. As Lillian-Yvonne Bertram wrote, commenting on Goldsmith's Facebook post in his own defense: "'It is a horrific American document, but then again it was a horrific American death' (Goldsmith, via Facebook.) No. It was a horrific *Black* American death."[17] Juxtaposing the commentary of Hong and Bertram reveals the volatility of the debate: where Hong demands that contemporary writers and editors take non-white points of view into account, giving equal space to poets of color, Bertram suggests that the African American experience is off limits for white writers like Goldsmith. Hong argues for breaking down racial barriers while Bertram demands recognition of racial difference. It is a complex and sensitive issue. Would American poetry be more inclusive if Allen's anthology had been?

Considering Allen's exclusion of people of color and women in tandem with the anthology's nationalism suggests they are analogous—the issue is exclusion[18]—and just as the cultural and political context of the late 1950s reveals something larger and more significant about the anthology's nationalism, looking more closely at *The New American Poetry*'s demographics and Allen's selection process brings the anthology's limitations as a model into focus while also suggesting why the anthology took its final form. The demographics of *The New American Poetry* are clear: 4 women

---

[15] Kaufmann, 73.

[16] As Brian Kim Stefans writes: "Place has also [...] recently been embroiled in accusations of racism for a project in which she republished the text of Margaret Mitchell's *Gone with the Wind* in 140-character tweets, using for her profile photograph a picture of black 'nanny' and a 'coon' drawing of the period, a project she claims is overtly anti-racist but which others have understood as akin to the exploitation in Kenny's Michael Brown piece." Brian Kim Stefans, "Open Letter to *The New Yorker*," *Arras.net*, October 4, 2015, http://www.arras.net/fscIII/?p=2467, November 18, 2017.

[17] Lillian-Yvonne Bertram, "The Whitest Boy Alive: Witnessing Kenneth Goldsmith," Poetry.org, May 18. 2015, https://www.poetryfoundation.org/harriet/2015/05/the-whitest-boy-alive-witnessing-kenneth-goldsmith, November 18, 2017.

[18] Nationalism and exclusion are always linked. As David Herd writes, citing Hannah Arendt, "national self-definition... results inexorably in exclusion and internment." Woznicki, 159.

6 POST-WAR TO POST-TRUTH: REASSESSING THE AMERICAN AVANT-GARDE... 173

and 1 poet of color out of 44 poets. By the standards of the time this would not necessarily have raised eyebrows.[19] Allen's response to Perloff, quoted above, suggests that Allen, unlike many anthologists today, did not think of diversity as a goal in itself. Fewer Americans did in the late 1950s. From the point of view of the twenty-first century, it is regrettable that Allen wasn't more inclusive, not only because more of us now understand the importance of diversity but also because Allen's anthology has so deeply influenced our conception of the avant-garde.

Looking back on the anthology now, *The New American Poetry* is remarkable for what it anticipated and helped bring into being—the dominance of free verse and the Beat and projective-type lyric in Anglophone poetry. This was evident almost immediately, so that Tallman could declare in 1972 that Allen's anthology had "won the battle"[20] over American poetry. But Allen's anthology is also remarkable for what it did not anticipate, or perhaps ignored. Considering the fact that a Civil Rights Commission was established in 1957, and the nation's fifth Civil Rights Act was passed in 1960, *The New American Poetry*'s almost complete lack of African American poets is puzzling. The same can be said for the anthology's myopia concerning the burgeoning feminist movement.

We can never know precisely why Allen wasn't more inclusive of women and people of color, but if we take his correspondence at face value, we must conclude that his choices were motivated by aesthetics rather than social issues.[21] The editor's correspondence shows that he was indeed aware of female poets and poets of color who could have been included, if diversity were a goal. As he wrote to Marjorie Perloff in the late 1990s:

---

[19] More recent anthologies are not necessarily more inclusive, but such imbalances are more likely to be called out today. See, for example, Jennifer K. Dick reviewing *Against Expression: An Anthology of Conceptual Writing*: "Finally, though I hate as a woman to be the one drawing attention to it, this is a book which contains only a little more than 25% of writings by women and yet is focused on the contemporary period where we are all aware that conceptual art and writing are certainly being practiced by as many women (if not more) as men today." Jennifer K. Dick, "The Pros and Cons of *Against Expression: An Anthology of Conceptual Writing*," *Drunken Boat*, http://www.drunkenboat.com/db15/against-expression.html, April 20, 2018.

[20] Warren Tallman to Donald Allen, November 26, 1972, Box 14, Folder 1, Donald Allen Collection, MSS 3, Special Collections & Archives, UC San Diego Library.

[21] See: Donald Allen to Marjorie Perloff, June 10, 1998, and June 19, 1999, Box 57, Folder 12, Donald Allen Collection, MSS 3, Special Collections & Archives, UC San Diego Library. And see: Joanne Kyger, Personal Interview, Email, January 13, 2014.

174   S. DELBOS

> When I was working on NAP I'd heard of [Steven] Jonas as a poet and had probably read a poem or two of his but decided I hadn't seen enough, and that I had more than enough of that trend in Kirby, Doyle and Ed Marshall, not to mention Ray Bremser... [Michael] Palmer multiplied Boston Jonas into a Cambridge coterie never heard of since because of my neglect... now they're all making a fuss about Jonas, Norman Pritchard, etc.[22]

It is interesting that Allen simultaneously claims to not have seen enough of Jonas's work and to have had more than enough of his style. This correspondence, in which the concept of racial inclusivity seems not to have occurred to Allen, corroborates Golding's observation that "the racial contours of *The New American Poetry* [did not] simply reflect the fact that there was no black avant-garde to be included – that, in Baraka's ironic phrasing, 'there were no other spooks.'"[23]

It is unlikely that LeRoi Jones was thinking about *The New American Poetry*'s lack of diversity in 1965 when he changed his name to Amiri Baraka and left Lower Manhattan for Harlem, where he spearheaded The Black Arts Movement. But African American poets of the time clearly felt—rightly—that the odds were stacked against them in terms of publication opportunities and all aspects of American life. The lack of diversity in *The New American Poetry* thus had a generative effect.[24] Nonetheless, Dorothy Wang describes Baraka as one of many African American poets who have been "relegated to the margins" since the emergence of the post-war avant-garde. Wang is particularly insightful about how "ideologies, institutional structures, and ingrained patterns of thought, especially if unexamined, come to have a life of their own" and how "the accretion of the power" of ideas about literature "and its reinforcement by countless individuals and structures" have led to what Hong calls delusions of whiteness in the avant-garde. Wang continues:

---

[22] Donald Allen to Marjorie Perloff, June 10, 1998, and June 19, 1999, Box 57, Folder 12, Donald Allen Collection, MSS 3, Special Collections & Archives, UC San Diego Library.

[23] Golding, 196.

[24] Even this is a troubled distinction, however. Steve Evans has written, in the context of feminist poetry, about how the reaction to the "patriarchal" poetry of *The New American Poetry* helped generate feminist poetry but also suggests that poets such as Kathleen Fraser had to choose between poetry that was concerned with linguistic innovation and poetry that was concerned with feminist issues. Steve Evans, "After Patriarchal Poetry: Feminism and the Contemporary Avant-Garde. Introductory Note," *Differences: A Journal of Feminist Cultural Studies*, 12.2, Summer, (2001): i.

6 POST-WAR TO POST-TRUTH: REASSESSING THE AMERICAN AVANT-GARDE... 175

And it is as much the case with Conceptual Writing as it is with High Modernism. The linkages between Yone Noguchi and Ezra Pound, between Jose Garcia Villa and Edith Sitwell, between Amiri Baraka and Ed Dorn (between Baraka and Jack Spicer, between Baraka and Frank O'Hara, and on and on) are forgotten or treated as incidental curiosities.[25]

Wang is correct to point out that current conditions in American poetry are systemic. Such eloquent repudiations of the status quo are encouraging, as their publication suggests that progress has been made since World War II, even though American poetry and society at large still have a long way to go. A look at the contemporary poetry publishing landscape shows that non-white, non-male and non-binary writers occupy a much more central position than they did during the 1950s. This suggests that the framework of *The New American Poetry* is less relevant than ever and speaks to a democratization of American poetry as channels of publication and distribution have become more available to poets of all races and genders. The lack of women and people of color in Allen's anthology is not exactly analogous. But arguments about the avant-garde's lack of inclusion in regard to both women and people of color, and how *The New American Poetry* has played a role in that disparity, follow similar lines of thinking. At the same time, the insightful scholarship on how female poets like Joanne Kyger created their own paths toward publication and reception in the second half of the twentieth century shows at least that an important conversation is taking place.

In her later years, Kyger did not object to her exclusion from *The New American Poetry*,[26] but critics such as Linda Russo have suggested how the consequences of the exclusion of someone like Kyger do not only affect a single poet. According to Russo, the male-dominated framework of Allen's anthology has tended to obscure the work of important female poets, both of the post-war period and of generations since, in ways that we have only recently begun to comprehend. During the late 1950s and early 1960s, Russo writes, "there were few poetry magazines (two in fact) and only one small press edited by a woman."[27] While there are certainly more

---

[25] Dorothy Wang, "From Jim-Crow to 'Color-Blind' Poetics: Race and the So-Called Avant-Garde," *The Boston Review*, March 10, 2015, http://bostonreview.net/poetry/dorothy-wang-race-poetic-avant-garde-response, December 29, 2017.

[26] Joanne Kyger, Personal Interview, Email, January 13, 2014.

[27] Linda Russo, "The Limited Scope of the Recuperative Model: A Context for Reading Joanne Kyger," *Jacket 2*, April 2000, www.jacketmagazine.com/11/kyger-russo.html, October 23, 2017.

176 S. DELBOS

poetry magazines and presses run by women today, when organizations such as VIDA: Women in Literary Arts actively monitor gender balance in the publishing world, Russo suggests that we are still far from reversing the damage already done by less-than-inclusive anthologies and the critical narrative that has descended from them. She states, "what is *missing* from an anthology *has* disappeared," and further, "the nomenclature and gene-alogies that *The New American Poetry* created and preserves and through which we see poetic production and assign significance shows itself to be a problem for locating, and so talking about, women writers of that generation."[28] Allen's anthology created not just the picture of post-war avant-garde poetry but the frame as well.

Russo interrogates Denise Levertov's contribution to the "Statements on Poetics" in Allen's anthology, the only such statement written by a woman. As Levertov writes in her statement: "It is given to the seer to see, but it is then his responsibility to communicate what he sees, that they who cannot see may see, since we are 'members one of another.'"[29] Russo is worth quoting at length on this point:

> Levertov's sentence, fraught with sexist semantics, points to the heart of this problem when the "seer," the potentially engendered constituent "members of one another," surfaces as pronominally male. A convention of English usage or a mechanism of exclusion? We get a sense, however, that this dis-tortion manifests itself visually in the non-appearance of women in the cat-egory "seer," and that this is the telos of a compulsion to disregard women when considering who composes 'the new.' Levertov, one of four women included in *The New American Poetry* (Helen Adam, Madeline Gleason, and Barbara Guest being the other three), is the only of that group to espouse a "poetics." Cast into increasingly myopic focus by an instrument tuned to see masculine production where poetic production is sought, one sees four women, then one woman, then only the seer "he" and no women at all.[30]

Russo is not the only critic to note that the male gaze is central to *The New American Poetry*. It is certainly the defining factor of a poem like Paul Blackburn's "The Once-over," in which a "tanned blonde" riding the subway "has had it from" most of the men in the subway car, who project

---

[28] Russo, "The Limited Scope of the Recuperative Model."
[29] Allen, 412.
[30] Russo, "The Limited Scope of the Recuperative Model."

6 POST-WAR TO POST-TRUTH: REASSESSING THE AMERICAN AVANT-GARDE... 177

onto her their sexual fantasies.[31] Andrew Mossin has written insightfully about the way that male subjectivity plays out in poetic form in Allen's anthology,[32] and Michael Davidson has described Olson's "Projective Verse" as "phallocentric."[33] In addition, critics such as Ann Vickery have taken up issues of race and gender in language poetry as it stemmed from Allen's anthology,[34] and innovative writers including Rachel Blau DuPlessis, Kathleen Fraser and Megan Swihart Jewell have written of how *The New American Poetry* was inspiring despite its "defining innovation as a largely male practice."[35]

The fact that this criticism of Allen's anthology and its legacy regarding women stretches back at least to the 1990s suggests that the debates about women in avant-garde poetry have received wider attention for a longer period and have progressed further than debates about race, which seem to be just getting started, despite the fact that the conversation about identity and representation in the western canon goes back at least to the late 1980s.[36] Yet the predominance of white men in Allen's anthology remains influential because there has been no competing model of the avant-garde that has been anywhere near as significant, despite the growing feeling that, as David Wheatley has written, "the default neutral position under which texts are assumed to be spoken by white male heterosexuals no longer fits the contemporary poem, nor is this a useful model for reading poems in a heteroglossic society."[37] That deeply engrained default neutral position is caused by much more than a single poetry anthology, especially one which the editor predicted would be "of

---

[31] Allen, 76.

[32] Andrew Mossin, *Male Subjectivity and Poetic Form in "New American" Poetry* (New York: Palgrave, 2010).

[33] Davidson, 3.

[34] As Timothy Yu writes, citing Vicker: "Gender has been a vexed question throughout the history of language poetry; although a number of women, including Lyn Hejinian, Susan Howe, and Rae Armantrout, were often grouped under the language writing umbrella, the domination of the group by men was pronounced enough that Charles Bernstein asked Armantrout to write an essay on the question, 'Why Don't Women Do Language-Oriented Writing?' – later reprinted in Silliman's anthology *In the American Tree*." Timothy Yu, "Ron Silliman and the Ethnicization of the Avant-garde," *Jacket*, 2009, http://jacketmagazine. com/39/silliman-yu.shtml#fn9, December 28, 2017.

[35] Woznicki, 140.

[36] Fukuyama, *Identity*, 102.

[37] Wheatley, 5.

178 S. DELBOS

interest for a couple of years – then to be replaced by another view."[38] *The New American Poetry* has not been replaced by another view, of course. It has—with all its shortcomings—remained an influential model in part because critics have not moved beyond it.

Critics have played a crucial role—before and after Allen's anthology—in policing the borders of the avant-garde.[39] Jones/Baraka, whom Hong considers a token inclusion in *The New American Poetry*, has been pigeonholed as a "radical man of letters"[40] and "a poet and playwright of pulsating rage,"[41] his contributions to expanding the form and idiom of Anglophone poetry obscured by his activism. Allen's anthology is not solely responsible for the shortcomings of today's avant-garde, and David Kaufmann's argument that conceptual writing is not inherently racist "in any important or interesting way"[42] but rather suffers from "tone-deafness"[43] can be extended to *The New American Poetry*. Certainly the anthology's outsized influence is due to a larger network of poets, editors and critics who have consciously accepted its status quo and have chosen to perpetuate it. Seeing around a foundational text like Allen's can be difficult, but we are now in a position to do so, more than 60 years after its publication. *The New American Poetry* has had vast influence, not control.

Nonetheless, recognizing the lack of inclusion in *The New American Poetry* is necessary, and doing so should inspire us to seek out the significant poetry written by women and people of color who have been largely excluded from the dominant critical narrative. Bob Kaufman, Steven

---

[38] Donald Allen to Cid Corman, July 18, 1958, Box 11, Folder 12, Donald Allen Collection, MSS 3, Special Collections & Archives, UC San Diego Library. The fact that Allen did not predict *The New American Poetry* would be so influential does not completely exonerate the book from charges of exclusionism. Allen's 1982 revision of the anthology, *The Postmoderns: The New American Poetry Revised*, did nothing to rework the racial or gender imbalance.

[39] As Kaufmann writes: "But there is no reason to single out the avant-gardes for their racial and religious exclusion. Modernism, of which the avant-gardes were merely an important subset, was based on a sentimentalizing racism and an often vicious, visceral racialized anti-Semitism." Kaufmann, 74.

[40] "Amiri Baraka, radical playwright and poet, dies aged 79 in Newark," *The Guardian*, January 9, 2014, https://www.theguardian.com/books/2014/jan/09/amir-baraka-playwright-poet-dies, January 31, 2017.

[41] Margalit Fox, "Amiri Baraka, Polarizing Poet and Playwright, Dies at 79," *The New York Times*, January 9, 2014, https://www.nytimes.com/2014/01/10/arts/amiri-baraka-polarizing-poet-and-playwright-dies-at-79.html, January 31, 2017.

[42] Kaufmann, 5.

[43] Kaufmann, 76.

Jonas, Ted Joans, Tom Postell, Oliver Pitcher, A. B. Spellman, Norman Pritchard, Rosalie Moore, Jeanne McGahey, Amelia MacIntyre and Lenore Kandel are just a few interesting and engaging poets who only appear to readers looking beyond Allen's presentation of the post-war Anglophone avant-garde as dominantly white and male. This should logically lead to more inclusivity in poetry publications, as contemporary editors seek to avoid the mistakes of their predecessors. But the reception of several recent poetry anthologies shows this has not been the case. In actuality, some of the most prominent defenders of the post-war avant-garde have aligned with more conservative critics in calls to preserve the canon that solidified in the second half of the twentieth century, after the impact and acceptance of *The New American Poetry*. The formalist framework of this canon—which remains influential despite dramatic shifts in the landscape of American poetry—has led several mainstream critics to discourage, on supposedly aesthetic grounds, recent gestures toward further inclusion in American poetry.

6.2 A DEGREE OF VARIATION: FORM AND SUBJECTIVITY IN AVANT-GARDE AMERICAN POETRY

The New American Poetry helped validate form as the differentiator of innovative verse, and it also helped compartmentalize American poetry into geographically and stylistically specific groups of poets scattered across the American continent and distinct from the rest of the Anglophone world. But for many contemporary poets and critics, issues of form, once the center of debates about value in poetry, have begun to seem like outdated concerns.[44] At the same time, Allen's groupings of poets have fractured into a multiplicity of personal, sexual, gender and racial identities through which many of today's newer poets identify themselves and their work. Identity politics reverberate through contemporary American poetry, and previously oppositional critics have seemingly aligned against further inclusion in the canon, while a younger group of poets and critics, many of them women and people of color, are upending the foundations

---

[44] This section focuses more on critics than poets, but for an example of poets focusing more on identity than traditional ideas about experimentation and formal mastery, see the Palestinian-American poet Noor Hindi's recent poem, published in *Poetry*, "Fuck Your Lecture on Craft, My People Are Dying," https://www.poetryfoundation.org/poetrymagazine/poems/154658/fuck-your-lecture-on-craft-my-people-are-dying, May 15, 2021.

of the American avant-garde, including Allen's anthology, in favor of a discourse that puts less emphasis on formal innovation and more emphasis on identity and the inclusion of voices that have been overlooked in part—but only in part—because of *The New American Poetry*.

In the course of these debates, dominant concepts of form, content and subjectivity, which stem in large part from Allen's anthology and can be traced through more recent avant-gardes including language poetry and conceptual writing, are being renovated to acknowledge the impossibility of absolutely objective, impersonal poetry and to promote the author as representative witness rather than privileged maker or conceptual designer. While these debates began during the final days of the Cold War—the late 1980s and early 1990s—and are rooted in outdated binary conceptions from that period,[45] they have performed the crucial role of highlighting real imbalances in American poetry, many of which are a hangover from the models of mid-twentieth century, including *The New American Poetry*. Besides conceptual writers like Goldsmith and Place, several recent poetry anthologies have been flash points of controversy. Examining the discourse around these individuals and publications reveals just how deeply the current landscape of American poetry is influenced by larger societal shifts and also suggests the tenacity with which an older generation of critics holds to a formalist framework of American poetry, which includes the binaries of avant-garde and academic, and tends to discount the work of poets who are less concerned with experimentation and traditional demonstrations of formal mastery.

When *American Hybrid*, an anthology that cited *The New American Poetry* explicitly and was dedicated to blending the two perceived stylistic camps in American poetry, was published in 2010, some critics argued that it was representative of a trend in American anthologies to exclude poets of color from the discourse. As Craig Santos Perez wrote, referring to Cole Swensen, one of the anthology's editors: "Swenson's 'Legacy' is a white poetic legacy, a white reading of 20th century American Poetry...

---

[45] One early example of this debate is John Yau's condemnation of what he identified as the Orientalism at the heart of Eliot Weinberger's anthology *American Poetry Since 1950: Innovators and Outsiders* (which, incidentally, contains only 5 women out of 35 poets, a fact Yau points out). See: John Yau, "Neither Us Nor Them," *American Poetry Review* 23.2 (1994): 45. Alan Filreis comments: "Yau's counterdicta resemble the multi-culturalist rejoinder to the Right... One might say that this fight is being waged at or for the heart of modernism's liberalism." Alan Filreis, "Neither Us Nor Them," *Al Filreis Blog*, September 18, 2007, http://afilreis.blogspot.com/2007/09/neither-us-nor-them.html, April 18, 2018.

6 POST-WAR TO POST-TRUTH: REASSESSING THE AMERICAN AVANT-GARDE... 181

'American Hybrid' should have more accurately been titled 'White American Hybrid.'"[46] Laying blame for the current situation, Perez points to Ron Silliman "for propagating the simplistic binary reading of poetic history into quietude & avant garde… Silliman forced white writers into the binary of Ransom or Goldsmith, creating white cultural-aesthetic anxiety, which necessitated the formation of an 'ideal hybrid.'"[47] Perez is referring to categories of American poetry that Silliman often mentions on his blog[48] and which characterize what he sees as an essential difference among American poets. The concept of a hybrid American poetics originated well before Silliman or Swenson, of course, as critics predicted the emergence of this style as early as 1964.[49] But the key point here is that Perez doesn't mention the content or form of the poems in his arguments; he objects to the anthology's lack of diversity.

Regarding *American Hybrid*'s central argument—that the binary between academic and avant-garde has begun to break down—Perez suggests this binary is a front for the more pervasive organizing principle of American poetry: racial hierarchy. This signals the important ways the critical discourse has shifted in recent decades from questions of form to questions of identity, and it also suggests that many readers now expect anthologists to focus on diverse inclusivity rather than—or even while—focusing on the exclusivity of formal mastery or bold experimentation. This is a development Allen could not have predicted and one that has affected several recent anthologies.

Rita Dove's *The Penguin Anthology of Twentieth-Century American Poetry* (2011) also highlighted the pervasive whiteness of American poetry for many readers, perhaps conversely, because its inclusion of a significant number of African American poets inspired complaints from several prominent white critics.[50] Dove's anthology was negatively reviewed by both

---

[46] Craig Santos Perez, *The Poetry Foundation*, April 14, 2010, "Whitewashing American Hybrid Aesthetics," https://www.poetryfoundation.org/harriet/2010/04/whitewashing-american-hybrid-aesthetics, December 20, 2017.

[47] Craig Santos Perez, *The Poetry Foundation*, April 14, 2010, "Whitewashing American Hybrid Aesthetics," https://www.poetryfoundation.org/harriet/2010/04/whitewashing-american-hybrid-aesthetics, December 20, 2017.

[48] Ron Silliman, *Silliman's Blog*, July 7, 2010, http://ronsilliman.blogspot. com/2010/07/i-know-whenever-i-use-phrase-school-of.html, December 30, 2017.

[49] Chad Walsh, "The war between Iambs and Ids," *Book Week*, July 26, 1964, 9.

[50] Evie Shockley situates the controversy surrounding Dove's anthology prominently within the debate about race and the canon from the second half of the twentieth century.

Helen Vendler and Marjorie Perloff, two eminent critics who have each advocated different, complementary strands in American poetry. Vendler, at Harvard, has spent decades writing about and teaching the work of Robert Lowell, Wallace Stevens and others, while Perloff, an early advocate of language poetry and conceptual writing, has long been a vocal supporter and theorizer of the avant-garde. So it surprised many readers when Perloff and Vendler published negative reviews of Dove's anthology for essentially the same reason. Both critics objected to the contents of the book, and both explicitly connected their arguments to subjectivity and form. In her review of the anthology, Vendler cited its "Multicultural inclusiveness," writing that Dove had "decided... to shift the balance, introducing more black poets and giving them significant amounts of space, in some cases more space than is given to better-known authors. These writers are included in some cases for their representative themes rather than their style."[51] Here Vendler declares her allegiance to a certain conception of the American canon and draws a distinction between theme and style, while suggesting that the latter is more important as a criterion for value in poetry.

Perloff also takes issue with the form of the poems in the anthology, lamenting the fact that they do not seek to shift what she calls the "paradigm" of "a certain kind of prize-winning, 'well-crafted' poem."[52] She goes on to question the racial inclusivity of the anthology: "One surmises from the table of contents of this chronological survey that Dove, from her perspective as a woman of color, has included many more poets of color than is usually the case."[53] Later in the same review she writes: "identity politics has produced a degree of variation, so that we have Latina poetry, Asian American poetry, queer poetry, the poetry of the disabled, and so on."[54] This is not a new complaint for Perloff, who wrote in 2005 that identity-based poetry is antithetical to avant-garde poetry, while ignoring the authoritative role of the critic in labelling poets and groups:

Shockley, "Shifting the (Im)balance: Race and the Poetry Canon," *The Boston Review,* June 6, 2013. http://bostonreview.net/poetry/shifting-imbalance, January 3, 2018.

[51] Helen Vendler, "Are these the Poets to Remember?" *New York Review of Books,* November 24, 2011, http://www.nybooks.com/articles/2011/11/24/are-these-poems-remember/, December 31, 2018.

[52] Marjorie Perloff, "Poetry on the Brink," May 18, 2012, *The Boston Review,* http://bostonreview.net/forum/poetry-brink, December 31, 2017.

[53] Perloff, "Poetry on the Brink."

[54] Perloff, "Poetry on the Brink."

6 POST-WAR TO POST-TRUTH: REASSESSING THE AMERICAN AVANT-GARDE... 183

In recent years, ideological and identity-based movements have sometimes been labeled "avant-garde": for example, the Black Arts movement, the feminist performance art of the '70s, or the "new" Asian-American poetries. But the "breakthrough" of such movements tends to be short-lived, the aim of the groups concerned being ironically counter-avant-garde in their drive to win acceptance within the larger public art sphere.[55]

In the same essay, Perloff expresses regret about how language poetry was "pressed to be inclusive" by "the juggernaut of Political Correctness" in the 1990s. More recently, she has said, "It's just not a great moment for poetry" because "the criterion for poetry is very romantic again, filled with the witnessing of personal pain and suffering, whether in relation to gender or race or disability, and so on."[56] While many readers and critics have moved beyond form to questions of identity and representation, Perloff seems to want to maintain critical standards that judge poetry on the skill and innovation of its creator, which reveal themselves through form. In this she finds common ground with Vendler.

Vendler's emphasis on form rather than content as the criterion for value judgments about poetry has been a cornerstone of what she calls "a properly aesthetic criticism"[57] which recognizes that "an ultimate disregard for 'surface' in favor of a presumed 'depth' goes absurdly counter to the primary sensuous claim of every work of art, the claim made precisely by its 'surface' (these words, these notes, and no others)... Form, after all, is nothing but content-as-arranged."[58] Similarly, the poets that Perloff has championed over her long, estimable career have tended to emphasize form in terms of the materiality of language, which is another way of describing the surface Vendler refers to here. Both Perloff and Vendler object to the African American poets in Dove's anthology not because they're African American but because their poetry supposedly does not display formal mastery or experimentation. The argument from both

---

[55] Marjorie Perloff, "Avant-Garde Tradition and Individual Talent: The Case of Language Poetry," *Dans Revue française d'études américaines*, https://www.cairn.info/revue-francaise-d-etudes-americaines-2005-1-page-117.htm#no3, April 15, 2018.

[56] Jeremy Sigler, "A Conversation with Marjorie Perloff," *Tablet Magazine*, April 1, 2019, https://www.tabletmag.com/jewish-arts-and-culture/282087/marjorie-perloff, April 2, 2019.

[57] Helen Vendler, *The Music of What Happens: Poems, Poets, Critics* (Cambridge: Harvard University Press, 1988), 2.

[58] Vendler, *The Music of What Happens*, 3.

184   S. DELBOS

Vendler and Perloff is essentially conservative: the canon has been established and many of the outsider poets of the post-war avant-garde have achieved greater acceptance, their masterful, formally challenging poetry now considered more easily digestible. And there we should set the limits.

How the form and content of a poem overlap and whether they are mutually exclusive have been topics of debate among poets and critics at least since Allen's anthology, which emphasized the formal choices of its poets by the inclusion of the "Notes on Poetics" section. One result was that by 1962, a British anthologist could write persuasively that "Contemporary American poetry… seems to be wandering off in the direction of the decorative, where style and technique is all."[59] As Hickman has argued, "the question of form in its narrowest sense is the most visible measure of *The New American Poetry*'s impact."[60] The fact that both Perloff and Vendler can agree that the value of a poet's work is purely aesthetic rather than social is an important distinction between older and younger critics and poets today and suggests the ways that these established critics are replaying old debates. While *The New American Poetry* helped focus the discourse on the form rather than the content and social ramifications of the poetry, this was a method appropriated from conservative critics of the 1940s and 1950s who used form as a stalking horse to dismiss poetry with objectionable left-leaning content. When critics like Vendler and Perloff today use formal considerations as a way to discount poetry from supposedly unsophisticated poets of color, the debate seems to have come full circle. An awareness of the fact that the canon is overwhelmingly male shows how this focus on form also perpetuates the myth of the male genius,[61] praising the masterful practitioner while relegating poets who privilege social rather than formal issues to minority positions of less power and influence.

The personal nature of these debates and *The New American Poetry*'s long-standing model of editorial imbalance make it difficult to maintain impartiality. Ken Chen, for example, cites William Logan's negative review of Dove's anthology—in which Logan actually gives Dove "credit" for including "poets often ignored because of race or gender"[62] and spends

---

[59] Woznicki, 88.

[60] Woznicki, 96.

[61] Emily Atkin, "The Sexism of 'Genius,'" *The New Republic*, March 15, 2018, https://newrepublic.com/article/147463/sexism-genius-death-stephen-hawking, April 1, 2018.

[62] William Logan, "Guys and Dove," *The New Criterion*, June 2012, https://www.new-criterion.com/issues/2012/6/guys-dove, April 18, 2018.

6 POST-WAR TO POST-TRUTH: REASSESSING THE AMERICAN AVANT-GARDE... 185

more time lambasting Dove's prose style than her choice of poets—to argue that American poetry is segregated by race rather than form:

> The critical consensus between Vendler, Perloff, and Logan shows that our poetry wars are not really positioned around aesthetic camps (say, experimental versus mainstream poetics), but by hierarchies of racial segregation. The Penguin anthology, for example, included many Language poets, the very poets traditionally thought to be too subversive for Official Verse Culture.[63]

This may be an exaggeration, especially considering the degree to which language poetry has been canonized over the past two decades. It's hard to imagine that Vendler, Perloff or Logan would actually advocate racial segregation, and perhaps it's more accurate to say that these critics—of whom Logan, born in 1950, is the youngest by two decades—have starkly different values than critics who came of age at the height of debates about canonical inclusion. Logan's review of Dove's anthology shows that he is clearly aligned with aesthetics rather than what he refers to as "sociology":

> When sociology masquerades as aesthetics, your fairness seems immediately unfair to everyone left out... The blogs have been alight with rage over the absence of Appalachian poets, disabled poets, cyber poets, performance poets, avant-gardists of every stripe, and many other groups implicitly maligned... No art is an equal-opportunity art. Talent is always asymmetrically distributed.[64]

It is debatable whether this reveals, as Chen suggests, a hierarchy of racial segregation, but Logan here certainly expresses his belief in a hierarchy of values and a preference for the aesthetic rather than the social function of poetry.

---

[63] Chen continues: "If for Perloff, the Dove anthology triggered vitriol for 'includ[ing] many more minority poets than is usually the case,' this is only to say that most American poetry anthologies omit people of color – even anthologies that one would imagine would be racially marked, like *American Hybrid* (four people of color out of 78), *The New American Poetry of Engagement: A 21st Century Anthology* (five poets of color out of 50), *Beneath a Single Moon: Buddhism in Contemporary American Poetry* (no people of color), and *American Poetry Since 1950: Innovators and Outsiders* (two black poets out of 35 total)." Ken Chen, "Authenticity Obsession, or Conceptualism as Minstrel Show," *The Margins*, June 11, 2015, http://aaww.org/authenticity-obsession/, November 18 2017.

[64] Logan, "Guys and Dove."

186   S. DELBOS

But whether or not Logan, Perloff and Vendler intend to promote racial segregation is beside the point for many younger critics who align pure aestheticism with white privilege. Timothy Yu distinguishes between "those networks and scenes which are organized by and around the codes of oppressed peoples, and those other 'purely aesthetic' schools."[65] The arguments against critics like Logan, Vendler and Perloff—that their focus on aesthetics and poetic form ignores crucial issues of race and representation—are essentially the same as those against conceptual poets: their lack of concern with oppression and their supposedly impersonal poetics stem from a position of privilege that allows them to believe they can work with even the most offensive content without being implicated in it because that content is pre-existing. As Goldsmith has said, "my books are about the apparatus rather than the content."[66]

Are concerns about poetic form or apparatus antithetical to concerns about race? How did an intense interest in poetry's formal aesthetics come to seem like an excuse for excluding people of color? These questions are rooted, at least in part, in Cold War divisions. Back in 1984, Ron Silliman wrote in his introduction to *In the American Tree*: "While the old dichotomy of 'academic'... and 'non-academic'... has not disappeared, it now sits in a very different context... any debate over who is, or is not, a better writer... is, for the most part, a surrogate social struggle."[67] More recently, according to Terence Diggory, "the so-called 'canon wars' have proved to be a battle in the larger war of 'identity politics,' waged on the field of aesthetics."[68] But we cannot discount the crucial role that poetic form has played in these debates, and specifically what Blasing calls the "academic... [belief] in the inherent virtue of one form or another,"[69] a debate in which Allen's anthology was deeply engaged, as are critics like Logan, Perloff and Vendler. The frame of the debate has shifted, however, and many critics today see race as the most significant issue of contemporary poetry and one that continues to be avoided by established critics for whom "race alone seems unspeakable."[70] These younger critics, like Wang, argue that

---

[65] Timothy Yu, "Ron Silliman and the Ethnicization of the Avant-garde," *Jacket*, 2009, http://jacketmagazine.com/39/silliman-yu.shtml#fn9, December 28, 2017.

[66] Kenneth Goldsmith, Seminar at The Academy of Fine Arts in Prague, January 29, 2019.

[67] Silliman, *In the American Tree*, xxii.

[68] Woznicki, 74.

[69] Blasing, 27.

[70] Dorothy Wang, *Thinking Its Presence: Form, Race, and Subjectivity in Contemporary Asian American Poetry* (Stanford: Stanford University Press, 2013), XXII.

6 POST-WAR TO POST-TRUTH: REASSESSING THE AMERICAN AVANT-GARDE... 187

race has been separated from considerations of American poetry due to a focus on form by critics and writers like Goldsmith, compartmentalizing the current discourse into "reductive binary categories."[71]

Goldsmith has called conceptual writing "postidentity literature,"[72] a statement that Wang has suggested betrays a "myopic cluelessness about the privileges of his own subject position."[73] Indeed, it's not hard to see the racial privilege from which Goldsmith could write: "If my identity is really up for grabs and changeable by the minute – as I believe it is – it's important that my writing reflect this state of ever-shifting identity and subjectivity."[74] It is also clear how this idea comes logically out of language writing and conceptual art while dovetailing with the approach of critics like Logan, Perloff and Vendler who privilege aesthetics above all. For these critics, the best poets escape subjectivity through formal means and only lesser poets remain mired in subjectivity, theme and social issues. Despite the protestations of Goldsmith and Perloff, however, personal subjectivity is inherent in conceptual writing, as it was in language writing and the breath-based poetry that makes up much of *The New American Poetry.*

Subjectivity and how it is expressed through a poem's form and content have been a subject of debate in American poetry at least since Olson's "Projective Verse,"[75] in which Olson quotes Robert Creeley's argument that "form is never more than an extension of content."[76] This idea originated in a letter to Olson in which Creeley also sounds off against the seeming "objectivity" of mainstream verse, echoing Eliot when he writes "no such thing as 'objectivity' for the man who wants to do a good job."[77] As Rifkin notes, when Creeley turned this letter into an essay, "he [made] the connection between objectivity and the professional self-interests of mainstream literary culture more explicit: 'objectivity has become the

---

[71] Wang, *Thinking its Presence*, XXIII.

[72] Kenneth Goldsmith, *Uncreative Writing* (New York: Columbia University Press, 2011), 85.

[73] Wang, *Thinking Its Presence*, 15.

[74] Goldsmith, *Uncreative Writing*, 84.

[75] Olson's essay emerged during the same decade as the concept of individual identity was introduced to American psychology and parenting through Erik Erikson's book *Childhood and Society* (1950), which defined the concept of the "identity crisis." See Fukuyama, *Identity*, 9.

[76] Allen, 387.

[77] Rifkin, 35.

188   S. DELBOS

apparent trademark of the careful mind.'"[78] So for Creeley and Olson, insisting on the subjectivity of form and content was one way to differentiate themselves from mainstream post-war poetry. Their insistence has become much more consequential.

Denise Levertov echoed and updated Creeley's idea in an essay about organic form in 1965, writing "form is never more than a *revelation* of content."[79] Like Creeley and Olson, Levertov privileges the content of the poem as originary. Clearly this was a reaction to what they saw as the academic poets of their time, who largely worked with received forms which were developed well before the moment of composition. By suggesting that the form of the poem must be dictated by the content, Creeley, Olson and Levertov promoted the poet as an individual privileged with talent and trained in language enough to recognize the rightful form of the poem as it emerges and to guide its course through the unmapped frontiers of language. These poets privilege the search for form as the poet's primary objective, and the result, at least for Olson, is what Edward Foster has called a "profoundly subjective poetics."[80] So while attempting to downplay the notion of received form, Creeley, Olson and Levertov dramatically emphasized the importance of organic form, while playing up the authority of the poet, which Allen's inclusion of the "Notes on Poetics" also promotes. Aesthetically minded critics like Logan, Vendler and Perloff would agree: form and style, whether avant-garde or traditional, rather than theme and content, differentiate the best poets from the good poets and should be the central criteria for critical judgment. A great poet can write a great poem about anything.

But this distinction between form and content does not account for the fact that, as Wang has written, "a poem's use of form is inseparable from the larger social, historical, and political contexts that produced the poet's subjectivity."[81] That is, whether the poet is the expert who charts the fresh form of each poem, the minor poet who handles meter with a heavy hand or anywhere between, we must look to contexts beyond that poet—their identity and the conditions that formed it—to fully understand their formal choices. This is discouraged both by the subjective physicality of

---

[78] Rifkin, 50.
[79] Denise Levertov, *New & Selected Essays* (New York: New Directions, 1992), 73.
[80] Foster, 60.
[81] Wang, *Thinking its Presence*, XXII

6 POST-WAR TO POST-TRUTH: REASSESSING THE AMERICAN AVANT-GARDE... 189

projective verse and Goldsmith's contention that conceptual writing is post-identity.

Form for Olson was an extension of content, but it was also an expression of the physicality of the poet himself, because, for Olson, "poetry depended for its life on the rhythms, music, diction of the individual poet."[82] It was this personal, expressive, breath-based poetry that Silliman would refer to as "aging" by the 1980s,[83] an opinion that fueled many of the innovations of language poetry, which would go on to influence writers like Goldsmith.[84] But we are now in a position to see how little these recent avant-gardes have actually moved beyond the subjectivity of the author-as-creator and the primacy of form. The problem of subjectivity, or what Olson referred to as the "lyrical interference of the individual as ego,"[85] is an obstacle that every avant-garde since World War II has unsuccessfully attempted to surmount, mostly by utilizing novel approaches to form and composition. Bruce Andrews has written that the desire to transcend the expressive subjectivity of preceding poetry was a key element of language writing: "reading can be set loose... from the usual demands for a Psychology-Centered Subjective Expressiveness on the part of the Author (that all-purpose glue the traditional reader is supposed to identity with)" and to shatter the illusion of "the comforting distance that nurtured our little dream of subjective centeredness and mastery and protected independence."[86] Similarly, Barrett Watten has critiqued Olson's "romantic subjectivity" in which "the emotive voice, the 'I,' is perceptible

[82] Foster, 17.

[83] Silliman, *In the American Tree*, 584. Nonetheless, Silliman's recognition of how the poets in *The New American Poetry* possess a sense of the "materiality of language" would remain an important factor for language poetry. See: Ron Silliman, "Four Contexts for Three Poems," *Conjunctions* 49 (2007): 298.

[84] Elaborating on the links between conceptual writing and earlier American avant-gardes, Goldsmith has stated: "Yet there's some sort of openness in the poetry world concerning writing that I haven't been able to find elsewhere. Some of the Language poets, in particular, sort of blew apart notions of prescriptive lineation in favor of margin-to-margin madness. I'm thinking of works like Ron Silliman's *Tjanting*." Christopher Higgs, "You Take Your Love Where You Get it: An Interview with Kenneth Goldsmith," *Paris Review*, April 2, 2013, http://www.theparisreview.org/blog/2013/04/02/youtake-your-love-where-you-get-it-an-interview-with-kenneth-goldsmith/, May 15, 2019.

[85] Allen, 395.

[86] Bruce Andrews, "The Poetics of L=A=N=G=U=A=G=E," *UbuWeb*, http://www.ubu.com/papers/andrews.html, April 9, 2018.

as a person behind the words."[87] Numerous other critics and supporters of language poetry, such as Douglas Messerli, have described the way that this type of writing goes beyond the subjectivity of the post-war avant-garde:

> While these writers thus participate in the climate of the poetics of Charles Olson's process-oriented writing... and the disjunctive procedures of the poets associated with the New York School, they have eschewed the myth-making and personalization of poetry practiced by these and other modern poets.[88]

To what degree language poetry achieved impersonal objectivity is debatable, but examining the movement through the lens of recent controversies in the American avant-garde shows how the desire for objectivity in poetry has inspired avant-gardes since the 1970s in a way that actually aligns these recent avant-gardes with modernism.

Language poetry wanted to inherit the alternative values of the poets in Allen's anthology, while doing away with the subjective referentiality of the projective and Beat lyric, or what Steven McCaffery has called the "referential fallacy of language." According to McCaffery, rather than deal with the thoughts and perceptions of the poet, "writing must stress its semiotic nature through modes of investigation and probe, rather than mimetic, instrumental indications."[89] While this seeks to limit the subjectivity of the individual poet in favor of foregrounding the materiality of language, it never does away with the subjectivity of the one who does the probing. So for language poets the poets in *The New American Poetry* were correct in their awareness and concern for the materiality of language but were wrong to ground that awareness in speech-based writing. But the failure of language poets to convincingly do away with subjectivity is grounded in the fact that emphasizing the materiality of language is just another way to emphasize form and the choices of the poet. Pointing this out in an investigation of form that equates new formalism with language poetry, Blasing writes:

---

[87] Foster, 12.

[88] Douglas Messerli, "'Language' Poetries," *The PIP Blog*, February 24, 2013, http://pippoetry.blogspot.com/2013/02/language-poetries.html, April 15, 2018.

[89] Steve McCaffery, *North of Intention: Critical Writings 1973–1986* (New York: Roof Books, 2000), 13–29.

6 POST-WAR TO POST-TRUTH: REASSESSING THE AMERICAN AVANT-GARDE...   191

A poetic that appeals to the "discipline" of "mathematics" is blind to the issue of rhetoric and duplicates Pound's "discipline," for it does not ask: Who chooses the arbitrary mathematical constraint that will maximally motivate each sign if not the "ego?" What carries out such tiresome plans to the bitter end but "habit?" What purpose to such work but "self-indulgence?"... Indeed, a procedural nonreference seems to me to be an extreme case of formalism.[90]

Here Blasing suggests the ways that even non-traditional or constraint-based approaches to writing exercise the same subjectivity—often even more subjectivity—as working in traditional form. Although she is specifically addressing language poetry here, Blasing's arguments apply equally to conceptual writing. As Dworkin writes, "impersonal procedures tend to magnify subjective choices."[91]

The critical narrative surrounding conceptual writing suggests that focusing on concept and appropriated text rather than personal experience and chosen language updates the notion of the individual writer to what Perloff calls "unoriginal genius."[92] Dworkin labels this "non-expressive poetry,"[93] which Goldsmith claims expresses "sentiments... as a result of the writing process rather than by authorial intention,"[94] which should protect the conceptual writer from charges of racial insensitivity while also distinguishing this type of writing from that which is grounded in a concern for social issues and identity. And yet, when Goldsmith writes that "context is the new content,"[95] this context surely includes the writer (or composer, to use Olson's word) who conceived of the concept which is so important that "if you get the concept... then you get the book, and you don't even have to read it."[96]

[90] Blasing, 25.

[91] Craig Dworkin, "The Fate of Echo," in *Against Expression: An Anthology of Conceptual Writing*, eds. Craig Dworkin and Kenneth Goldsmith (Evanston: Northwestern University Press, 2011), xxxix.

[92] See: Marjorie Perloff, *Unoriginal Genius: Poetry by other Means in the New Century* (Chicago: University of Chicago Press, 2010).

[93] Craig Dworkin, *Introduction to the UbuWeb Anthology of Conceptual Writing*, UbuWeb, http://www.ubu.com/concept/, December 31, 2018.

[94] Goldsmith, *Uncreative Writing*, 4.

[95] Goldsmith, *Uncreative Writing*, 3.

[96] "Against Expression: Kenneth Goldsmith in Conversation," *The Academy of American Poets,* June 17, 2011, https://www.poets.org/poetsorg/text/against-expression-kenneth-goldsmith-conversation, December 31, 2017. Dworkin cautions readers against taking statements like this at face value, however: "Noting a method – transcribed radio reports, parsed grammar, alphabetized answers, et cetera – is no substitute for carefully reading the textual

Contradicting Goldsmith's claims, Kaufmann has argued that "Uncreative Writing, or at least some of it, is all about subjectivity and expression"[97] and that it "emphasizes what Richard Wollheim called the pre-executive function of the artist: her choices, rather than her skills,"[98] an argument that can also be applied to language poetry, following Blasing. The centrality of the author in conceptual writing likely plays a role in the vehemence of recent controversies regarding race and the avant-garde. There is a tension inherent in the way that conceptual writing seeks to avoid authorial subjectivity while simultaneously calling attention to the author as framer and performer. Clearly, conceptual writers have not been able to avoid the "lyrical interference of the individual as ego"[99] any more than Olson. Of course this does not necessarily make them racist, but it does contradict their claims of immunity to charges of racism due to the impersonality of their work. It also calls into question the veracity of critics who privilege form and aesthetics over subjectivity as the distinguishing qualities of the best poetry. If no poetry is truly objective because form is always rooted in subjectivity, these critics need new reasons for protesting the inclusion of minority voices in contemporary anthologies.

Surveying the major controversies of American poetry in the twenty-first century makes it clear that issues of race, identity and subjectivity have taken center stage while an older generation of critics clings to the formalist framework established after World War II. It is also clear that now more than ever editors need to be aware of the racial and gender imbalances of their publications, as these imbalances will no longer pass unnoticed, nor should they. For many of today's younger critics, *The New American Poetry* is not an emblem of the avant-garde's breakthrough into the public consciousness but a monument to the continued exclusion of minority voices. These developments are indicative of more than a new chapter in the culture wars or a reconsideration of one influential poetry anthology. They represent the slow collapse of the formalist framework that Allen's anthology helped establish.

---

details of a work." Craig Dworkin, "The Fate of Echo," in *Against Expression: An Anthology of Conceptual Writing*, eds. Craig Dworkin and Kenneth Goldsmith (Evanston: Northwestern University Press, 2011), xxxvii.

[97] Kaufmann, 5.

[98] Kaufmann, 6.

[99] Craig Dworkin, "The Fate of Echo," in *Against Expression: An Anthology of Conceptual Writing*, eds. Craig Dworkin and Kenneth Goldsmith (Evanston: Northwestern University Press, 2011), xliii.

CHAPTER 7

Conclusion: The Slow Collapse of the Formalist Framework

Tracking current controversies in the avant-garde shows just how far we've come from promising post-war ideas about a community of love through poetry. But it also shows how the cooked and raw binary, outdated as it may be, continues to influence older generations of influential critics who agree on the importance of a formalist framework for judging poetry despite the fact that they favor different poets. Allen's anthology, which insisted that the poets included were anti-academic but were also intimately concerned with form, won entrance into the formalist framework for poets who had until then generally been considered too wildly informal to merit serious scholarly attention. Allen's host of "new American" publications in the decades after 1960 further entrenched these poets in their position on one side of the binary. But this framework, with its insistence on formal mastery and experimentation, does not take into account the work of poets who are more concerned with giving voice to issues of race and identity.[1] The myopia of critics in the 1950s, who could not or would not take avant-garde poets into account, has developed into a

---

[1] Recent critics such as Natalia Cecire have questioned our understanding of the term "experimental" as a specific mode of writing while acknowledging that "the version of experimentalism that emerges when names get named is tacitly US-centric, as reflected in the importance of Allen's *New American Poetry* anthology – emphasis on 'American' – in back-of-the-envelope genealogies." Natalia Cecire, *Experimental: American Literature and the Aesthetics of Knowledge* (Baltimore: Johns Hopkins University Press, 2019), 28.

© The Author(s), under exclusive license to Springer Nature Switzerland AG 2021
S. Delbos, *The New American Poetry and Cold War Nationalism*, Modern and Contemporary Poetry and Poetics, https://doi.org/10.1007/978-3-030-77352-6_7

193

194   S. DELBOS

critical model that cannot or will not take poets of color and identity-based and socially minded poets into account. But this framework, founded on outdated principles and binaries, has begun to collapse as American poetry and society become more diverse and pluralistic than ever before.

Commenting in the 1980s on what he saw as the problem of hermeticism in American poetry, Nathanial Tarn lamented the loss of Whitman's sense of the marriage between poet and reader[2] due to language writing's emphasis on the materiality rather than the sense of language. In recent years conceptual writing has emphasized this even further, so that for conceptual poets the idea of a readership no longer really exists.[3] Tarn, in contrasting language poetry with writing produced by MFA programs, suggested that both sides of the divide in American poetry were guilty of hermeticism and betraying the reader. Indeed, poets who are no longer concerned with their reading public have retreated from the communal sense of poetry that was hinted at in the mid-twentieth century, a communal sense that, at its best, might have included poets and readers from all walks of life. Donald Allen's emphasis on the formal divide helped code this aesthetic binary into American poetry. The academy's gradual acceptance of the poets in Allen's anthology, and more recently language poetry and conceptual writing, is due at least in part to the fact that this poetry fits into the dominant formalist framework *The New American Poetry* helped establish.

The formalist framework of American poetry, which has begun to fracture despite the efforts of critics such as Logan, Perloff and Vendler, has room enough for both apparent poles of poetry, from Lowell to Ginsberg, from Stevens to Bernstein to Goldsmith and conceptual writing, which Perloff connects to the formal gestures of modernism, so that an entire

---

[2] "When we lost the Whitmanian notion that there should be marriage between poet and people, poet and public, or poet and 'reader,' if you will, we entered incest. And the great nuclear breeder of incest has been the university… Those who, for worse rather than better, have gotten baptized as 'language poets' are in every way as divorced from a 'readership,' as I understand it here, as the MFA writer – indeed, many of them may be MFA writers, for all I know." Nathanial Tarn, "Is There, Currently, an American Poetry?," Republished in *Dispatches from the Poetry Wars*, March 14, 2019, https://www.dispatchespoetrywars.com/wp-content/uploads/2019/03/Tarn-Is-there-an-American-Poetry-1986-red.pdf, April 22, 2019.

[3] According to Goldsmith, "this work demands a thinkership, not a readership." Katharine Elaine Sanders, "So What Exactly Is Conceptual Writing: An Interview with Kenneth Goldsmith," *BOMB Magazine*, October 2, 2009, https://bombmagazine.org/articles/so-what-exactly-is-conceptual-writing-an-interview-with-kenneth-goldsmith/, April 22, 2018.

7 CONCLUSION: THE SLOW COLLAPSE OF THE FORMALIST FRAMEWORK   195

century of poetry fits into a single model of two opposing camps. This concern with form leaves much outside its purview, however, beginning at least with the politically active, left-leaning transnational poets of the 1920s, 1930s and 1940s, continuing to the poets of the Civil Rights Movement, poets of the Black Arts Movement and feminist poets, and more recently the whole plethora of identities from which poets write and wish to be read. These poets' concerns with race, identity, subjectivity and social themes have been looked down upon from critics on both sides of the divide who consider form preeminent.

In the early twenty-first century, the questionable dichotomy of academic and avant-garde has become one in which readers are seemingly forced to choose between traditional formal mastery and supposedly impersonal textual appropriation, a model that does not do justice to the increasing diversity of American poetry. Meanwhile, this contemporary dichotomy is simply replaying, in slightly altered form, the debates of the mid-twentieth century. Is Goldsmith truly a new kind of post-identity poet or are his avant-garde strictures simply a new kind of conservatism? In a description of mainstream mid-twentieth-century poetics, Foster describes Robert Frost in a way that harmonizes with Goldsmith's comments about not having to actually read conceptual writing, suggesting the two poets have more in common than most would realize: "Frost grounded his poems in 'the sound of sense,' taking from the spoken language tones and cadences that seemed meaningful in themselves; one didn't have to hear the actual words, that is, in order to understand and be affected by the literal argument of the words."[4] While neither writer would agree, Frost's insistence on the sound of sense and Goldsmith's insistence on the primacy of concept share similar characteristics: one doesn't have to read Goldsmith's writing to understand and be affected by his concept.

The formalist argument is that by sublimating everything to form, poets avoid the subjectivity that makes social poetry less sophisticated. But it should be clear at this point that critical judgments about poetry that privilege form over content and theme are inadequate, especially because recent avant-gardes have not transcended subjectivity, despite their best efforts. These formal arguments have always been used as a way to benignly discount politically questionable poetry. That may no longer be possible in today's less hierarchical literary and political discourse.

---

[4] Foster, 84–85.

196   S. DELBOS

Debates about identity and subjectivity in twenty-first-century American poetry echo debates in contemporary American culture at large. What Perloff calls "a degree of variation"[5] created by the insistence on highlighting the differences among American poets stems from conditions in American society and politics. As Francis Fukuyama writes: "Again and again, groups have come to believe that their identities – whether national, religious, ethnic, sexual, gender, or otherwise – are not receiving adequate recognition."[6] This also applies to Anglophone poetry.

Despite the best efforts of some critics, the simplistic Cold War binary of academic and avant-garde has become a much more fragmented and complex landscape, where differences are insisted upon, often at the cost of recognizing underlying similarities and shared stylistic or thematic traits. The question we must pose about Anglophone poetry today is the same one we must pose about American society. Perhaps it remains unanswerable for the time being: will this emphasis on difference ultimately lead to a more variegated whole, a unity that takes into account the important distinctions among its members? Or will it destroy any sense of unity where one may have existed? Fukuyama suggests that the solution is not to abandon the idea of identity but "to define larger and more integrative national identities that take into account the de facto diversity of liberal democratic societies."[7] The constellating of the traditional publishing hierarchy makes this possible in poetry, but it also suggests that the very idea of an organized canon may begin to lose currency. Ideally, however, future conceptions of the canon will do away with national divisions in favor of a more inclusive framework that also takes into account the vital contributions of women and people of color and does not seek to separate concepts of form and content. One hopes—and senses—that the increasing plurality of poetry and criticism will only continue, despite or perhaps because of the fact that we are unlikely to see the towering tenured figures

[5] Perloff, "Poetry on the Brink."

[6] Francis Fukuyama, "Against Identity Politics: The New Tribalism and the Crisis of Democracy," *Foreign Affairs*, September/October 2018, https://www.foreignaffairs.com/articles/americas/2018-08-14/against-identity-politics-tribalism-francis-fukuyama, February 1, 2019.

[7] Francis Fukuyama, "Against Identity Politics: The New Tribalism and the Crisis of Democracy, *Foreign Affairs*, September/October 2018, https://www.foreignaffairs.com/articles/americas/2018-08-14/against-identity-politics-tribalism-francis-fukuyama,   May 1, 2019.

7 CONCLUSION: THE SLOW COLLAPSE OF THE FORMALIST FRAMEWORK   197

of Vendler and Perloff's or Logan's generations again, considering the current state of American higher education.

But in the heat of these debates, it is imperative that any critique of the past is subtle and considered. To blame contemporary problems in American poetry solely on *The New American Poetry* is misleading. As David S. Reynolds has written, historians and literary critics must "adhere to the historical record instead of imposing today's views on the past,"[8] and in the same way, according to Fukuyama:

> Identity politics for some progressives has become a cheap substitute for serious thinking about how to reverse the thirty-year trend in most liberal democracies toward greater socioeconomic inequality... University curricula can be more readily altered to include readings of women and minority authors than can the incomes or social situations of the groups in question.[9]

To change poetry, we must change society. But too often in contemporary debates, emotion trumps critical examination and investigation. As Alcalay writes: "Such false debates come at the cost of deeper explorations, refinement of positions, and possibilities for re-imagining and re-defining. Such structures mirror the constraints and privatizing forces within official political, academic, and media frameworks."[10] While American poetry is beginning to account for shortcomings of race and gender, numerous important issues remain relatively unexamined. As Christopher Nealon has pointed out, "the matter of capital"[11] is just one topic that has often been ignored in discussions of American poetry that have focused on form, while Alcalay works to call the reader's attention to "class issues."[12] The arguments in this book should expand, not limit or simply refocus, our perception of the forces at work in creating and codifying American poetry since the Cold War. A deeper, more critical understanding of the genesis of Allen's anthology and its continued effects helps us to more fully comprehend our own moment. It may also serve as a guide to future anthologists, critics and poets. And while poets of color and female poets

---

[8] David S. Reynolds, *Walt Whitman's America: A Cultural Biography* (New York: Alfred A. Knopf, 1995), xii.

[9] Fukuyama, *Identity*, 115.

[10] Alcalay, 152.

[11] Christopher Nealon, *The Matter of Capital: Poetry and Crisis in the American Century* (Cambridge: Harvard University Press, 2011), 1.

[12] Alcalay, 152.

continue to claim their rightful place in the canon, they must not repeat the mistakes of previous outsiders who now police their hard-won ground and exclude the next group or generation seeking recognition.

The New American Poetry reflected and revised many of the social and political values of its time: it suggested new lifestyles and ways of conceiving of literature and also echoed the nationalism, sexism and racial segregation of the 1950s. The lack of racial and gender inclusivity in the twenty-first-century American avant-garde was foreshadowed by Allen's anthology, and recognizing this shows the necessity of updating our understanding of the dynamics of avant-garde writing and canon formation in the second half of the twentieth century and today. We need new, less formalist, homogeneous, hierarchical and hegemonically masculine ways to talk about Anglophone poetry since World War II, and we must recognize how central women and poets of color have been in developing this poetry, despite the fact that they have not always been represented, either in anthologies or in the critical narrative. To remain relevant, the contemporary critical discourse must recognize where Anglophone poetry and society are now and seek to be as innovative as the best poetry always has been.

Appendices

Appendix I: Interview with Joanne Kyger, Email, January 10, 2014

Although you weren't included in The New American Poetry, *you did have a relationship with Donald Allen, I believe. Did you know him while he was making the anthology, or did you have any sense of his vision of how the energies of post-war American poetry seemed to be coalescing in the late 1950s?*

I met Don, briefly, at The Place on Grant Avenue, in 1958, I think. He was in town visiting poets. I knew him as the editor of the great issue of *Evergreen Review* #2, "The San Francisco Scene," which came out in 1957. Having moved up from Santa Barbara in the early spring of 1957, *Evergreen Review* #2, with its pictures of local poets, became a very special guide to me with its introduction to the "scene" by Kenneth Rexroth, and all the other writers. Most of whom I eventually met. It was like a Stars of West Coast Poetry Handbook, and I found all the poetry accessible and exciting. I had already been "schooled" in Williams and Pound and Eliot in Santa Barbara by Hugh Kenner.

Although The New American Poetry *is often credited with being a kind of liberal breakthrough in American poetry, very few women (or African Americans) were included. Does this accurately represent the state of American poetry at the time? Can you in any way account for this ratio?*

© The Author(s), under exclusive license to Springer Nature
Switzerland AG 2021
S. Delbos, *The New American Poetry and Cold War Nationalism*,
Modern and Contemporary Poetry and Poetics,
https://doi.org/10.1007/978-3-030-77352-6

200 APPENDICES

Well I think the editorial selection was a reflection of where the direction of American poetry Don Allen was interested in was going, with much emphasis on the exciting and creative scene happening in the Bay Area. Don had gone to Berkeley graduate school and knew Spicer and Duncan from that time, so he was familiar with the Berkeley–SF energy in the arts. He did include Denise Levertov, Madeline Gleason, from Mill Valley, and Barbara Guest, a friend of his. I'm not sure where else his tastes would have taken him. I don't think African American poetry was recognized as such at that time, something that LeRoi Jones was able to guide to more prominence, as Amiri Baraka.

Why wasn't your work included in the anthology?

I submitted some poems for the anthology, but really hadn't written anything as yet that had any cohesive strength. He did include me in the U.K. Penguin *New American Poetry* which came out a few years later. And he did go on to publish my first book *The Tapestry and the Web* in 1965.

Allen famously mapped out American poetry according to geographical and stylistic distinctions like The New York School. Were these categories apparent to you before the publication of the anthology? Did you find them appropriate? Revelatory? Insightful?

I was aware of "New York" poets, and of course the Black Mountain School. But his geographical distinction were still abstract to me at the time.

What do you recall of the reception of the anthology, both by yourself and your peers? Now it is considered a landmark book. Did it give you the impression of being especially significant in 1960?

I was living in Kyoto during 1960–64, so the only poets that were really impressed/inspired by the anthology around me were Snyder and Cid Corman. But I'm sure it made a big difference to the American poets who were included. The hold of the "academic" writing of the time and its corner on the publications and publishing of poetry was another mind/language altogether. City Lights and New Directions were the only open channels for the "new American" writing.

This period of "the anthology wars" is suffused with military vocabulary and the sense of very clear demarcations between competing poetic "camps." Is this an accurate picture of how things were in American poetry in 1960?

As I mentioned before, I was living in Japan, so my poetry connections came from San Francisco – Spicer, Duncan, and friends my age, George Stanley, Ebbe Borregaard, Stan Persky, etc. And wherever the wayward John Wieners was going...

APPENDICES 201

Appendix II: Interview with Edward Field, Email, January 14, 2014

What werethe circumstances of your inclusionin The New American Poetry? *Did you submit your poems to DonaldAllen? How did you first hear about the anthology?*

I never submitted. I hadn't even heard about the anthology. I assume that Frank O'Hara told Don Allen to include me, and I think he took the poems from my manuscript, which I'd sent to Grove. So the whole thing was out of my hands. I'd never have thought of including myself with that group, and I'd never have chosen those poems. So I was surprised to hear about it.

Was there a sense in New York in the late '50s and early '60s of Grove Press being a vital force in New York literature?

Grove did stand for the avant-garde, along with New Directions press, and a lot of writers sucked up to Barney Rosset. I'd published quite a bit in *Evergreen Review*, his magazine, but I didn't hang out in that world and don't know that Frank and Don Allen were friends. I only met Don Allen in San Francisco later when he was into heavy Buddhism up the coast.

You mention in a YouTube clip about being hung up with the poetry of the 1930s. Did you have a feeling in the 1950s that writing Socialist or Proletarian verse was possible? It seems to me that a whole generation of poets from the '30s were swept off the table in the '50s.

It was really through Robert Friend who was a lefty that I felt attracted to the literary left, though I was never part of it. I especially liked Auden and MacNeice and Spender. But I was more involved with the artists of the '30s through my friend Herman Rose than the poets. But I did somehow want to be "a poet of the people" and even got jobs in warehouses and factories. And then surprisingly, when I met O'Hara, who had an entirely different mindset, comfortable with corporate America, I discovered his crowd also liked Herman Rose, and Alice Neel, even though Frank's crowd rejected most of the rest of the lefty world.

Allen famously mapped out American poetry according to geographical and stylistic distinctions like The New YorkSchool. Were these categories apparent to you before the publication of the anthology? Did you find them appropriate? Revelatory? Insightful?

A lot of the poets were new to me, but the categories roughly made sense. Before then, I'd only thought of American poetry as divided into the Beats in San Francisco, formalist poets who taught in universities and

202 APPENDICES

published in the literary quarterlies, and everybody else, individuals like May Swenson and me. I was surprised to learn about the influence poets like Charles Olson had – I'd known nothing about him before. I confess that I lived in a world of my own.

What do you recall of the reception of the anthology, both by yourself and your peers? Now it is considered a landmark book. Did it give you the impression of being especially significant in 1960?

I was surprised by the reception. It was nice to be included but I was still alien to that world.

You were also included in DaisyAldan's A New Folder. *How did you come to be included in that anthology, and how would you contrast the process of your inclusion and the reception of that anthology with Allen's anthology?*

Aldan's anthology is virtually unknown compared to Allen's anthology.

Why do you think that is, based on your own experience with both?

Daisy's anthology was more inclusive of the poets in New York than Donald Allen's was. She and I met at readings and parties. Coming from such a small press, Tiber Press, it couldn't get the same attention as a book from Grove, which got national attention.

Did inclusion in Allen'santhology have a significant impact on your "career" as a poet? For example, you went on to publish two books with Grove. Was this a direct result of your inclusion in the anthology?

Grove didn't want to publish me but was willing to submit my ms. for the Lamont Award. When I won, they were committed to publishing me. And since the book did so well they brought out my second book, which also did well. Nevertheless, I was reminded by the editor, Richard Seaver, that I had not earned my share of the overhead.

This period of "the anthologywars" is suffused with military vocabulary and the sense of very clear demarcations between competing poetic "camps." Is this an accurate picture of how things were in American poetry in 1960?

There was another anthology that came out just after Allen's that included all the well-known (conventional) poets appearing in literary magazines of that time, who were left out of the Allen anthology, and a literary war seemed to break out between the two camps. It was fun, and gave poetry publicity, but didn't change anything. We all went on writing our own poetry.

It is said that you began writing poetry when a Red Cross worker handed you an anthology. Which anthology was it?

APPENDICES **203**

Louis Untermeyer's *Great Poems of the English Language*. But it was the Oscar Williams *Anthology of Modern Poetry* that was my Bible once I started writing poetry seriously.

Appendix III: Interview with Donald Hall, Email, February 11, 2014

Dear Mr. Delbos,

It is strange to be asked about "the anthology wars" in 2014!

I had forgotten the distinction between "raw and cooked." I think that the two-Business is silly. Actually, nobody talks about it any more.

I knew Tom McGrath pretty well. His poetry had nothing to do with either so-called camp. I knew that he was, or had been, a communist. I knew that the subject was congressionally worrisome. When we talked, we never talked about his politics – simply because it was a boring subject. Back in the late 1940s the left-wing, and even communist, notions were common at Harvard. Myself, I was asked to join the Party because of my politics. Before I graduated in 1951, the un-American Activities Committee quieted things down! It was not a great big deal.

Robert Pack knew a publisher and arranged for the anthology. Then he realized that he did not know enough about poetry at the moment. He asked Louis to join with him. Louis was a friend of mine and I knew much more than he did. I had been editing the *Paris Review* for quite a while, which extended my acquaintance. Also I had spent a couple of years at Oxford and had a good idea of what was happening in England. I don't remember Pack's introduction but he had least to do with the choices, of the three of us. I remember: I found Snodgrass, who had no book. We had a meeting at Pack's New York apartment. Pack was enthusiastically against Snodgrass. He went off to the bathroom and Louis and I agreed that Snodgrass was in. We told Pack when he came back.

The definite article [in *The New Poets of England and America*] was criticized! When there was a second edition, Louis dropped out – largely because he didn't want to work with Pack. For the same reason, I did the English part alone, and Pack the American. I did not want to work with him. The division among the three of us was not hateful. I suppose each of us knew he was right.

Pack and Simpson and I did not edit with any notion of a conflict with another school of poets. Pack and I had never heard the name Allen Ginsberg. Louis had known him at Columbia, where he was writing little

204 APPENDICES

Elizabethan ballads – nothing like "Howl." None of us knew anything of Snyder or Robert Duncan. If we had known the work of many of them, probably we would not have put it in anyway. We were more conventional – but we didn't know about them, so he never had a chance to judge.

Let me give you a funny example. When we first finished the choices, one of our poets was John Ashbery. Then the anthology was too long, the publisher told us, and we cut it down – alas omitting Ashbery. It was two to one, and I was the one. Therefore John Ashbery got picked for the Donald Allen book, and thus (as it were) became a Beat poet. Don Allen's book printed all sorts of different poets, many totally un-Beat. Pretty much our bunch was called "academic" and a lot of them, including more conventional, "Beat." Remember that "academic" had nothing to do with teaching at colleges. It was like the Royal Academy of Art in England, and that meant academic in a kind of conventional sense of belonging to an established group.

Really there was not a winner in the anthology wars. People who were not poets tried to keep the "battle" alive. I suppose it was amusing to take sides. The poets were ecumenical. Denise Levertov was supposed to be Beat. Once Robert Bly took me around to meet her in the Village, and her husband hid himself away, and would not talk with me. Denise and I were friendly. Later, when she was poetry editor of the *Nation*, she asked me to do a review of Charles Olson. There was the ecumenism. Snyder and Creeley and I became close friends. And I met other of these Allen anthologies [*sic*], we got along fine.

When I was teaching at Michigan I invited Allen [Ginsberg] to come and read, and we enjoyed it. On the platform, after I had introduced him, Allen said that "Once we were the greatest enemies in the poetry world" and now we kiss each other! (I don't remember that we kissed!) Once I was asleep and Allen was in town with Gary Snyder and they wrote lines of poetry for me, each side of one piece of paper, and shoved it under my door.

A few years after the "wars" I was able to edit an anthology for Penguin. What did I call it, *Poetry Since the War*? I can't remember. I was able to include a fair sampling of very different poets. I think that Allen was not in it until the second edition or printing. I was really pleased, because Penguin was still mostly English but international – throughout Australia and New Zealand and India – which made the newer American poetry known all over the world. I don't know anyone who has spoken to me, or

APPENDICES   205

written in print, anything about the so-called anthology wars for several decades.

I hope to be helpful,
Don Hall

Appendix IV: Interview with Robert Pack, Telephone, March 23, 2014

Can you provide some background information on the creation and publication of The New Poets of England and America? *Was it your intention to feature only poets writing in received forms?*

I look back on that youthful exuberant period in which I joined with friends, they were friends at that time, Donald Hall and Louis Simpson. I can't remember the exact occasion in which the three of us were talking and just decided it would be fun to put together an anthology. The basic sense was that there was a lot of good poetry being written. It was an anthology to toot our own horn. And we had the enthusiasm and the presumption of being young poets ourselves. I went to Dartmouth, and I'd gotten to know Robert Frost somewhat. I was an immense admirer of him then and I still am. At that time, my sense of the tradition, the great tradition of English writing, was poets who wrote in recognizable forms, so that has remained my preference. I have always found the challenge of form to be stimulating to the imagination.

At the time did you perceive of two opposing camps of American poetry?

I never did and still don't really think of them as opposing camps. That was I think a publicity response that kind of stuck when the Allen anthology came out. It was fun to get into debates about poetry and modernism, depending on one's attitude toward meter and rhyme and stanza form and all that. But anyone who would take a position in which poetry has got to be exclusively this or that, would be too narrow. My own point of view has mainly been that writing in forms is a stimulus to the imagination. You're pressing against something that makes it harder to write and for me the primary paradox is that anything that makes it harder to write might make it easier to write well. Attention to received forms only wasn't a conscious intention with the anthology.

Was American poetry distinct from British poetry in the 1950s?

I've always felt that British and American poetry was a single tradition. The Wordsworth tradition in response to nature and the English tradition of writing poetry in celebration of God, or in doubt about divinity, those

206   APPENDICES

issues crossed the ocean and I'd draw a line from Wordsworth to Frost and Wordsworth to Stevens, and to Emerson of course. All in all, it's a healthy dialogue between honoring tradition and understanding that tradition includes variants of what has been done. If you try too hard for newness, I think what you get is eccentricity. One needs to write with one's feelings, not in an embattled state with one's forebears. I think Bloom assumes that no writer can recover from his literary Oedipus complex. I don't think that's true. I think poets can love their sources and models. One of my favorite comments was when Frost was reviewing E. A. Robinson, a formalist: "He has an old-fashioned way of making things new." In my many years of teaching, if I have a complaint, it's that too often students are not sufficiently schooled in what poetry has been in the past. I'm not sympathetic to the doctrinaire approach of creating a dichotomy, and I remember not liking it at the time.

What's your opinion on the so-called anthology wars?

The war of the anthologies was more part of the history of publicity than a real phenomenon. It was unfortunate that there should be a war or cultural divide, with people saying I'm part of this group or that group. I think most good poets discover over the course of a lifetime what technique they can employ and what works for them and what doesn't. I don't think your practice follows your philosophy.

Was there a sense, in the late 1950s, that American poetry needed to be redefined, or was redefining itself, after World War II, and hence the "new" in both the title of your anthology and in The New American Poetry?

There probably was, but that was not my motivating attitude. I just was enthusiastic about what I considered to be variety in American writing. I haven't gone back recently to look at the collection, but I'll bet you that my batting average of included poets is not too bad, and that there were a lot of poets in that anthology who have gone on to have substantial careers. Stevens for example is both traditional and innovative. It doesn't have to be one or the other. Sometimes you want an open effect and sometimes you want it tighter. But for me the blank verse line is very compatible with colloquial diction. I don't think there's a war between high and low diction. They can merge and they can be appropriate under different circumstances.

Your introduction to New Poets of England and America: Second Selection*is quite eloquent and outspoken about how you saw the landscape of American verse. In it, you protest the division of American poetry into camps. You also insist that the poets included in your anthology utilize various modes* of "*experimentation with form.*" *Generally, you seem to imply that the perceived divisions in post-war American poetry are less than accurate. Do you still believe this to be the case? Why do you think these divisions, or the perception of them, have endured?*

When I look back at my own work, there is war poetry and poems in response to the Civil Rights Movement, but I wouldn't think of myself primarily as a social poet. There was one year where my poetry reading itinerary by chance took me to college campuses shortly after Allen Ginsberg had appeared on campus. What seemed to have stayed in the minds of the poets at these schools was Allen telling them "first thought, best thought." That was the formula, and it was one with which I heartily disagreed. The first idea is that the sun revolved around the earth. Not the best idea. Revision is a key aspect of composition. The revisionary imagination is part of the conceptual imagination. The idea there focuses on the definition of inspiration and spontaneity. My basic concept of spontaneity is expressed well in the Yeats poem called "Adam's Curse." That's my central belief: Spontaneity is an effect that comes last. You work to achieve the illusion of spontaneity.

What were the circumstances that led you to publish New Poets of England and America: Second Selection?

I think we did a second because the first edition did so well that the publisher was eager to follow up on its success. Maybe at that point I was responding to what had become the public controversy, the views about poetry being complex and coming out of the tradition and employing many of the formal elements that characterize the history of English and American poetry. That belief has been part of my life from the beginning, I guess. And what I'm remembering is that I used to get asked by people whether teaching took away time and incentive and effort from writing. I would answer that question by saying no, that teaching and writing for me went very well together because the kind of attention that I would give to a poem when teaching it in class provided me with a sense of audience, which was the audience I wanted to address myself, an audience that would appreciate the technical aspects of the poem and the complexity and formal aspects that also conveyed certain ideas. A poem is not just an expression of an opinion but the expression of an opinion or idea held with feeling. That feeling derives greatly from the sound and music of the poem. That's been an attitude I've carried with me through the years. I didn't feel the academic poet thing was a stigma but I do feel there was a turning or an opening toward embracing poetry that was in looser forms.

208 APPENDICES

And I think sometimes that works, but I think that when poets lose the techniques of tradition, there is a loss. There's a loss when poets don't use rhyme and meter and alliteration and all the musical aspects and those that are part of the great tradition of English and American poetry. The generation right before mine was not the generation of Frost, but Berryman and Roethke and Lowell and Richard Wilbur and Howard Nemerov. They are all traditionalists. In Roethke there is some opening of the form, but it's grounded in the tradition of a psychoanalytic understanding of the unconscious mind. Those were my immediate predecessors and among the contemporaries of mine, the poets that I most admire are Wilbur and Mark Strand. I don't know what category you'd put Strand in, but I find in his writing many if not all of the virtues of traditional form with some modifications. I just had the unpleasant experience of receiving a manuscript from a previous student of mine who wanted me to write a blurb. My personal inclination was yes I'd love to do that, but when I read it, it seemed so fragmented, so unsatisfying as a narrative that I couldn't do it. There wasn't enough pleasure or coherence or meaning behind it. It's possible that there's something that I'm missing, that there are some values that I'm not temperamentally tuned into appreciating. And you're right to raise the question of there being a lasting difference in taste and concepts of poetry that might very well go back to the value of the anthologies, and that might make your writing about it worthwhile.

Who won the anthology wars?

Today we have poets who are writing in open form and what we call traditional forms. In that sense both sides won. Nobody knocked out the other, nor would it have made any sense to try to come to a reductive exclusionary point of view.

Appendix V: Interview with Basil and Martha King, Telephone, April 7, 2018

Basil, you created the cover for LeRoi Jones's Preface to a Twenty Volume Suicide Note *as well as several covers for* Yugen. *How did that come about?*

Basil: We came back to New York City in 1959 and by that time Fielding Dawson had met Roi. He came over and said "man you've got to meet this guy, you're really going to love each other." At that time LeRoi was married to Hettie. We went over to their place on a Friday and we didn't leave until Monday morning. The first cover I did for him was for Ron Lowensohn [Ron Lowensohn, *Watermelons*, 1959]. Ron had been a good

APPENDICES   209

friend in San Francisco, so that was the first, then I did a few covers for *Yugen*, and the cover for *Preface to a Twenty Volume Suicide Note*. All the covers I did, I made the cover especially for them. I worked for them, I didn't just hand them something of mine.

That type of collaboration between artists and writers and other creative people seems to have been especially common in those days. Was that the sense you had?

Basil: We were just people with the same interest. And people had different approaches. Jonathan Williams for example wanted to do really beautiful books. With LeRoi and *Yugen*, we'd get together and have coffee and a couple of joints and staple the thing together. We didn't have money. Then with something like The New York Poets Theatre, people would pitch in not because they were going to take it to Broadway, but because it was fun and interesting and there was an energy there.

Martha: Because there were so few of us, there was a real mutual interest. Like Hilda Morley said about New York in the 1930s, if you didn't really want be here, you left. There was nothing here for you. It was the same for us: there was nothing here for us. No one had any interest in art in any commercial way.

Basil: [Adolph] Gottlieb told me he won a prize when he was 24 years old and got $10,000. He said "I thought I'd be set for life." Then he didn't sell a painting for 25 years! But he stayed and he worked. They got married, their wives taught school, they went to Wellfleet for the summer, but they didn't have kids because they said they couldn't afford it. That was the Depression generation.

Martha: When we were in New York in the '50s and early '60s there was a lot of poverty. Scrounging was so possible. We're not talking about lofts with jacuzzis. It was grungy but possible to make do with a part-time job. The Holy Grail was to get on unemployment.

Basil: It was a different life. You'd go down 2nd Avenue and they threw out so much, spinach tops and stuff and you'd pick them up for free. Chicken parts were nine cents a pound. You could make a huge stew for a buck and have people over for dinner. That sort of intimacy bred a lot of exchanges among artists and writers. There was cooperation and collaboration, and life was a lot more communal. Today that's a rarity. People are so paranoid today. You ask to go to someone's studio today and they think you're going to steal their ideas. Once the corporations moved in and starting buying paintings, the whole thing changed.

210 APPENDICES

So yes, there was collaboration. In New York, Frank O'Hara was the catalyst. He had his hands on the first generation and the second generation abstractionists. He was quite marvelous the way he could bring people together. Fortunately, I got to know him very well.

Frank O'Hara was encouraging for you as you transitioned from abstraction to figurative art, is that correct?

Basil: Yes. Frank O'Hara saved my potatoes. When I gave up abstract painting I was 27 or 28 years old and I'd been doing it since I was a teenager at Black Mountain. I was becoming known for it. And I woke up one morning and thought "I don't want to be a third-generation abstract expressionist." I'd seen a fourth-generation Cubist exhibit and it was just ghastly. But then I didn't know what to paint. I went through a year and a half of sitting and not knowing what to do. Then one day I was walking past St. Mark's and thinking "you're a has-been who has never been." Well, there was one store there, a print shop and he sold stationary and things like that. I bought 500 sheets of the cheapest paper possible and I just started drawing circles. I must have drawn about 2000 circles until I drew a flower and then I got back to work. At that time Frank would come over sometimes once a month and see what I was up to.

Right around that time Jay Milder had his show and all of New York went Pop. It was unreal. Everything came down and everything went up. It took quite a while to get there. Frank was very encouraging.

Martha: I've been going through some of his old work, and it's kind of amazing that Baz went through a period where he was minimalist.

Basil: I went up to David McKee's gallery and he said "I've got something to show you." He showed me a painting of two people sitting in a room. He said "who do you think did it?" I said "Franz Kline." And he put up a Kline and there was the structure. There was a room with two people in it, 10 years before he started the black and white. That's where we are as painters I think.

After Black Mountain you initially went to San Francisco before relocating to New York City. Did you have similar experiences there?

Basil: I never really met any painters in San Francisco. [Richard] Diebenkorn and them were quite shut up. I just wanted to start painting. I wasn't writing at the time. I said to Martha "we've got to get back to New York." But the poetry scene was very vital. Spicer, Duncan, Rexroth, Blaser, and others. But Spicer and Duncan snarled at each other. I don't know if it was jealousy or competition. They loved each other but they'd sit there and snarl at each other.

APPENDICES **211**

Allen Ginsberg kept to himself. When I met him he was working at Greyhound. When I got to San Francisco after Black Mountain closed, Creeley had written a letter to Allen saying that I was coming. After I met him he said "I'm reading a poem at a high school in two days, I hope you can come." He read "Howl" for the second time. I still get goose pimples. Rexroth gave him a great introduction.

Martha, I'd like to ask you about a quote from a piece you and Basil wrote about Charles Olson. You wrote: "Charles is my father's age. I always connected them. My father loves Eliotand fears Pound, and Olsonthe opposite, but politically, I call them both jingoists." Could you talk more about this?

Martha: I was connecting my father and Olson and I stick by the word jingoist. There was a romantic concept about America being an exceptional place on earth. That was something they both held very much in their mindset and I'm sure that Olson's interest in politics came out of wanting to influence that, especially during the FDR era. My father was an FDR Democrat too. It is nationalistic, but in a very romantic way, that there's a new world and a new way to be a human being and America's got an edge on it. There was a whole body of intellectuals and artists whose feelings about America were influenced by that.

Paul Metcalf is in that same vein. It's not exactly *Stars and Stripes Forever*. It's a nationalism but a looking back kind of valorization of agricultural values and being close to the earth. Think about Olson's attachment to a town that was foreign to him, Gloucester. I mean, I'm more from Gloucester than he was!

Basil: That was one of the things that absolutely annoyed Charles, that his parents were immigrants. He would not eat leftovers. The whole idea of poverty frightened him.

Basil, in Warp Spasm, *you write: "For a very short time New York City and Black Mountain held the arts in the palms of their hands. But it wasn't my time, it wasn't for me, not then. I saw my commitment." What did you mean by this?*

Martha: You were already feeling the limitations of pure abstract expressionism for you.

Basil: I always felt that my abstract expressionist painting was student work. I was so influenced by Franz and Philip and Mark, I adored them and was very influenced. I worked for Rothko, Motherwell, Gottlieb, Barney Newman, stretching canvas, mixing paint and things like that. But I always felt that I was terribly influenced by them and they weren't completely mine. Even if people told me the opposite, I felt that.

212 APPENDICES

Black Mountain was a sanctuary. Most of the people there were working it out. For one thing they weren't known. The teachers, the professors, Merce and John, Vincente and Albers himself. You could see him working it out and Anni the same way, and Charles was doing that.

Creeley on the other hand came strangely formed. He said "one night I just sat down and it came." He did *For Love* in one night. He said "I had a joint, I sat down and boom. I couldn't stop!" You can't teach anybody to do it that way.

It was a fantastic place because everyone came there from all over and my feeling is, by the time it closed it was ready to close. It had done its job. Because San Francisco was open and New York was open. It did its job. You can't start something like that unless it's absolutely needed.

Were you at Black Mountain for Theatre Piece No. 1?

Basil: They had done it in the spring and I arrived in the fall. They were still talking about it. John and David Tudor later came back and did some wonderful things. David came out immaculately dressed in tails, and sat at the piano. He just sat there for a while, then stood up, bowed and left.

Do you remember when Donald Allen's anthology The New American Poetry *was published in 1960? Did you see the exhibition* The New American Painting, *at MOMA?*

Basil: I saw the show because I saw the show. Don's anthology, well you know, many friends were in it, so it meant a lot to me and to them. I was just busy. I didn't think of it historically in that way. Most of the people in it were pleased, but they weren't ecstatic.

Like Black Mountain, the older it gets, the more important people take it. Black Mountain is becoming a caricature. There was more of a change when abstract expressionists started to get really rich when people were moving out and becoming rich and buying fancy cars. Those were the big changes. The money available for art. Some people weathered it and a lot of people just went downhill with it. In terms of the poetry, it becomes more important now like Black Mountain.

Martha: It wasn't going to change their life the way that being a star painter would change you life so you could buy a house in the Hamptons. The people in *The New American Poetry* didn't suddenly get into *The New Yorker* and *The New York Times*. We still remained on the outside. It was a good thing and exciting, but it didn't really offer a change of life. Maybe some people got offers to teach because of it.

BIBLIOGRAPHY

Adams, Henry. *The Education of Henry Adams.* Boston and New York: Houghton Mifflin Company, 1918.

Alcalay, Ammiel. *A little history.* Los Angeles: Re : public, 2013.

Aldan, Daisy. *A New Folder: Americans, Poems and Drawings.* New York: Folder Editions, 1959.

Alexander, Charles. *Here the Country Lies: Nationalism and the Arts in Twentieth-Century America.* Bloomington: Indian University Press, 1980.

Allen, Donald. *The New American Poetry 1945–1960.* New York: Grove Press, 1960.

———. Donald Allen Collection, MSS 3, Special Collections & Archives, UC San Diego Library.

Allen, Donald and Creeley, Robert, eds. *The New Writing in the USA.* Middlesex: Penguin, 1967.

Allen, Donald and Tallman, Warren, eds. *The Poetics of the New American Poetry.* New York: Grove Press, 1973.

Allen, Donald, and Butterick George, eds. *The Postmoderns: The New American Poetry Revisited.* New York: Grove Press, 1982.

Anderson, Benedict. *Imagined Communities.* London: Verso, 1996.

Anderson, T.J. III. *Notes to Make the Sound Come Right: Four Innovators of Jazz Poetry.* Fayetteville: University of Arkansas Press, 2004.

Andrews, Bruce. "The Poetics of L=A=N=G=U=A=G=E." *UbuWeb.*http://www.ubu.com/papers/andrews.html. April 9, 2018.

© The Author(s), under exclusive license to Springer Nature Switzerland AG 2021
S. Delbos, *The New American Poetry and Cold War Nationalism,*
Modern and Contemporary Poetry and Poetics,
https://doi.org/10.1007/978-3-030-77352-6

214 BIBLIOGRAPHY

Atkin, Emily. "The Sexism of 'Genius.'" *The New Republic*. March 15, 2018. https://newrepublic.com/article/147463/sexism-genius-death-stephen-hawking. April 1, 2018.

Balliett, Whitney. *Collected Works: A Journal of Jazz, 1954–2000*. New York: St. Martin's Press, 2000.

Baraka, Amiri. *The Autobiography of LeRoi Jones*. New York: Freundlich, 1984.

Barolini, Helen. "The Shadowy Lady of the Street of Dark Shops." *Virginia Quarterly Review*. Spring 1998. http://www.vqronline.org/essay/shadowy-lady-street-dark-shops. May 1, 2015.

Belgrad, Daniel. *The Culture of Spontaneity: Improvisation and the Arts in Postwar America*. Chicago: The University of Chicago Press, 1998.

Bernstein, Charles. *A Poetics*. Cambridge: Harvard University Press, 1992.

Bernstein, Charles and Morris, Tracie. "Poetry Needs a Revolution that Goes beyond Style." *LitHub*. February 17, 2017. https://lithub.com/poetry-needs-a-revolution-that-goes-beyond-style/. March 24, 2018.

Bertholf, Robert J. and Gelpi, Albert, eds. *The Letters of Robert Duncan and Denise Levertov*. Stanford: Stanford University Press, 2003.

Bertram, Lillian-Yvonne. "The Whitest Boy Alive: Witnessing Kenneth Goldsmith." *Poetry Foundation*. May 18, 2015. https://www.poetryfoundation.org/harriet/2015/05/the-whitest-boy-alive-witnessing-kenneth-goldsmith. November 18, 2017.

Bidart, Frank and Gewanter, David, eds. *Robert Lowell Collected Poems*. New York: Faber and Faber, 2003.

Blasing, Mutlu Konuk. *Politics and Form in Postmodern Poetry*. Cambridge: Cambridge University Press, 1995.

Boatright, James. "Short Reviews." *Shenandoa* 12, no. 2 (1961): 13.

Bogan, Louise. "Verse." *The New Yorker*. 13 April (1957): 174.

———. "Verse." *The New Yorker*. 29 March (1958): 122–124.

———. "Verse." *The New Yorker*. 8 October (1960): 199–200.

Bohanon, Cecil. "Economic Recovery: Lessons from the Post-World War II Period." *Mercatus Center*. September 10, 2012. http://mercatus.org/publication/economic-recovery-lessons-post-world-war-ii-period. March 27, 2016.

Borzutzky, Daniel. "Delusions of Progress." *Poetry.org*. December 29, 2014. https://www.poetryfoundation.org/harriet/2014/12/delusions-of-progress. November 18, 2017.

Bourdieu, Pierre. *The Field of Cultural Production: Essays on Art and Literature*. New York: Columbia University Press, 1993.

Breslin, Paul. *The Psycho-Political Muse: American Poetry Since the Fifties*. Chicago: University of Chicago Press, 1988.

Brooks, Cleanth and Warren, Robert. *Understanding Poetry*. New York: Holt, 1938.

BIBLIOGRAPHY 215

Brodeur, Michael Andor "For a Singular Poet, an Overdue Fresh Look," *Boston Globe*, Sunday, October 18, 2015, N25.

Brunner, Edward. *Cold War Poetry: The Social Text of the Fifties Poem*. Urbana: University of Illinois Press, 2001.

Bureau of Labor Statistics. CPI Inflation Calculator. http://www.bls.gov/data/inflation_calculator.htm. May 1, 2015.

Butts, William. *Conversations with Richard Wilbur*. Jackson: University Press of Mississippi, 1990.

Calimach, Andrew. "The Beautiful Way of the Samurai: Native Tradition and Hellenic Echo." *The World History of Male Love*. 2008. http://www.gay-art-history.org/gay-history/gay-customs/japan-samurai-male-love/japan-samurai-homosexual-shudo.html. October 28, 2017.

Carlson, Marvin. *Performance: A Critical Introduction*. London: Routledge, 2003.

Carpenter, Humphrey. *A Serious Character: The Life of Ezra Pound*. Boston: Houghton Mifflin, 1988.

Carvel, Cody. "Robert Duncan...A Life in Poetry." *YouTube*. May 28, 2018. www.youtube.com/watch?v=WC1EwgBqEUU. March 15, 2019.

Cecil, David and Tate, Allen, eds. *Modern Verse in English: 1900–1950*. New York: Macmillan, 1958.

Cecire, Natalia. *Experimental: American Literature and the Aesthetics of Knowledge*. Baltimore: Johns Hopkins University Press, 2019.

Chapin, Katherine Garrison. "Fifteen Years of New Writing." *The New Republic* 144, no. 2 (1961): 25.

Chen, Ken. "Authenticity Obsession, or Conceptualism as Minstrel Show." *The Margins*. June 11, 2015. http://aaww.org/authenticity-obsession/. November 18 2017.

Clark, Tom. *Charles Olson: The Allegory of a Poet's Life*. Berkeley: North Atlantic Books, 2000.

Clay, Steven and Phillips, Rodney. *A Secret Location on the Lower East Side: Adventures in Writing, 1960–1980*. New York: The New York Public Library, 1998.

Clifford, James. *Routes: Travel and Translation in the Late Twentieth Century*. Cambridge: Harvard University Press, 1997.

Clippinger, David. "Neither Us nor Them: Poetry Anthologies, Canon Building, and the Silencing of William Bronk." *The Argotist Online*.http://www.argotistonline.co.uk/Clippinger%20essay.htm. December 19, 2016.

———. *The Mind's Landscape: William Bronk and Twentieth-century American Poetry*. Newark: University of Delaware Press, 2006.

Cockcroft, Eva. "Abstract Expressionism: Weapon of the Cold War." *Artforum* 15, no. 10 (1974): 39–41.

Colombo, John Robert. "Short Reviews." *Tamarack Review* 16. (Summer 1960): 22.

216 BIBLIOGRAPHY

Corbett, William. *All Prose: Selected Essays and Reviews*. Brooklyn: Pressed Wafer, 2018.

Corman, Cid. Cid Corman Collection. The Poetry Collection of the University Libraries, University at Buffalo, The State University of New York.

Corso, Gregory. *Gasoline*. San Francisco: City Lights, 1958.

———. "The Literary Revolution in America." *Litterair Paspoort*. 100. Amsterdam. (November 1957): 193–196.

Corso, Gregory and Höllerer, Walter. *Junge Amerikanische Lyrik*. Munich: Hanser, 1961.

Conrad, CA. "Kenneth Goldsmith Says He Is an Outlaw." *Poetry Foundation*. June 1, 2015. https://www.poetryfoundation.org/harriet/2015/06/kenneth-goldsmith-says-he-is-an-outlaw. January 4, 2018.

Cowley, Malcolm. "The Little Magazines Growing Up." *The New York Times*. September 14, 1947. https://www.nytimes.com/1947/09/14/archives/the-little-magazines-growing-up-the-little-magazines.html. April 15, 2018.

———. "The Time of the Rhetoricians." *New World Writing* 5. New York City: The New American Library of World Literature, Inc., 1954.

Creeley, Robert. *A Quick Graph: Collected Notes & Essays*. San Francisco: Four Seasons Foundation, 1970.

———. *Selected Poems of Robert Creeley*. Berkeley: University of California Press, 1991.

Davidson, Michael. *Guys Like Us: Citing Masculinity in Cold War Poetics*. Chicago: University of Chicago Press, 2004.

———. *The San Francisco Renaissance: Poetics and Community at Mid-century*. Cambridge: Cambridge University Press, 1989.

Davis, Douglas M. "Where the Poet Finds Fertile Ground." *The National Observer*. July 11, 1966: 24.

Dewey, Anne and Rifkin, Libbie, eds., *Among Friends: Engendering the Social Site of Poetry*. Iowa City: University of Iowa Press, 2013.

Dewhurst, Robert. *Supplication: Selected Poems of John Wieners*. Seattle: Wave Books, 2015.

Dick, Jennifer K. "The Pros and Cons of *Against Expression: An Anthology of Conceptual Writing*." *Drunken Boat*. http://www.drunkenboat.com/db15/against-expression.html. April 20, 2018.

Dickey, James. "The Death and Keys of the Censor." *The Sewanee Review* 69, no.2 (1961): 318–332.

Diggory, Terence. *Encyclopedia of the New York School Poets*. New York: Facts on File, 2009.

Droitcour, Brian. "Reading and Rumor: The Problem with Kenneth Goldsmith." *Art in America*. March 8, 2015. http://www.artinamericamagazine.com/news-features/news/reading-and-rumor-the-problem-with-kenneth-goldsmith/. December 30, 2017.

BIBLIOGRAPHY 217

Duberman, Martin. *Black Mountain: An Exploration in Community*. Evanston: Northwestern University Press, 2009.

Duncan, Robert. *Collected Essays and Other Prose*. Ed. James Maynard. Berkeley: University of California Press, 2014.

———. *The Collected Later Poems and Plays*. Ed. Peter Quartermain. Berkeley: University of California Press, 2014.

———. *The H.D. Book*. eds. Michael Boughn and Victor Coleman. Berkeley: University of California Press, 2011.

———. Robert Duncan Collection. The Poetry Collection of the University Libraries, University at Buffalo, The State University of New York.

Dworkin, Craig. "The Fate of Echo." *Against Expression: An Anthology of Conceptual Writing*, ed. Craig Dworkin and Kenneth Goldsmith. Evanston: Northwestern University Press, 2011.

———. *Introduction to the UbuWeb Anthology of Conceptual Writing. UbuWeb*. http://www.ubu.com/concept/. December 31, 2018.

Edmond, Murray. "Trade and True: Anthologies Fifty Years after Donald Allen's *The New American Poetry*." *ka mate ka ora: a new zealand journal of poetry and poetics*. March 2010, http://www.nzepc.auckland.ac.nz/kmko/09/ka_mate09_edmond.pdf. February 8, 2019

Ellingham, Lewis and Killian, Kevin. *Poet Be Like God: Jack Spicer and the San Francisco Renaissance*. Hanover: Wesleyan University Press, 1998.

Emerson, Ralph Waldo. *Essays and Lectures*. New York: Viking Press, 1983.

Epstein, Andrew. *Attention Equals Life: The Pursuit of the Everyday in Contemporary Poetry and Culture*. Oxford: Oxford University Press, 2016.

———. "Frank O'Hara's 'For Bob Rauschenberg, on his Birthday.'" *Locus Solus: The New York* School Poets. October 22, 2016. https://newyorkschoolpoets. wordpress.com/2016/10/22/frank-oharas-for-bob-rauschenberg-on-his-birthday/. March 20, 2018.

Evans, Steve. "After Patriarchal Poetry: Feminism and the Contemporary Avant-Garde. Introductory Note." *differences: A Journal of Feminist Cultural Studies*. 12.2 (Summer 2001): i.

Farago, Jason. "A Flag Is a Flag Is a Flag." *The New York Review of Books*. March 22, 2018. http://www.nybooks.com/articles/2018/03/22/jasper-johns-flag-is-a-flag/. March 23, 2018.

Fenton, James A. "The Writer as Professor." *New World Writing 7*. New York City: The New American Library of World Literature, Inc., 1955.

Field, Douglas. *American Cold War Culture*. New York: Columbia University Press, 2006.

Field, Edward. Personal Interview. Email. January 14, 2014.

Filreis, Alan. *Counter-Revolution of the Word: The Conservative Attack on Modern Poetry 1945–1960*. Chapel Hill: University of North Carolina Press, 2008.

218 BIBLIOGRAPHY

———. "Neither Us Nor Them." *Al Filreis Blog*. September 18, 2007. http://afilreis.blogspot.com/2007/09/neither-us-nor-them.html. April 18, 2018.

Flood, Alison. "US poet defends reading of Michael Brown autopsy report as a poem." *The Guardian*. March 17, 2015. https://www.theguardian.com/books/2015/mar/17/michael-brown-autopsy-report-poem-kenneth-goldsmith. December 31, 2017.

Foster, Edward Halsey. *Understanding the Black Mountain Poets*. Columbia: University of South Carolina Press, 1995.

Fox, Margalit. "Amiri Baraka, Polarizing Poet and Playwright, Dies at 79." *The New York Times*. January 9, 2014. https://www.nytimes.com/2014/01/10/arts/amiri-baraka-polarizing-poet-and-playwright-dies-at-79.html. January 31, 2017.

Franks, Pamela. *The Tiger's Eye: The Art of a Magazine*. New Haven: Yale University Press, 2002.

Fukuyama, Francis. "Against Identity Politics: The New Tribalism and the Crisis of Democracy." *Foreign Affairs*. September/October 2018. https://www.foreignaffairs.com/articles/americas/2018-08-14/against-identity-politics-tribalism-francis-fukuyama. February 1, 2019.

———. *Identity: Contemporary Identity Politics and the Struggle for Recognition*. London: Profile Books, 2018.

Ginsberg, Allen. *Howl and Other Poems*. San Francisco: City Lights, 1956.

Gizzi, Peter. *The House that Jack Built: The Collected Lectures of Jack Spicer*. Hannover, NH: Wesleyan University Press, 1998.

Glass, Lorin. *Counterculture Colophon. Grove Press, The Evergreen Review, and the Incorporation of the Avant-Garde*. Stanford: Stanford University Press, 2013.

Goddard, J.R. "There Are No Schools – Just Kindergartens." *The Village Voice*. May 11 (1961): 9.

Golding, Alan. *From Outlaw to Classic: Canons in American Poetry*. Madison: University of Wisconsin Press, 1995.

———. "*The New American Poetry* Revisited, Again." *Contemporary Literature* 39.2 (1998): 187

Goldsmith, Kenneth. "Paragraphs on Conceptual Writing. *Epc.Buffalo.edu*. http://epc.buffalo.edu/authors/goldsmith/conceptual_paragraphs.html. November 18, 2017.

———. Seminar at The Academy of Fine Arts in Prague. January 29, 2019.

———. *Uncreative Writing*. New York: Columbia University Press, 2011.

Gooch, Brad. *City Poet: The Life and Times of Frank O'Hara*. New York: Harper, 2014.

Goodman, Paul. "Advance Guard Writing, 1900–1950." *Kenyon Review*, Summer, 1951. JSTOR. http://www.jstor.org/discover/10.2307/4333252. January 23, 2014.

Greene, Roland, et al., eds. *The Princeton Encyclopedia of Poetry & Poetics.* Princeton: Princeton University Press, 2012.

Guilbaut, Serge. *How New York Stole the Idea of Modern Art.* Chicago: University of Chicago Press, 1985.

Guillory, John. *Cultural Capital: The Problem of Literary Canon Formation.* Chicago: University of Chicago Press, 1993.

Hall, Donald, ed. *American Poetry.* London: Faber and Faber, 1969.

———. *Claims for Poetry.* Ann Arbor: University of Michigan Press, 1982.

———. *Contemporary American Poetry.* Harmondsworth: Penguin, 1962.

———. *Death to the Death of Poetry.* Ann Arbor: University of Michigan Press, 1997.

———. Personal Interview. Email. February 11, 2014.

———. *Poetry and Ambition: Essays 1982–1988.* Ann Arbor: University of Michigan Press, 1988.

Hall, et al, eds. *The New Poets of England and America.* New York: Meridian Books, 1957.

Hall, Donald and Pack, Robert. *New Poets of England and America: A Second Selection.* Cleveland: The World Publishing, 1962.

Hallberg, Robert Von. *American Poetry and Culture 1945–1980.* Cambridge: Harvard University Press, 1988.

Hamil, Sam and Morrow, Bradford. *The Collected Poems of Kenneth Rexroth.* Port Townsend: Copper Canyon Press, 2003.

Hammer, Langdon. *James Merrill: Life and Art.* New York: Knopf, 2015.

Hampson, Robert and Montgomery Will. *Frank O'Hara Now: New Essays on the New York Poet.* Liverpool: Liverpool University Press.

Hegel, Georg Wilhelm Friedrich. *On Christianity: Early Theological Writings.* Trans., T. M. Knox. New York: Harper & Brothers, 1961.

Helmore, Edward. "Gone with the Wind tweeter says she is being shunned by US arts Institutions," *The Guardian.* June 25, 2015. http://www.theguardian. com/books/2015/jun/25/gone-with-the-wind-tweeter-shunned-arts-institutions-vanessa-place. June 26, 2015.

Hentoff, Nat. *At the Jazz Band Ball: Sixty Years on the Jazz Scene.* Berkeley: University of California Press, 2010.

Hicock, Bethany. *Elizabeth Bishop's Brazil.* Charlottesville: University of Virginia Press, 2016.

Higgs, Christopher. "You Take Your Love Where You Get it: An Interview with Kenneth Goldsmith." *Paris Review.* April 2013. http://www.theparisreview. org/blog/2013/04/02/youtake-your-love-where-you-get-it-an-interview-with-kenneth-goldsmith/, January 3, 2018.

Hindi, Noor. "Fuck Your Lecture on Craft, My People Are Dying." https://www. poetryfoundation.org/poetrymagazine/poems/154658/fuck-your-lecture-on-craft-my-people-are-dying. May 15, 2021.

220 BIBLIOGRAPHY

Hobbs, Stuart D. *The End of the American Avant Garde*. New York: New York University Press, 1997.

Hoover, Paul. *Postmodern American Poetry: A Norton Anthology*. New York: W.W. Norton, 2013.

Hong, Cathy Park. "Delusions of Whiteness in the Avant-Garde." *Lana Turner Journal*. http://www.lanaturnerjournal.com/print-issue-7-contents/delusions-of-whiteness-in-the-avant-garde. May 2, 2015.

———. "There's a New Movement in American Poetry and It's Not Kenneth Goldsmith." *The New Republic*. October 1, 2015. https://newrepublic.com/article/122985/new-movement-american-poetry-not-kenneth-goldsmith. October 28, 2017.

Horowitz, Michael. *Children of Albion: Poetry of the Underground in Britain*. London: Penguin, 1969.

Iber, Patrick. "Literary Magazines for Socialists Funded by the CIA, Ranked." *The Awl*, August 24, 2015. https://www.theawl.com/2015/08/literary-magazines-for-socialists-funded-by-the-cia-ranked/. January 6, 2018.

Ifill, Sherrilyn. "It's time to face the facts: Racism is a national security issue." *The Washington Post*. December 18, 2018. https://www.washingtonpost.com/opinions/its-time-to-face-the-facts-racism-is-a-national-security-issue/2018/12/18/f9746466-02e8-11e9-b5df-5d3874f1ac36_story.html?utm_term=.839176a9259b. March 21, 2018.

Jarman, Mark and Mason, David. *Rebel Angels: 25 Poets of the New Formalism*. Ashland: Story Line Press, 1998.

Johnson, David K. *The Lavender Scare: The Cold War Persecution of Gays and Lesbians in the Federal Government*. Chicago: University of Chicago Press, 2004.

Johnson, Kent. "Dispatch #20 – Unfree poetry for brave Marxists." *Dispatches from the Poetry Wars*. September 14, 2017. https://www.dispatchespoetry-wars.com/dispatches/dispatch-20-unfree-poetry-brave-marxists/. October 15, 2017.

Johnson, Nicholas. "Gael Turnbull: Internationalist poet whose Migrant Press pointed the way to the British poetry renaissance." *The Independent*. July 7, 2004. https://www.independent.co.uk/news/obituaries/gael-turnbull-550057.html. March 12, 2017.

Jones, LeRoi. "Putdown of the Whore of Babylon." *Yugen 7 (1960): 4*.

Juliette Lee, Sueyeun. "Shock and Blah: Offensive Postures in 'Conceptual' Poetry and the Traumatic Stuplime." *Evening Will Come*. May 2014. http://www.thevolta.org/ewc41-sjlee-p1.html. December 30, 2017.

Kalaidjian, Walter. *Languages of Liberation: The Social Text in Contemporary American Poetry*. New York: Columbia University Press, 1989.

Kaufmann, David. *Reading Uncreative Writing: Conceptualism, Expression and the Lyric*. Cham: Palgrave Macmillan, 2017.

BIBLIOGRAPHY 221

Kennedy, John F. "Radio and television address on civil rights, 11 June 1963." John F. Kennedy Presidential Library and Museum. http://www.jfklibrary.org/asset-viewer/archives/JFKPOF/045/JFKPOF-045-005. February 26, 2018.

Kimmelman, Burt. "*The New American Poetry*'s Objectivist Legacy: Linguistic Skepticism, the Signifier and Material Language." *The New American Poetry 50 Years Later*, ed. John R. Woznicki. Lanham, Lehigh University Press, 2014.

———. "Who is There?: Revisiting Michael Brown's Autopsy Report and Reassessing Conceptual Poetry Two Years after 'Interrupt 3.'" *Dispatches from the Poetry Wars*. August 25, 2017. http://dispatchespoetrywars.com/commentary/2017/08/revisiting-michael-browns-autopsy-report-reassessing-conceptual-poetry-two-years-interrupt-3-burt-kimmelman/. January 25, 2018.

King, Basil. Personal Interview. Telephone. April 7, 2018.

King, Martha. "Three Months in 1955: A Memoir of Black Mountain College." *Jacket 2*. 2010. http://jacketmagazine.com/40/king-martha-black-mountain.shtml. March 23, 2018.

———. Personal Interview. Telephone. April 7, 2018.

Kirchick, James. "The Dark History of Anti-Gay Innuendo." *Politico*. February 13, 2019. https://www.politico.com/magazine/story/2019/02/13/the-dark-history-of-anti-gay-innuendo-224930. February 14, 2019.

Klein, Marcus. *Foreigners: The Making of American Literature 1900–1940*. Chicago: University of Chicago Press, 1981.

Klíma, Ivan. *The Spirit of Prague*. London: Granta, 1994.

Krenn, Michael L. *Fall-out Shelters for the Human Spirit: American Art and the Cold War*. Chapel Hill: University of North Carolina Press, 2005.

Kyger, Joanne. Personal Interview. Email. January 13, 2014.

Leary, Paris and Kelly, Robert, eds. *A Controversy of Poets*. Garden City: Anchor Books, 1965.

Lee, David Neil. *The Battle of the Five Spot: Ornette Coleman and the New York Jazz Field*. Hamilton: Wolsack and Wynn, 2014.

Lehman, David. *The Last Avant-Garde*. New York: Anchor Books, 1995.

Lennox, Sara. "Constructing Femininity in the Early Cold War Era." The University of Michigan Press. https://www.press.umich.edu/pdf/0472113844-ch4.pdf. March 20, 2018

Lerner, Rachel Katz. "Rexroth's 'The Dragon and the Unicorn." *Jacket 2*, December 24, 2012. http://jacket2.org/article/rexroths-dragon-and-unicorn. September 20, 2015.

Levertov, Denise. *New & Selected Essays*. New York: New Directions, 1992.

Levertov, Denise and Williams, William Carlos. *The Letters of Denise Levertov and William Carlos Williams*. Christopher MacGowan, ed. New York: New Directions, 1998.

222 BIBLIOGRAPHY

Lhamon, W.T. *Deliberate Speed: The Origins of a Cultural Style in the American 1950s*. Cambridge: Harvard University Press, 1990.

Lipton, Lawrence. *The Holy Barbarians*. New York: Julian Messner, 1959.

Litweiler, John. *Ornette Coleman: A Harmolodic Life*. New York: William Morrow and Company, 1993.

Logan, William. "Guys and Dove." *The New Criterion*. June 2012. https://www.newcriterion.com/issues/2012/6/guys-dove. April 18, 2018.

Longenbach, James. *Modern Poetry After Modernism*. Oxford: Oxford University Press, 1997.

Low, Trisha. "On Being-Hated: Conceptualism, the Mongrel Coalition, the House That Built Me." *Open Space*. May 20, 2015. https://openspace.sfmoma.org/2015/05/on-being-hated-conceptualism-the-mongrel-coalition-the-house-that-built-me/. December 28, 2017.

Lowell, Robert. "National Book Award Acceptance Speech." *The National Book Awards*. http://www.nationalbook.org/nbaacceptspeech_rlowell.html#.Vllc7_mrTIU. January 20, 2015

Lowenfels, Walter. "Poetry and Politics." *Liberation*. June (1959): 12.

Lucas, John. "Gael Turnbull: Poet and doctor who promoted the cause on both sides of the Atlantic." *The Guardian*. July 12, 2004. https://www.theguardian.com/news/2004/jul/12/guardianobituaries.booksobituaries. March 12, 2017.

Luce, Henry. *The American Century*. New York: Farrar and Rinehart, 1941.

Lynes, Russell. "Highbrow, Lowbrow, Middlebrow." *Harper's*. http://harpers.org/archive/1949/02/highbrow-lowbrow-middlebrow/. May 1, 2015.

Macdonald, Dwight. "Masscult and Midcult." *The Partisan Review* 27, no. 4 (1960): 203–233.

Mariani, Paul. *William Carlos Williams: A New World Naked*. New York: Norton, 1981.

Maud, Ralph. *Poet to Publisher: Charles Olson's Correspondence with Donald Allen*. Vancouver: Talonbooks, 2003.

Mauren, Peter. *Easy Essays*. *Easyessays.org*. http://www.easyessays.org. May 15, 2015.

May, Elaine Tyler. *Homeward Bound: American Families in the Cold War Era*. New York: Basic Books, 1988.

May, Lary. *Recasting America: Culture and Politics in the Age of Cold War*. Chicago: University of Chicago Press, 1989.

McCaffery, Steve. *North of Intention: Critical Writings 1973–1986*. New York: Roof Books, 2000.

McCormack, Tom. "The 1913 Armory Show: America's First Art War. *Art 21*. http://www.art21.org/texts/the-culture-wars-redux/essay-the-1913-armory-show-americas-first-art-war. May 1, 2015.

McGee, Micki. *Yaddo: Making American Culture*. New York: Columbia University Press, 2008.

BIBLIOGRAPHY 223

McHugh, Vincent. "What IS That New, Unlabeled Streak Across the Sky Saying?" *San Francisco Sunday Chronicle* (San Francisco, CA), June 12, 1960.

McReynolds, David. "After the Beat Generation: Hipsters Unleashed." *Liberation*, June (1959): 8.

Merrill, Thomas F. "'The Kingfishers:' Charles Olson's 'Marvelous Maneuver.'" *Contemporary Literature*. 17.4 (Autumn, 1976) 506.

Messerli, Douglas. "'Language' Poetries." *The PIP Blog*. February 24, 2013. http://pippoetry.blogspot.com/2013/02/language-poetries.html. April 15, 2018.

Meyer, Steven P. and Steinberg, Jeffrey. "The Congress for Cultural Freedom: Making the Postwar World Safe for Fascist 'Kulturkampf.' *The Executive Review*.http://www.larouchepub.com/other/2004/site_packages/3125ccf_kulturkampf.html. January 6, 2018.

Mills, C. Wright. *White Collar: The American Middle Classes.* Oxford: Oxford University Press, 1956.

Messerli, Douglas. *From the Other Side of the Century: A New American Poetry 1960–1990.* Los Angeles: Sun & Moon Press, 1994.

Mossin, Andrew. *Male Subjectivity and Poetic Form in "New American" Poetry.* New York: Palgrave, 2010.

Monod, David. "He's a Cripple an' Needs my Love: Porgy and Bess as Cold War Propaganda." Giles Scott-Smith and Hans Krabbendam, eds. *The Cultural Cold War in Western Europe.* London: Frank Cass, 2003.

Monroe, Harriet. "Colonialism Again." *Poetry*. X. May, 1917. 94. http://www.poetryfoundation.org/poetrymagazine/browse/10/2#!/20571230/2. March 23, 2015.

Museum of Modern Art. *The New American Painting as Shown in Eight European Countries 1958–1959.* New York: Museum of Modern Art, 1959.

Myers, Marc. *Why Jazz Happened.* Berkeley: University of California Press, 2013.

Nealon, Christopher. *The Matter of Capital: Poetry and Crisis in the American Century.* Cambridge: Harvard University Press, 2011.

Nelson, Deborah. *Pursuing Privacy in Cold War America.* New York: Columbia University Press, 2001.

O'Hara, Frank. "Bob Rauschenberg," *ARTnews* 53.9 (January 1955): 47.

———. *The Collected Poems of Frank O'Hara.* ed. Donald Allen Berkeley: University of California Press, 1995.

———. "Personism: A Manifesto," *Yugen* 7. 1961, 27–29.

———. *Selected Poems.* New York: Alfred A. Knopf, 2008.

———. *The Selected Poems of Frank O'Hara.* New York: Vintage Books, 1974.

Olson, Charles. The Charles Olson Research Collection. Archives & Special Collections at the Thomas J. Dodd Research Center. University of Connecticut Libraries.

224 BIBLIOGRAPHY

————. "Projective Verse." *The New American Poetry*. Ed. Donald Allen. New York: Grove Press, 1960.

————. *The Maximus Poems*. Ed. George Butterick. Berkeley: University of California Press, 1980.

Orr, David. "Michael Derrick Hudson Posed as a 'Yi-Fen Chou': Did the Name Sell His Poem?" *The New York Times*. September 9, 2015. http://www.nytimes.com/2015/09/10/books/michael-derrick-hudson-posed-as-a-yi-fen-chou-did-the-name-sell-his-poem.html?_r=0. September 11, 2015.

Orton, Fred. *Figuring Jasper Johns*. London: Reaktion Books, 1994.

Orwell, George. "Notes on Nationalism." http://orwell.ru/library/essays/nationalism/english/e_nat. April 21, 2016.

Parkinson, Thomas. "A Look at American Poetry Since 1945: Some Funny, Some Satiric and Many from San Francisco." *San Francisco Examiner* (San Francisco, CA), July 10, 1960.

Pearce, Roy Harvey. *The Continuity of American Poetry*. Princeton: Princeton University Press, 1961.

Perelman, Bob. "On Don Allen, 'The New American Poetry.'" *Jacket*. https://jacket2.org/article/don-allen-new-american-poetry. October 31, 2013.

Perloff, Marjorie. "Avant-Garde Tradition and Individual Talent: The Case of Language Poetry." *Dans Revue française d'études américaines*.https://www.cairn.info/revue-francaise-d-etudes-americaines-2005-1-page-117.htm#no3. April 15, 2018.

————. *Frank O'Hara: Poet among Painters*. Chicago: University of Chicago Press, 1977.

————. "Poetry on the Brink." May 18, 2012. The Boston Review. http://bostonreview.net/forum/poetry-brink. December 31, 2017.

————. "'Transparent Selves:' The Poetry of John Ashbery and Frank O'Hara." *The Yearbook of English Studies*. Vol. 8. American Literature Special Number (1978): 171–196.

————. *Unorginal Genius: Poetry by other Means in the New Century*. Chicago: University of Chicago Press, 2010.

————. "Whose New American Poetry?" November 13, 2013. http://epc.buffalo.edu/authors/perloff/anth.html. November 17, 2017.

Perez, Craig Santos. *The Poetry Foundation*. April 14, 2010. "Whitewashing American Hybrid Aesthetics." https://www.poetryfoundation.org/harriet/2010/04/whitewashing-american-hybrid-aesthetics. December 20, 2017.

Place, Vanessa. "No More." *Poetry.org*. March 2013. https://www.poetryfoundation.org/poetrymagazine/poems/56142/no-more. November 18, 2017.

Plagens, Peter. "Whose Art Is it Anyway?" *The Nation*. October 12, 2006. https://www.thenation.com/article/whose-art-it-anyway/. January 9, 2018.

Podhoretz, Norman. "The Know-Nothing Bohemians." *Partisan Review*. Vol. 25 no. 2. (Spring 1958): 305–318.

BIBLIOGRAPHY 225

Pound, Ezra. *Literary Essays of Ezra Pound*. New York: New Directions Publishing.

———. *The Cantos of Ezra Pound*. New York: New Directions 1993.

Quinn, Justin. *Between Two Fires: Transnationalism and Cold War Poetry*. Oxford: Oxford University Press, 2015.

Rasula, Jed. *American Poetry Wax Museum: Reality Effects 1940–1990*. Urbana, IL: NCTE, 1996.

Ramazani, Jahan. *A Transnational Poetics*. Chicago: University of Chicago Press, 2009.

———. "Poetry and Race: An Introduction." *New Literary History* 50, no. 4 (2019): vii–xxxvii. doi:https://doi.org/10.1353/nlh.2019.0050.

Reynolds, David S. *Walt Whitman's America: A Cultural Biography*. New York: Alfred A. Knopf, 1995.

Rexroth, Kenneth. *An Autobiographical Novel*. New York: New Directions, 1991.

———. "Jazz Poetry." *Bureau of Public Secrets*. http://www.bopsecrets.org/rexroth/essays/jazz-poetry.htm. March 23, 2018.

———. *The Complete Poems of Kenneth Rexroth*. Port Townsend: Copper Canyon Press, 2003.

———. *The New British Poets*. New York: New Directions, 1947.

———. *The View Outside the Window: Selected Essays*. New York: New Directions, 1987.

———. "Rukeyser: A Partisan of Love," *Los Angeles Times* (Los Angeles, CA), March 2, 1989.

———. "Some Thoughts on Jazz as Music, as Revolt, as Mystique." Bureau of Public Secrets. http://www.bopsecrets.org/rexroth/jazz.htm. November 22, 2013.

———. "The New American Poetry." *Bop Secrets*. http://www.bopsecrets.org/rexroth/essays/american-poetry.htm. October 31, 2013.

Riach, Alan. "What Can We Learn from Ed Dorn?" *The National*. April 1, 2016. www.thenational.scot/culture/alan-riach-what-can-we-learn-from-edward-dorn.15780. April 1, 2016.

Rifkin, Libbie. *Career Moves: Olson, Creeley, Zukofsky, Berrigan, and the American Avant-garde*. Madison: University of Wisconsin Press, 2000.

Richman, Robert. *The Direction of Poetry: An Anthology of Rhymed and Metered Verse Written in the English Language Since 1975*. Boston: Houghton Mifflin, 1988.

Roland, Philip. "In Conversation with Cid Corman." *Flashpoint Mag*. September 19, 2000. http://www.flashpointmag.com/corman1.htm. October 31, 2013.

Rosenburg, Harold. "The American Action Painters." *Art News* 51, no. 8 (1952): 22

Ross, Clifford, ed. *Abstract Expressionism: Creators and Critics*. New York: Harry N. Abrams, Inc., 1990.

Rosset, Barney and Allen, Donald, eds. *The Evergreen Review* 1, no. 1 (1957).

226 BIBLIOGRAPHY

Rosset, Barney. *Evergreen Review* 1, no. 2 (1957).

―――. *Evergreen Review* 1, no. 3 (1957).

―――. *Evergreen Review* 1, no. 4 (1957).

Rother, James. "Anthology Wars." *Contemporary Poetry Review.* http://www.cprw.com/Rother/newengland2.htm. October 31, 2013.

Rubin, Andrew N. *Archives of Authority: Empire, Culture and the Cold War.* Princeton: Princeton University Press, 2012.

Russo, Linda. "The Limited Scope of the Recuperative Model: A Context for Reading Joanne Kyger." *Jacket* 11. April 2000. www.jacketmagazine.com/11/kyger-russo.html. October 23, 2017.

Sanders, Katharine Elain. "So What Exactly Is Conceptual Writing: An Interview with Kenneth Goldsmith." *BOMB Magazine.* October 2, 2009. https://bombmagazine.org/articles/so-what-exactly-is-conceptual-writing-an-interview-with-kenneth-goldsmith/. April 22, 2018.

Sandler, Irving. *A Sweeper Up after Artists.* New York: Thames and Hudson, 2012.

―――. *The Triumph of American Painting: A History of Abstract Expressionism.* New York: Harper & Row, 1970.

―――. *Abstract Expressionism and the American Experience: A Reevaluation.* New York: Hudson Hills, 2009.

Sapolsky, Robert. "This Is Your Brain on Nationalism: The Biology of Us and Them." *Foreign Affairs.* March/April (2019): 47

Saunders, Stonor Frances. *The Cultural Cold War: The CIA and the World of Arts and Letters.* New York: The New Press, 2001.

―――. "Modern Art Was CIA Weapon." *The Independent.* October 22, 1995. http://www.independent.co.uk/news/world/modern-art-was-cia-weapon-1578808.html. October 31, 2013.

Schneider, David. *Crowded by Beauty: The Life and Zen of Poet Philip Whalen.* Oakland: University of California Press, 2015.

Schugurensky, Daniel. "1940: Bertrand Russell Unwelcome to Teach in New York." *History of Education: Selected Moments of the 20th Century.* http://schugurensky.faculty.asu.edu/moments/1940russell.html. October 28, 2017.

Schweitzer, Andras. "This isn't the start of a new cold war – the first one never ended." *The Guardian.* December 13, 2016. https://www.theguardian.com/commentisfree/2016/dec/13/cold-war-never-ended-west-russia. March 12, 2018.

Shapiro, Alan. "The New Formalism." JSTOR. http://www.jstor.org/discover/10.2307/1343578. June 21, 2014.

Shapiro, Harvey. "Rebellious Mythmakers." *The New York Times Book Review.* Aug 28 (1960): 6

Shaw, Lytle. *Frank O'Hara: The Poetics of Coterie.* Iowa City: University of Iowa Press, 2006.

BIBLIOGRAPHY   227

Shockley, Evie. "Shifting the (Im)balance: Race and the Poetry Canon." *The Boston Review.* June 6, 2013. http://bostonreview.net/poetry/shifting-imbalance. January 3, 2018.

Sigler, Jeremy. "A Conversation With Marjorie Perloff." *Tablet Magazine.* April 1, 2019. https://www.tabletmag.com/jewish-arts-and-culture/282087/marjorie-perloff. April 2, 2019

Silliman, Ron, "Four Contexts for Three Poems," *Conjunctions* 49 (2007): 298.

———. *In the American Tree.* Orono: National Poetry Foundation, 1986.

———. *The New Sentence.* San Francisco: Roof, 2003.

———. "On Robert Duncan, The Opening of the Field." *Jacket 2.* https://jacket2.org/article/robert-duncan-opening-field. December 24, 2013.

———. *Silliman's Blog.* July 7, 2010. http://ronsilliman.blogspot.com/2010/07/i-know-whenever-i-use-phrase-school-of.html. December 30, 2017.

———. "The World of Poetry is Changing." *Silliman's Blog.* June 10, 2013. http://ronsilliman.blogspot.com/2013/06/the-world-of-poetry-is--changing.html. December 24, 2013.

Silverberg, Mark. *The New York School Poets and the Neo-Avant-Garde: Between Radical Art and Radical Chic.* New York: Routledge, 2010.

Simon, John. "Sleight of Foot." *Audit* I.6 (1960): 3.

Smith, Rod, Baker, Peter and Harris, Kaplan. *The Selected Letters of Robert Creeley.* Berkeley: University of California Press, 2013.

Spicer, Jack. *My Vocabulary Did This to Me: The Collected Poetry of Jack Spicer.* eds. Peter Gizzi and Kevin Killian. Middletown: Wesleyan University Press, 2008.

———. *One Night Stand and Other Poems.* San Francisco: Gray Fox Press, 1980.

Stearns, Harold. *Civilization in the United States: An Inquiry by Thirty Americans.* New York: Harcourt, Brace and Company, 1922.

Steele, Timothy. *Missing Measures: Modern Poetry and the Revolt Against Meter.* Fayetteville: University of Arkansas Press, 1990.

Stefans, Brian Kim. "Open Letter to *The New Yorker.*" *Arras.net.* October 4, 2015. http://www.arras.net/fscIII/?p=2467. November 18, 2017.

Steinberg, Leo. *Other Criteria.* New York: Oxford University Press, 1972.

Stevens, Mark and Swan, Annalyn. *De Kooning: An American Master.* New York: Alfred A. Knopf, 2004.

Stewart, Michael Seth. *Stars Seen in Person: The Selected Journals of John Wieners.* San Francisco: City Lights Books, 2015.

Stich, Sidra. *Made in U.S.A. An Americanization in Modern Art, the '50s and '60s.* Berkeley: University of California Press, 1987.

Stoltzfus, Ben. *The Target: Alain Robbe-Grillet, Jasper Johns.* Cranbury: Rosemont, 2006.

Swensen, Cole and St. John, David, eds. *American Hybrid.* New York: W.W. Norton, 2009.

Talese, Gay. *Thy Neighbor's Wife.* Garden City: Doubleday, 1980.

228 BIBLIOGRAPHY

Tarn, Nathanial. "Is There, Currently, an American Poetry?. Republished in *Dispatches from the Poetry Wars*. March 14, 2019. https://www.dispatchespoetrywars.com/wp-content/uploads/2019/03/Tarn-Is-there-an-American-Poetry-1986-red.pdf. April 22, 2019.

Thomson, Ian. "Cold War Dante: How a Medieval Christian Poet Inspired a Texan, Neo-Dadaist Maverick." *Times Literary Supplement*. September 15, 2017, 5.

Torgerson, Eric. "Cold War in Poetry: Notes of a Conscientious Objector." *The American Poetry Review* (July/August 1982): 31.

Torra, Joseph. "A Formal Rack/-et": On Stephen Jonas' Exercises for Ear." *Stylus: The Poetry Room Blog*. March 2, 2015. http://woodberrypoetryroom.com/?p=736. March 17, 2018.

Trenin, Dmitri. "Welcome to Cold War II." *Foreign Policy*. March 4, 2014. https://foreignpolicy.com/2014/03/04/welcome-to-cold-war-ii/. January 9, 2018.

Tooze, Adam. "Is this the end of the American century?: America Pivots." *The London Review of Books*. April 4, 2019. https://www.lrb.co.uk/v41/n07/adam-tooze/is-this-the-end-of-the-american-century. April 5, 2019.

Turnbull, Gael. "A Visit to WCW: September, 1958." *The Massachusetts Review*. 3.3 (Winter 1962): 297–300.

———. *While Breath Persist*. Erin, Ontario: The Porcupine's Quill, 1992.

Untermeyer, Louis. *Modern American Poetry*. http://www.bartleby.com/104/1000.html. December 13, 2014.

Vendler, Helen. "Are these the Poets to Remember?." *New York Review of Books*. November 24, 2011. http://www.nybooks.com/articles/2011/11/24/are-these-poems-remember/. December 31, 2018.

———. *The Music of What Happens: Poems, Poets, Critics*. Cambridge: Harvard University Press, 1988.

Von Eschen, Penny M. *Satchmo Blows up the World: Jazz Ambassadors Play the Cold War*. Cambridge MA: Harvard University Press, 2004.

Wagstaff, Christopher. *A Poet's Mind: Collected Interviews with Robert Duncan, 1960–1985*. Berkeley: North Atlantic Books, 2012.

Wagner, Geoffrey. "The New American Painting." *The Antioch Review*. 14. 1. Spring, 1954. 3–13. JSTOR. http://www.jstor.org/discover/10.2307/4609685. January 5, 2013.

Wakoski, Diane. "Picketing the Zeitgeist." *The American Book Review*. 8.4 (May–June 1986): 3.

Wald, Alan. *American Night: The Literary Left in the Era of the Cold War*. Chapel Hill: University of North Carolina Press, 2012.

Walsh, Chad. "The war between Iambs and Ids." *Book Week*. July 26, 1964: 9.

Wang, Dorothy J. "From Jim-Crow to 'Color-Blind' Poetics: Race and the So-Called Avant-Garde." *The Boston Review*. March 10, 2015. http://bostonreview.net/poetry/dorothy-wang-race-poetic-avant-garde-response. December 29, 2017.

———. *Thinking Its Presence: Form, Race, and Subjectivity in Contemporary Asian American Poetry.* Stanford: Stanford University Press, 2013.

Watten, Barrett. "The Lost America of Love: A Genealogy," *Genre* XXXIII Fall-Winter, (2000): 287.

Webster, Noah. *Dissertations on the English Language: with Notes, Historical and Critical.* Boston: Isaiah and Company, 1789.

Weddle, Jeff. *Bohemian New Orleans: The Story of the Outsider and Loujon Press.* Jackson: University Press of Mississippi, 2007.

Weinberger, Eliot. *American Poetry Since 1950.* New York: Marsilio Publishers, 1993.

Weinberten and Higgerson, Richard M. *Poets of the New Century.* Boston: David R. Godine, 2001.

White, Edward. *The Tastemaker: Carl Van Vechten and the Birth of Modern America.* New York: Farrar, Straus and Giroux, 2014.

Whitfield, Stephen J. *The Culture of the Cold War.* Baltimore: Johns Hopkins University Press, 1991.

Wiebe, Robert H. *Who We Are: A History of Popular Nationalism.* Princeton: Princeton University Press, 2002.

Wilkinson, Alec. "Something Borrowed." *The New Yorker.* October 5, 2015. http://www.newyorker.com/magazine/2015/10/05/something-borrowed-wilkinson. May 1, 2016.

Wilcox, Bradford. "The Evolution of Divorce." *National Affairs.* http://www.nationalaffairs.com/publications/detail/the-evolution-of-divorce. March 12, 2014.

Wilkinson, Alec. "Something Borrowed." *The New Yorker.* October 5, 2015. https://www.newyorker.com/magazine/2015/10/05/something-borrowed-wilkinson. December 29, 2017.

Williams, Tyrone. "Individuality vs. Individualism: Coteries, Affiliations, and Loners." *Poetry Magazine.* October, 2013. http://www.poetryfoundation.org/harriet/2013/10/individuality-vs-individualism-coteries-affiliations-and-loners/. October 31, 2013.

Williams, William Appleman. *The Tragedy of American Diplomacy.* New York: W.W. Norton, 1959.

Williams, William Carlos. *The Autobiography of William Carlos Williams.* New York: Random House, 1951.

———. "The Poem as a Field of Action." *The Poetry Foundation.* October 13, 2009. http://www.poetryfoundation.org/learning/essay/237854. May 1, 2015.

Wilson, Sloan. *The Man in the Gray Flannel Suit.* New York: Simon and Schuster, 1955.

230 BIBLIOGRAPHY

Woolf, Douglas. "Radioactive Generation." *Inland*. Autumn (1960): 33–34.

Woznicki, John R. *The New American Poetry: Fifty Years Later*. Bethlehem: Lehigh University Press, 2013.

Wright, Anne and Rose Maley, Saundra, eds. *A Wild Perfection: The Selected Letters of James Wright*. New York: Farrar, Strauss and Giroux, 2005.

Wright, James. "The Few Poets of England and America." *The Minnesota Review* 1/2 (Winter, 1961): 248.

Yau, John. "Neither Us Nor Them." *American Poetry Review* 23.2 (1994): 45.

Yu, Timothy. "Ron Silliman and the Ethnicization of the Avant-garde." *Jacket*. 2009. http://jacketmagazine.com/39/silliman-yu.shtml#fn9. December 28, 2017.

Zahn, Curtis. "An Inch of Culture." *Trace* 39 (September–October 1960): 40–44.

Zimple, Lloyd. "They Also Serve Who Only Lie in Wait." *The Nation*. September 26, 1959.

"Against Expression: Kenneth Goldsmith in Conversation." *The Academy of American Poets*. June 17, 2011. https://www.poets.org/poetsorg/text/against-expression-kenneth-goldsmith-conversation. December 31, 2017.

"Amiri Baraka, radical playwright and poet, dies aged 79 in Newark." *The Guardian*. January 9, 2014. https://www.theguardian.com/books/2014/jan/09/amir-baraka-playwright-poet-dies. January 31, 2017.

"Édouard Roditi, 1910–1992." *The Poetry Foundation*.https://www.poetryfoundation.org/poets/edouard-roditi. April 2, 2018.

"Gael Turnbull 1928–2004." *The Poetry Foundation*.https://www.poetryfoundation.org/poets/gael-turnbull. January 24, 2018.

"Grace Hartigan." *The Telegraph*. November 18, 2008. http://www.telegraph.co.uk/news/obituaries/3479770/Grace-Hartigan.html. May 1, 2015.

"Helen Adam." *Wikipedia*. http://en.wikipedia.org/wiki/Helen_Adam. May 1, 2015.

"Neo-Dada." *The Art Story*. http://www.theartstory.org/movement-neo-dada.htm/. March 15, 2018.

Parapolitics: Cultural Freedom and the Cold War Haus der Kulturen der Welt. https://www.hkw.de/en/programm/projekte/2017/parapolitics/parapolitics_start.php. January 6, 2018.

The National World War II Museum. "By the Numbers: The US Military." http://www.nationalww2museum.org/learn/education/for-students/ww2-history/ww2-by-the-numbers/us-military.html. January 23, 2015.

The New American Painting. Exhibition catalogue. New York: The Museum of Modern Art: 1959.

Index[1]

A

Abstract expressionism, 2, 19, 34, 79, 80, 84, 157, 158, 211

Academic poetry, 12, 28, 32, 70, 108, 162

Activist Group, 49

Adam, Helen, 30, 46, 110, 116, 125, 132, 139, 140

Adams, Henry, 108

African Americans, 46, 47, 49, 50, 170–174, 181, 183, 199, 200
poets, 46, 50, 170, 173, 174, 181, 183

Albers, Anni, 212

Albers, Josef, 212

Alcalay, Ammiel, 74, 197

Aldan, Daisy, 48, 48n142, 60–63, 73, 127, 202

Allen, Donald, 1–9, 2n6, 12–17, 13n14, 15n24, 16n26, 53–61, 60n27, 87–90, 88n4, 98–102, 106–108, 131–136, 134n4, 137n19, 138–142, 140n29, 144–147, 149–166, 150n64, 168–181, 178n38, 184, 186, 188, 190, 192–194, 193n1, 197–202, 204, 212

Alvarez, A., 19, 20, 20n43
The New Poetry, 19

America, 8, 10, 26, 32, 36, 38, 41, 43, 45, 46, 49, 50, 54–72, 79, 82, 87–129, 138n21, 142, 143, 147, 158, 164, 201, 205–208, 211

American Century, 54, 157n85

American Flag
on the cover of the *New American Poetry*, 8, 144, 157, 159
painted by Jasper Johns, 158, 159
Pledge of Allegiance, 159
as a symbol, 132, 143, 158, 159

American Hybrid, 24, 25, 180, 181, 185n63

---

[1] Note: Page numbers followed by 'n' refer to notes.

© The Author(s), under exclusive license to Springer Nature Switzerland AG 2021
S. Delbos, *The New American Poetry and Cold War Nationalism*, Modern and Contemporary Poetry and Poetics, https://doi.org/10.1007/978-3-030-77352-6

232   INDEX

Anderson, Benedict, 143, 144, 150
Andrews, Bruce, 189
Anglophone, 3, 7, 9, 11–53, 81, 83,
    122, 129, 131–144, 146, 149,
    154, 156, 157, 162, 164–166,
    168, 172, 173, 178, 179,
    196, 198
    poetry, 3, 7, 9, 11–53, 83, 122,
        129, 131–144, 154, 156, 166,
        168, 172, 173, 178, 196, 198
Anthologies
    anthology wars, 6, 10, 28, 58, 63,
        64, 84, 159, 200,
        202–206, 208
    of poetry, 2, 7, 10, 11, 18–28, 40,
        44, 52, 107, 137n19, 141,
        155, 160, 164, 169, 177, 179,
        180, 185n63, 192
Ark, The, 73
Artisan, 104, 146
Ashbery, John, 26, 33, 35, 36, 73, 92,
    150, 204
Auden, W. H., 33, 34, 94, 95,
    138n21, 142, 201
Avant-garde aesthetics, 8

B
Baraka, Amiri, 46, 47, 60, 74, 76, 77,
    110, 166, 170, 174, 175, 178,
    178n40, 200
Barr, Alfred H., 79
Beats and Beat publications, 20, 21,
    23, 26, 31, 36, 50, 55, 59,
    68n58, 71–73, 75, 108, 109,
    117, 118, 122, 150, 153,
    153n75, 154, 162n97, 173, 190,
    201, 204
Beckett, Samuel, 144
Bernstein, Charles, 2, 4n10,
    177n34, 194
Berryman, John, 20, 30, 208

Bertram, Lillian-Yvonne, 172
Binary, Cold War, 84, 180
Bishop, Elizabeth, 59, 81
Black Arts Movement, 51, 174,
    183, 195
Blackburn, Paul, 73, 119, 146, 176
Black Mountain College, 26, 56, 93,
    126, 147
Black Mountain Review, The, 146,
    147, 150, 150n64
Blaser, Robin, 92, 110, 210
Blasing, Mutlu Konuk, 186, 190–192
Bloom, Harold, 206
Bogan, Louise, 17n29, 32, 33, 35,
    48n142, 51, 61, 67, 68, 100,
    124, 128, 150, 212
Borregaard, Ebbe, 92, 200
Botteghe Oscure, 17n30, 146
Boyd, Bruce, 30, 113, 125
Bremser, Ray, 69, 112, 174
Breton, André, 142, 161
British poetry, 4, 7, 8, 20, 20n43, 23,
    40–42, 131, 132, 139, 139n23,
    140n31, 141, 205–206
Brook Farm, 105, 159
Brooks, Gwendolyn, 164
Brother Antoninus, 30, 31, 73, 88, 125
Broughton, James, 18, 62, 64, 73, 77,
    79, 92, 110n69, 134n4, 151
Brown, Michael, 51, 168,
    171, 172n16
"The Body of," 171
Bruce, Lenny, 127
Brunner, Edward, 2, 34, 123
Bunting, Basil, 144

C
Cage, John, 164
Canon, The, 9, 164, 168, 171, 179,
    182n50, 184, 196, 198
Carroll, Paul, 163

INDEX 233

Catholic Worker Movement, The, 88, 99, 104
Cecil, David, *see Modern Verse in English 1900–1950*
Chapin, Katherine Garrison, 88n4, 141
Chen, Ken, 184, 185
Christensen, Paul, 128
Christianity, *see* Georg Wilhelm Friedrich Hegel
CIA, *see* Congress for Cultural Freedom
City Lights Books, 127
Civil Rights, 49
  Movement, Acts, 3, 49, 164, 195, 207
Clay, Steven, 74
Clifford, James, 148
Clippinger, David, 151n66
Cockcrover, Eva, 80
Coffey, Brian, 145
Cold War
  cultural warfare, 2, 7–9, 29, 34, 39, 41, 44–46, 52–56, 63, 65, 70, 78, 80, 82–84, 92, 98, 99, 101, 102, 108, 109, 118, 129, 131, 132, 135, 144, 148, 149, 159, 162n97, 163, 164, 187, 192, 196
  poetry, 1, 22, 39, 53, 54, 162
Coleman, Ornette, 39
Collins, Jess, 110
Colombo, John Robert, 66, 68n58
Community, 56, 59, 74, 75, 78, 87–90, 93, 94, 96–113, 119, 120, 122, 124–126, 128, 133, 135, 139, 144, 145n47, 150, 152, 165
  of love, 7, 8, 87–129, 193
Conceptual writing, 4, 5, 5n11, 175, 178, 180, 182, 187, 189, 189n84, 191, 192, 194, 195

Congress for Cultural Freedom (CCF), 7, 54, 78, 80–83, 81n98, 83n101, 131
Conrad, CA, 168
Contact, 73, 146
Continuity, of American Poetry, *see* Roy Harvey Pearce
Cooked and Raw, 1, 4, 12, 25, 27, 34, 56, 63, 84, 162, 193, 203
Corbett, William, 71
Corman, Cid, 35, 60n27, 63, 136, 138, 139n22, 155, 200
Corso, Gregory, 14, 41, 58–60, 60n23, 61n27, 70, 73, 118, 126, 137, 137n19, 152, 153, 153n75
Counterculture, 7, 74
Cowley, Malcolm, 73, 73n69, 75
Crane, Hart, 98
Creeley, Robert, 98, 110, 112, 114–116, 125, 129, 133, 134, 136, 136n16, 140n29, 146, 147, 147n54, 151, 156, 187, 188, 204, 211, 212
Culture, 2, 7–9, 29, 34, 39, 41, 44, 46, 52–56, 63, 65, 70, 78, 80, 82, 84, 92, 98, 99, 101, 102, 108, 109, 118, 131, 132, 135, 144, 148, 149, 159, 162n97, 163, 164, 187, 192, 196
  warfare (*see* Cold War, cultural warfare)
Cunningham, Merce, 212

D
Daedalus, 81
Dahlberg, Edward, 76
Davidson, Michael, 65, 93, 159, 177
Davis, Douglas M., 37
Dawson, Fielding, 208
Day, Dorothy, 104
De Kooning, Willem, 55

234 INDEX

Democracy, 63, 65, 98–100, 144, 166, 197
Di Prima, Diane, 74
Diebenkorn, Richard, 210
Diggory, Terence, 186
Dimock, Wai Chee, 148
Divers Press, 136n16, 146
Dorn, Edward, 145, 175
Dove, Rita, 138n21, 181–185, 182n50, 185n63
Doyle, Kirby, 47, 174
Dragon and the Unicorn, The, *see* Kenneth Rexroth
Duerden, Richard, 110
Duncan, Robert, 7, 17, 21, 28, 34, 37, 49, 58, 61n27, 62, 72, 72n67, 73, 76, 82, 87–97, 99, 102, 107, 108, 110, 128, 136, 139, 140, 140n29, 146, 150, 152, 153, 153n75, 200, 204, 210
Dupee, F. W., 123
DuPlessis, Rachel Blau, 177
Dworkin, Craig, 4, 5n11, 191, 191n96

E
East-West division, 24
Eberhart, Richard, 60
Edmond, Murray, 19n38
Eigner, Larry, 73, 146, 151
Eliot, T. S., 40, 66, 135, 156, 187, 199, 211
Emerson, Ralph Waldo, 42, 206
English Poetry, *see* British poetry
Evergreen Review, 14, 50, 102, 152, 154, 199, 201
Everson, William, *see* Brother Antoninus
Exclusion, 8, 40, 50, 51, 63, 131, 139, 141, 165, 170, 172, 172n18, 175, 176, 178n39, 192
in poetry anthologies, 40, 141
Experimental poetry, 1, 144, 164, 170

F
Faas, Ekbert, 91
Fearing, Kenneth, 68, 68n58, 162
Female poets, 48, 49, 51, 140, 173, 175, 197
Feminism, 3
Fenton, James A., 32
Ferlinghetti, Lawrence, 18, 50, 57, 153
Field, Edward, 6, 58, 60, 75, 75n74, 92, 126, 201–203
Filreis, Alan, 67, 75n74, 100, 126, 162, 180n45
Fisher, Roy, 144
Five Spot, The, 56, 56n10
Folder, A New, anthology, see Daisy Aldan
Form
formal framework in criticism, 68
in poetry, 61n27, 87, 125, 128, 139, 160, 178–192, 195, 196, 205
Foster, Edward Halsey, 114, 188, 195
Fragmente, 146
Fraser, Kathleen, 174n24, 177
French Poetry, 162n97
Frost, Robert, 63n35, 67, 68, 195, 205, 206, 208
Fukuyama, Francis, 135, 196, 197

G
Gay men, *see* Homosexuality, in post-war poetry
Geography, 80, 149
organization of *The New American Poetry*, 149
GI Bill, 27, 33
Gill, Eric, 104, 105
Ginsberg, Allen, 9, 10, 20, 20n43, 22, 26, 28, 35, 37, 59, 60, 61n27, 64, 65, 69, 70, 72, 75, 89, 90, 92, 94, 97–99, 108, 112, 113, 136, 139n22, 152, 194, 203, 204, 207, 211

INDEX 235

Glass, Loren, 157n86
Gleason, Madeline, 46, 47, 73, 140, 176, 200
Goddard, J. R., 66
Golden Goose, The, 73
Golding, Alan, 5, 29, 31, 32, 50, 53n1, 96, 110, 110n69, 139, 153n75, 159, 170, 174
Goldsmith, Kenneth, 5, 5n11, 51, 168, 171, 172, 180, 181, 186, 187, 189, 189n84, 191, 192, 194, 194n3, 195
Gooch, Brad, *see* Frank O'Hara
Gottlieb, Adolph, 79n86, 209, 211
Grove Press, 1, 6, 13–15, 15n24, 78, 87, 127, 127n121, 133, 154, 157, 157n86, 165
Guest, Barbara, 46, 47, 116, 117, 176, 200
Guilbaut, Serge, 161n96

H
Hall, Donald, 6, 12, 24, 25, 27, 29–31, 33, 35, 36, 41, 45, 48n142, 57, 58, 60, 61, 71–73, 72n67, 75, 89n6, 123–125, 133, 158, 203–205
Hallberg, Robert Von, 165
Hammer, Langdon, *see* James Merrill
Harlem Renaissance, 164
Harrison, Katherine Chapman, 31
Hartigan, Grace, 56, 79n86
Heart's Needle, see W. D. Snodgrass
Hegel, Georg Wilhelm Friedrich, 88, 99, 105–107, 106n61, 106n62, 106n63, 120
Hentoff, Nat, 57
Herd, David, 31, 172n18
Hickman, Ben, 45, 138, 139, 143, 184
Hikmet, Nazim, 162
Hiss, Alger, 39

Hollander, John, 28
Holocaust, The, 119, 120
Homoeros, 96
Homophobia, 82, 92, 98
Homosexuality, 90–93, 96–98, 107, 127n121
in post-war poetry, 90, 98
in society, 92, 98
Hong, Cathy Park, 168, 170–172, 174, 178
Hoover, Paul, 24
Postmodern American Poetry, 24
Horowitz, Michal, 20n43
Children of Albion: Poetry of the Underground in Britain (1969), 20n43
Howl, *see* Allen Ginsberg
Hudson Review, The, 81
Hughes, Langston, 164

I
Identity
in poetry, 1, 30, 141, 158, 167, 169, 179, 183, 192, 196
in politics, 179, 182, 186, 197
Imagined Communities, see Benedict Anderson
In the American Tree, see Ron Silliman
Iron Curtain, The, 45, 82

J
Jabberwock 1959, 146
Jarrell, Randall, 34, 60
Jazz
influence on poetry, 56
Jewell, Megan Swihart, 177
Joans, Ted, 50, 179
Johns, Jaspet, 158–160
Johnson, David K., 91
The Lavender Scare, 7, 91, 98
Johnson, Kent, 83n101

236 INDEX

Jonas, Steven, 50, 139, 170, 174, 178–179
Jones, LeRoi, *see* Amiri Baraka

K

Kalaidjian, Walter, 68, 89
Kandel, Lenore, 179
Kaufman, Bob, 50, 153, 153n75, 178, 192
Kaufmann, David, 5, 171, 178, 178n39
Keene, John, 168
Kelly, Robert, 20–22
Kenyon Review, The, 81, 82, 92
Kerouac, Jack, 60, 61
Khrushchev, Nikita, 65
Kimmelman, Burt, 4n9, 4n10
King, Basil, 57, 80, 143
King, Martha, 6, 16n29, 142, 143, 146, 208–212
Kingfishers, The, *see* Charles Olson
Kinnell, Galway, 33
Kitchen debate, the, 48, 65, 101
Klein, Marcus, 162–164
Kline, Franz, 60, 79n86, 157, 210
Koch, Kenneth, 26, 33, 73, 136, 150
Korean War, 135
Kuhlman, Roy, 127n121, 157–159, 157n86
Kyger, Joanne, 6, 46, 47, 175, 199–200

L

Lamantia, Philip, 73, 94, 97, 112
Language poetry, 4, 4n10, 22–24, 99n40, 124, 177, 177n34, 180, 182, 183, 185, 189–192, 189n83, 194
Lavender Scare, 91, 98
Lawrence, D. H., 138, 142

Layton, Irving, 134, 141, 145
Leary, Paris, 20–22
Lennox, Sara, 47
Leo Castelli Gallery, The, 158
Levertov, Denise, 46, 47, 58, 61, 69, 70, 73, 132, 139–142, 139n22, 141n33, 156, 165, 176, 188, 200, 204
Life Studies, see Robert Lowell
Lipton, Lawrence, 57
Literary Revolution in America, The, *see* Gregory Corso
Literature, 6, 32, 33, 35, 42, 44, 55, 57, 97, 107, 108, 133, 135, 138, 138n20, 142, 144, 148, 149, 161, 164, 168n6, 174, 187, 198
Logan, William, 58, 138n21, 184–188, 194, 197
Lorca, Federico García, 142
Love, community of, *see* Community, of love
Lowell, Robert, 1, 4, 17, 20, 22, 27, 28, 30, 34, 56, 58–60, 63, 70, 76, 81, 125, 182, 194, 208
Lowenfels, Walter, 46, 169
Lowensohn, Ron, 208
Luce, Henry, 54
Lynes, Russell, 39

M

MacDiarmid, Hugh, 145
Macdonald, Dwight, 39, 92, 94
MacGreevy, Thomas, 145
MacIntyre, Amelia, 179
Major, Clarence, 50
Massachusetts Review, The, 136
Maurin, Peter, 104, 105
Maximus Poems, The, see Charles Olson
May, Elaine Tyler, 48, 123
May, Lary, 54

INDEX   237

McClure, Michael, 60n23, 61n27, 94, 112, 139n22
McGahey, Jeanne, 48, 179
McGrath, Tom, 107, 203
McHugh, Vincent, 141, 154
McKee, David, 210
McReynolds, David, 117
Meltzer, David, 110
Mencken, H. L., 108
Merrill, James, 22, 56, 59, 60, 81
Messerli, Douglas, 24, 190
Metcalf, Paul, 211
Migrant Books, *see* Gael Turnbull
Milder, Jay, 210
Mills, C. Wright, 127
Mingus, Charles, 56
Mitchell, Joan, 60, 172n16
Modernism/modernists, 44, 55, 71, 75n74, 128, 129, 149, 156, 161–163, 165, 169, 175, 178n39, 180n45, 190, 194, 205
Modern Verse in English 1900–1950, 40, 64
Monroe, Harriet, 42, 161
Moore, Rosalie, 48, 179
Morley, Hilda, 209
Mossin, Andrew, 53n1, 177
Motherwell, Robert, 79n86, 211
Museum of Modern Art, 79

N
Nation, The (fix in hall interview_), 68, 204
National Book Award, 56, 76
Nationalism, 3, 5, 8, 43–45, 52, 83, 102, 129, 131–166, 172, 172n18, 198, 211
Nealon, Christopher, 197
Neel, Alice, 201
Nemerov, Howard, 208

Neruda, Pablo, 162
New American Painting, 78, 212
New American Poetry, The, 6
    the cover of, 19, 157–159
    the poetics of the, 15, 30, 38, 142, 149, 159
    the postmoderns, 23, 138, 159, 178n38
    reviews of, 1
    revisited, 110n69, 159
New American Story, The, 15, 159
New British Poets, The, 140
New Criticism, 66, 88n4
New Directions, 18, 140n31, 200, 201
New Folder, Americans, 60
    Poems and Drawings (*see* Daisy Aldan)
New Poets of England and America, Second Selection of, 127, 158, 206–208
New Republic, The, 141
New World Writing, 73
New Writing in the USA, The, 15, 159
New York City, 48, 50, 56, 57, 74, 158, 161, 208, 210, 211
New Yorker, The, *see* Louise Bogan
New York Poets' Theatre, 57, 209
New York School, 5n11, 26, 59, 71, 141, 142, 150, 190, 200, 201
Newman, Barney, 211
Norse, Harold, 60
Nuyorican poetics, 51

O
O'Hara, Frank, 23, 26, 33, 56, 57, 61n27, 73, 78n82, 79, 92, 110–112, 126, 150, 175, 201, 210
Okigbo, Christopher, 145

238 INDEX

Olson, Charles, 3, 5, 5n11, 8, 16, 21,
27, 28, 35, 37, 41–43, 54, 55,
60, 61n27, 65, 73, 75, 75n75,
76, 78, 87, 92, 93, 97, 102, 110,
110n69, 132–135, 139n22, 142,
143, 145, 146, 147n54, 149,
154, 156, 161, 177, 187–192,
187n75, 202, 204, 211
Oneida Community, 105
Oppenheimer, Joel, 113, 124
Orlovsky, Peter, 92

P

Pack, Robert, 6, 12, 40, 57, 71, 72,
127, 203, 205–208
Paris Review, The, 81, 203
Partisan Review, The, 81
Patchen, Kenneth, 57, 68, 68n58, 162
Paul, Sherman, 96, 128
Paz, Octavio, 162
Pease, Donald E., 148
Penguin Anthology of Twentieth-
Century American Poetry, The, see
Rita Dove
Perelman, Bob, 129
Perez, Craig Santos, 180, 181
Perkoff, Stuart Z., 61n27, 119, 120
Perloff, Marjorie, 23, 26, 50, 170,
173, 182–188, 191, 194,
196, 197
Persky, Stan, 200
Personism, see Frank O'Hara
Phillips, Rodney, 74
Pitcher, Oliver, 179
Place, Vanessa, 4, 4n9, 5, 172n16, 180
Politics, 1–4, 8, 9, 39, 53, 53n1, 56,
66–70, 83, 88, 90, 98–100, 104,
105, 107, 124, 125, 127, 128,
135n8, 143, 164, 168n6, 171,
179, 182, 186, 196, 197,
203, 211

cold war, 1–4, 8, 39, 53, 56, 83, 98,
100, 104, 128
See also Dwight MacDonald
Pollock, Jackson, 19, 60
Postell, Tom, 179
Postmodern poetry, 169
Postmoderns, 15, 15n24, 24, 178n38
The New American Poetry Revised,
The, 15, 15n24, 138, 159,
160, 178n38
Pound, Ezra, 38, 63n35, 133, 135,
175, 191, 199
Prevert, Jacques, 141
Pritchard, Norman, 50, 170, 174, 179
Projective Verse, 5, 43, 75n75, 133,
177, 187, 189
Prospect, 146
Pulitzer Prize, The, 76

Q

Quinn, Justin, 20

R

Racism, 5, 12, 49, 52, 163, 171,
172n16, 178n39, 192
Ramazani, Jahan, 148, 149
Ransom, John Crowe, 60, 63, 81,
81n98, 82, 92, 126, 181
Rasula, Jed, 72
Raw and cooked, 1, 4, 12, 25, 27, 30,
34, 56, 63, 84, 162, 193, 203
Revolutionary
poetry, 167
Rexroth, Kenneth, 57, 59, 68n58,
99–108, 120, 140, 161, 162,
162n97, 199, 210, 211
Reynolds, David S., 117, 197
Riach, Alan, 145
Rifkin, Libbie, 98, 99n40, 187
Rivers, Larry, 56, 60

INDEX 239

Robinson, Edwin Arlington, 36, 206
Roditi, Édouard, 161
Roethke, Theodore, 59, 208
Rose, Herman, 201
Rosenberg, Harold, 55
Rosenthal, M. L., 68
Rosset, Barney, 13, 15, 15n24, 18,
  134n4, 201
Rothenberg, Jerome, 19n39
Rothko, Mark, 211
Roy Harvey Pearce, 45
Russell, Bertrand, 95
Russo, Linda, 175, 176

S
San Francisco scene, 50, 152, 199
Santayana, George, 108
Saunders, Frances Stonor, 80,
  81n98, 82
Schramm, Wilbur, 33
Schuyler, James, 33, 92, 141, 142
Scott, N., 66
Seaver, Richard, 202
Selby, Hubert, 127n121
  Last Exit to Brooklyn, 127n121
Sewanee Review, The, 81
Sherman, Jory, 93
Sherman, Paul, 96, 128
Silliman, Ron, 19, 20, 24, 37,
  140n29, 168, 168n6,
  177n34, 181, 186, 189,
  189n83, 189n84
Simon, John, 66, 68, 68n58, 112
Simpson, Louis, 12, 28, 30, 36, 41,
  58, 64, 71, 72, 158, 203, 205
Smith, Elihu Hubbard, 42
Smith, Sydney, 42
Snodgrass, W. D., 76, 77, 203
Snyder, Gary, 37, 58, 59, 61n27, 72,
  78, 97, 110, 119, 200, 204
Spellman, A. B., 179

Spicer, Jack, 50, 61n27, 92, 93,
  110–112, 139, 175, 200, 210
Stanley, George, 200
State Department, The, 80,
  83n101, 91
Stevens, Mark, *see* Willem De Kooning
Stevens, Wallace, 161, 182, 194, 206
Still, Clyfford, 79
St. John, Robert, *see* American Hybrid
Subjectivity, 5, 114, 169, 177,
  179–192, 195, 196
  in poetry, 179, 180, 182, 186,
    188–190, 192, 195, 196
  in politics, 196
Swan, Annalyn, *see* Willem De Kooning
Swenson, Cole, *see* American Hybrid
Swenson, May, 30, 202

T
Tale of Genji, The, 97
Tallman, Warren, 30, 38, 142,
  149, 173
Tarn, Nathanial, 128, 194
Tate, Allen, *see* Modern Verse in English
  1900–1950
Tiger's Eye, The, 56
Torgersen, Eric, 22
Tradition of the New, see Harold
  Rosenberg
Translation, 28, 28n66, 142, 149, 161
Transnationalism, 139n22, 143, 162
Transnational Poetics, A, see
  Ramazani, Jahan
Truman, Harry, 91
Trumbo, Dalton, 39
Tudor, David, 212
Turnbull, Gael, 132, 134, 136–139,
  136n16, 137n19, 139n22,
  139n23, 141, 142, 144, 146,
  149, 156, 165
Tzara, Tristan, 161

240 INDEX

U
Untermeyer, Louis, 42, 43, 203

V
Vendler, Helen, 182–188, 194, 197
VIDA
  Women in Literary, 176
Vincente, Esteban, 212

W
Walsh, Chad, 25, 33, 64
Wang, Dorothy, 174, 175, 186–188
Waste Land, The, 61n27, 156
Watten, Barrett, 96, 99n40, 128, 189
Weinberger, Eliot, 24, 180n45
Welch, Lew, 78
Whalen, Philip, 97, 112, 121, 122
Wheatley, David, 20, 164, 177
White citizens, 46–52
Whitman, Walt, 36, 38, 42, 57, 68,
  90, 98, 100, 108, 142, 194
Wieners, John, 26, 50, 92, 110, 200
Wilbur, Richard, 37, 59, 208
Williams, Jonathan, 73, 92, 117, 118,
  136n16, 139n22, 209
Williams, Oscar, 203

Williams, William Appleman, 104
Williams, William Carlos, 41–44, 57,
  71, 133, 136, 141n33, 156, 164
Wollheim, Richard, 192
Woolf, Douglas, 141
Wordsworth, William, 205, 206
World War II, 2–4, 4n10, 9, 12, 32,
  33, 43, 49, 53, 54, 79, 90, 103,
  104, 108, 123, 125–128, 131,
  143, 144, 146, 147, 156–158,
  162, 167, 175, 192,
  198, 206–207
Woznicki, John, 5, 53n1, 135, 139n23
Wright, James, 22, 29, 36, 37,
  59, 89n6
  reviews, 29

Y
Yaddo, 133
Yu, Timothy, 177n34, 186
Yugen, 57, 74, 76, 209

Z
Zahn, Curtis, 66
Zen Buddhism, 122
Zimpel, Lloyd, 73

Printed in the United States
by Baker & Taylor Publisher Services